SANDEEP JAUHAR

intern

Sandeep Jauhar, M.D., Ph.D., is the director of the Heart Failure Program at Long Island Jewish Medical Center. He writes regularly for *The New York Times* and *The New England Journal of Medicine*. He lives with his wife, Sonia, and their children, Mohan and Pia, in New York City.

intern

intern

A DOCTOR'S INITIATION

SANDEEP JAUHAR

FARRAR, STRAUS AND GIROUX · NEW YORK

FARRAR, STRAUS AND GIROUX
18 West 18th Street, New York 10011

Portions of this book originally appeared in different form in *The New York Times*, *The New England Journal of Medicine*, and *The Lancet*.

The Library of Congress has cataloged the hardcover edition as follows:
Jauhar, Sandeep, 1968–
    Intern : a doctor's initiation / Sandeep Jauhar.— 1st ed.
        p.   cm.
    Includes bibliographical references (p.   ).
    ISBN 13: 978-0-374-14659-7 (hardcover : alk. paper)
    ISBN-10: 0-374-14659-4 (hardcover : alk. paper)
        1. Jauhar, Sandeep, 1968–   2. Medical students—United States—Biography.
    3. Interns (Medicine)—United States—Biography.   4. Residents (Medicine)—
    United States—Biography.   I. Title.
        [DNLM: 1. Jauhar, Sandeep, 1968–   2. Physicians—Personal Narratives.
    3. Internship and Residency—Personal Narratives.   WZ 100 J4095 2008]

R154.J39 A3 2008
610.92—dc22
[B]

                                                            2007009161

Paperback ISBN-13: 978-0-374-53159-1
Paperback ISBN-10: 0-374-53159-5

Designed by Gretchen Achilles

www.fsgbooks.com

3   5   7   9   10   8   6   4   2

This is a work of nonfiction. The author has changed the names and identifying characteristics of most people. Dialogue is recounted from the author's memory.

FOR SONIA, RAJIV, AND DAD
BUT MOST OF ALL, FOR MOHAN—ALWAYS, ALWAYS

contents

II. CRACKING UP

III. RECONCILIATION

prologue: captive

The cardiac monitors are whistling like blowpipes and the ventilators are playing the kazoo. I pull open a sliding glass door and close it behind me. In the dark, I can barely make out the patient's face. It is delicate, wrinkled, almost peaceful. The ventilator that has sustained her for nine days sits unplugged in a corner, next to a small aluminum sink and a pullout toilet. Clear plastic bags of medicated fluids are hanging on a metal pole next to her bed. On the wall is a cheap print of a coastal village with yachts floating on azure blue water. I gaze at it for a moment. Right now, at four o'clock in the morning, it seems impossibly far away.

The data from the monitor swirl in my head like a maelstrom. I'm not sure what it all means, but I do know that right now the patient's blood pressure is normal and her heartbeat is a regular picket fence. I sigh, relieved. Nothing more for me to do tonight.

Then she opens her eyes. "Welcome, Doctor. Will you have a drink?" She points in the dark toward the fully stocked bar. "You know where everything is. And fix me one as well."

I ask her where she is. "My apartment," she replies, bewildered. She seems to know nothing about being sick or in the hospital.

I stare at her quietly. "It's too much trouble for these people," she says.

"Which people?" I ask.

"The people . . . People . . . It's too much trouble."

I assume she means the nursing staff. "Are they coming into your room?" I ask.

"I don't know," she replies. "Coming here, coming there . . . coming anyplace."

The monster has come back. Only hours earlier it took up residence in Mr. Schilling down the hall. I found him sitting at the side of his bed, his sheets soaked with blood. "Get me out of here!" he roared. "You're keeping me here against my will." The head of his penis was lacerated. A nurse explained that he had pulled out his catheter.

"You can't keep me here! I don't belong in jail." Earlier he had spoken to me quite normally of his grandchildren and his country club. Now he was a raving lunatic.

"I am a doctor!" I shouted, grabbing the lapels of my white coat. "This is a hospital, not a jail!"

"It is a jail," he cried, "and you are the warden!"

I ordered him sedated, and though I was confident that he would soon be his normal self again, I stopped outside his room to ponder what Dr. Carmen had told us residents that morning. "Get this patient out of the unit as soon as possible," he warned. "People like him don't do well here."

No one could ever say what exactly caused the monster to appear, but something about the environment of the intensive care unit makes some people lose their minds. Perhaps it is sensory deprivation—being kept in a windowless room, away from family and familiar things. Or perhaps it is the sensory overload—being tethered to noisy machines running all day and night. Perhaps it is sleep deprivation or pain. I had read about brainwashing experiments on American POWs: in environments of intense isolation and immobility, they often experienced psy-

chotic reactions. But that was the jungles of Southeast Asia. This is a respected hospital on the Upper East Side of Manhattan.

"I wish I could be a better host, but I've been under the weather,"
my patient explains, and I nod cautiously. For a moment I wonder
whether perhaps I am the one who is hallucinating. Maybe she is sitting in her living room. Maybe I am about to pour her a drink.

"You've been sick, but you're getting better now," I tell her, hoping
to jog her memory.

She looks through me. Even in the gray light, her eyes appear
bloodshot. "Yes, Doctor," she says. "Now please fix me that drink."

I squeeze the bag of saline hanging next to the bed. "Thank you,"
she says sweetly, and then goes off to sleep.

I head back to the conference room. Through a window the moonlight is shimmering off the East River. A barge floats by, loaded with
crates. The steady current provides comfort, especially now, the nether
time, when it is too late to go to sleep and too early to be awake.

The door to the conference room closes behind me like a trapdoor.
I dim the lights; in the middle of the night, bright lights are almost unbearable. I gaze at the grid on the whiteboard. Twenty beds, eighteen
patients, a nearly full unit. Scribbled in each square is a list of scut
work. Still so many tasks to finish. Still so much to do before morning
rounds.

I can hear the alarms behind the door. Some are low-pitched, like
the sounds a head submerged underwater would make: *glug, glug,
glug*. Others are high-frequency chimes. Sometimes they ring out of
sync, like dueling banjos. Out of the din I hear the Berkeley Campanile
announcing the turning of the hour. It is a sound from a different time,
a different place. I am surprised that I still remember it.

I start running around the conference table, hopping up and down,
shadowboxing. My fists are furiously pumping up and down as I fling
away the tension that has accumulated over the past few weeks here. I
am running, running—now sprinting. My legs seem to possess a spirit
of their own. I am back on the Fire Trail, racing around the reservoir,
punishing my calves on the steep, crevasse-ridden hills. Now I am slip-

ping on the polished tile floor, punching stiffly at the air while "Sympathy for the Devil" plays in my head. I am running, running, trying to escape: the patients, the monster, this hospital, this life. Perhaps Mr. Schilling was right. Perhaps this is a prison. Perhaps we are all being kept here against our wills.

I don't know how much more of this I can take.

internship:
an introduction

The education of a doctor which goes on after he has his degree is, after all, the most important part of his education.

—JOHN SHAW BILLINGS, *THE BOSTON MEDICAL AND SURGICAL JOURNAL*, 1894

E very profession has an apprenticeship, and the apprenticeship in medicine is called *residency*. The first year of residency is known as *internship*, when new medical school graduates rotate through different hospital settings—outpatient clinic, intensive care unit, cancer ward—to learn how to treat patients and see how medicine really works. This introduction to the profession is a legendarily brutal year, for many doctors the most trying of their professional lives. Working eighty or more hours per week and staying up every fourth night or so on call, most spend it in a state of perpetual exhaustion, as near ascetics with regard to family, friends, food, sex, and other pleasures. The intensity of the training has inspired a kind of awe among medical students, perhaps not unlike that of minor league baseball players waiting for their chance to go to the majors. Medical school is the farm team; internship is the show.

I was an intern a decade ago now, but I still remember it the way soldiers remember war. After our son Mohan was born, my wife, Sonia, also a doctor, referred to the newborn period as a kind of internship, and it definitely wasn't easy, staying up night after night. But taking care of a newborn was very different from internship. In internship, when you were awakened in the middle of the night you had to be prepared to deal with almost anything—and in the worst possible state, too. It didn't matter if you felt like you were going to drop. You still had to be at the top of your game.

After the internship year, a doctor can work as a general practitioner, but the skill set that has been acquired is so limited that most people go ahead and finish residency—several more years of training, depending on the clinical specialty—to become full-fledged physicians. In my field, internal medicine, which has a three-year residency, second-year (or junior) residents supervise interns. Third-year (senior) residents supervise interns and junior residents. Together, interns and residents constitute the hospital (or "house") staff. After finishing residency, many physicians elect to do a fellowship: one to four (or more) years of training, depending on the field, to further specialize. By the time they get to the senior level, that of attending physician, many doctors are already in their mid-thirties.

This book is about my residency at a prominent teaching hospital in New York City. The story goes up to the point when I decided to pursue a fellowship in cardiology, my specialty, and thus covers the most formative period of my education as a doctor. For me it was a disillusioning time; I spent much of it in a state of crisis and doubt. I had trained as a physicist before entering medical school, and ten years of uncertainty about my choice of a profession came out all at once. In his path-integral formulation of quantum mechanics, Richard Feynman hypothesized that when a particle travels from point A to point B, it traverses many different paths to arrive at its destination. This certainly seemed to apply to my journey into medicine. Because I had lived another, more sedate, professional life, the one I had to endure in the hospital was even more difficult to bear.

My goal in writing this book is to give others a sense of that confusing, tumultuous time, my initiation into the guild of which I am now a proud member. My hope is that readers, on their own journeys—many of them in the medical profession—will draw lessons and perhaps even inspiration from my experiences. The experiences will be especially relevant, I think, to medical students preparing to make their own forays into the hospital. Laymen often view doctors as Type A overachievers with little self-doubt. I hope this book will serve to dispel that myth.

Everything that appears on these pages actually happened to me. However, most names and identifying details have been changed to preserve confidentiality; in some places, time has been compressed or the order of events has been changed for the sake of narrative cohesion; and in rare cases I have used composite sketches to better represent my experience. I write only of my own experiences, but I am sure that most residents have undergone similar ones. Doctors' professional lives are built brick by brick, case by case, but the foundation, residency, is much the same.

Not long ago, when I was interviewing a student for a residency spot at the hospital where I now work, the applicant said, "Perhaps the easiest decision a doctor can make is to become one." I must have frowned, for that definitely had not been the case for me. I was a reluctant traveler when I started on my journey into medicine, and this ambivalence surely affected how I coped with it. For much of internship I felt buried—in a waking hell under the weight of my own (and others') expectations. Only when I learned to accept my limitations—and the workings of the strange new culture I found myself in—was I able to start digging my way out and emerge a less conflicted physician, if not exactly doubt-free.

Thankfully, I am finished with my apprenticeship, and I can say with pride that I made it. I now work as a cardiologist at a large teaching hospital on Long Island. Some days it feels strange being an attending physician, and other days so perfectly reasonable, like it was preordained. For the most part, I am happy. I enjoy my job, taking care of critically ill patients with heart failure. But so much about medicine still troubles me; sometimes I still want to muddle through things; sometimes I'm still not sure cardiology was the right choice. At one time I didn't know how to read a chest X-ray. I worried about being a code leader. I wasn't sure if I even believed in critical care. Now I make my living practicing it. It isn't something I ever expected I'd be able to do, and yet now I am doing it. I have made the leap. But I will never forget the journey.

switching horses

escape

There is no short cut, nor "royal road," to the attainment of medical knowledge. The path which we have to pursue is long, difficult, and unsafe. —JOHN ABERNETHY, ENGLISH SURGEON, HUNTERIAN ORATION, 1819

I had been an intern less than an hour, and already I was running late. The sloping footpath leading up to the hospital was paved with gray cobblestones. My feet ached as my oversize leather sandals slipped on the rounded irregular rocks. The hospital was an old building browned by the passage of two centuries, with spidery cracks in its façade. Founded in 1771, New York Hospital is the second-oldest hospital in the United States, a mecca for doctors and patients from all over the world. I had been in the building once before, six months ago, for a residency interview. I spun through a revolving brass door, nearly running into the burly security guard reading the *New York Post*. He looked up from the tabloid just long enough to point me in the direction of the elevator.

The tiled corridors were dark and dull, mixing shadow and light. I darted past the chapel, past the café, around the information desk, which sat in the middle of the huge atrium like a fort, and entered a bank of elevators. Hanging on a wall was a portrait of a gray-haired lady in a blue dress sitting in dignified repose before an open book. She was a graduate of the medical school, class of 1899, ninety-nine years ago, who built a medical college for women in Northern India, on the banks of the Ganges, near where my father had his early college education. Nearby was a metal tablet in bas-relief: "She cared for all in need. For each, she made time to guide, to teach, and to heal."

When I arrived on the fourth floor, other interns were still filing into the auditorium. A woman handed me a manila folder, and I went inside and sat down. The orientation packet contained several essential documents: a house-staff phone card, directions for obtaining autopsies, instructions on how to use the hospital dictation system, and the residency contract. I leafed through it quickly. My salary was going to be $37,000 a year, about eight dollars an hour, I calculated, given the number of hours I was going to be working, but I didn't mind. Though I was a year shy of thirty, it was more than double what I had ever made.

My classmates, though younger than I, appeared older than I expected, casually dressed, all thirty-five of them, in khakis and polo shirts, faded jeans and sequined tops. Some of them evidently knew each other, because they were already chatting in small, insulated groups. They were from some of the best medical schools in the country: Harvard, Yale, Cornell, Columbia. Though I too had gone to a top school—Washington University in St. Louis—I had been feeling insecure about the prospect of working with them. For months I had feverishly been reading Harrison's tome on internal medicine and review articles in *The New England Journal of Medicine* to prepare for this day.

Someone in the front row stood up and turned to face us. It was Shelby Wood, the hospital's residency director. He was a serious-looking man of medium build, with straight brown hair and a long, aquiline nose. He was wearing a white coat and a fat blue tie that might have been in fashion twenty years earlier. My elder brother, Rajiv, a cardiology fellow at the hospital, six years ahead of me in his medical training (though only two and a half years older), had warned me that Dr. Wood was a bit of a grouch, but had added that he was also fair and decent and a strong advocate for his house staff. Wood, I was to learn, hailed from the old school, where you were expected to live and breathe medicine, stay late in the hospital, neglect your family for the sake of your patients, and emerge on the other side a seasoned physician.

He cleared his throat and began to speak. His voice was deep but incongruously soft, and because I was sitting in the back of the sixty-seat auditorium, I only managed to catch snippets of his remarks. It was going to be a busy year, he said, as thirty-five heads stared motionlessly back at him. We were expected to devote ourselves fully to medicine. "You don't learn French by taking classes at Hunter College. You learn it by going to Paris, sitting in the cafés, talking to people." Likewise medicine: we would learn it by living it. "You are now ambassadors for the profession," he said gravely. "So don't let the students hear you complain. It sets a bad example." If everything went as planned, he added, by next June we'd be ready to supervise the next batch of interns.

I glanced over at the pretty brunette sitting next to me. She looked back at me, rolled her eyes, and opened her mouth in mock panic.

Then Wood dropped the bomb. Every intern starting on the wards or in the intensive care units was required to come to the hospital every single day, including weekends, for the first six weeks. The only exceptions were interns starting in the outpatient clinic, which was only open from nine to six; they would have no evening call and weekends off for the first month. I later learned that this regimen was a long-standing tradition at the hospital, the most efficient way to get everyone up to speed. To me it seemed brutal, like a kind of hazing, not to mention a violation of residency work-hour limits set forth by the Bell Commission in New York in the mid-1980s. Uneasy murmurings reverberated through the auditorium as new interns rustled through their packets. I scanned the master schedule before breathing a sigh of relief. Along with six classmates, I was slated to start in the clinic.

"We are here to help you," Wood said, raising his voice over the light chatter. "You should feel free to call on us anytime, day or night. The only mistake you can make is not asking for help."

I was reminded of a residency interview in Chicago a few months earlier. The interviewer, a portly senior physician with an abundance of facial hair, had posed the following scenario: A nurse pages me in the middle of the night to tell me that a patient who just had hip surgery is short of breath. What would I do? "Go see the patient," I said. I had enough sense to know that there was only one right answer to that question. Walking to the room, what would I be thinking about? "Pulmonary embolism," I replied. Blood clots in the lung are a feared complication after hip surgery. When I arrive in the room, the patient is in distress. His heart is beating 130 times per minute and the oxygen tension in his blood is low. Now what? I went over the treatment options in my head—blood thinner, supplemental oxygen, arterial blood gas— but it seemed the examiner wanted me to say something else. I'd heard about the notorious "July phenomenon," in which hospital mortality supposedly increases every summer with the entry of new and inexperienced hospital staff. "I'd call a senior resident," I finally answered. Why? "Because I could be missing something." My interviewer nodded; I had passed the test. Like all residency directors, he was looking for a soldier, not a cowboy.

Now it was late June, and we were the new hospital staff. For the rest of that first morning, we sat through a series of tag-team lectures. A woman from the blood bank talked about blood transfusions. A pathologist talked about the importance of autopsies. A psychologist spoke about work-related stress and told us that confidential counseling was available. A lawyer from risk management, the department that defended the hospital against lawsuits, informed us that at some point in our careers every one of us was likely to be sued, and that we could even be sued during residency. She offered some advice: Document your decision-making; document when a patient refuses treatment; never admit wrongdoing; never talk to an opposing attorney; and, finally, be nice to your patients. Doctors who were nice to their patients were rarely sued, even in cases of egregious malpractice. I looked around the room, trying to gauge the reaction of my classmates, frankly surprised that such a cynical thing was being taught on the first day of residency. No one's eyes met mine.

At the midmorning break, I went outside. Stepping through the humid air was like sweeping away static. The sidewalk was buzzing in a kind of Brownian motion, with pedestrians sidestepping me as though I were a moving obstacle. A long line snaked from an aromatic hot dog stand. Buses and taxicabs were letting people off in front of the hospital. An ambulance whizzed by on the main thoroughfare, sirens blaring, lights flashing. The noise fed my sense of wonder. I had grown up in a quiet Southern California suburb, craving the excitement of a big city. Berkeley and St. Louis had their pockets of vitality, but nothing like this. Even the smell of the neighborhood—a mix of pizza, garbage, cigarette smoke, and fragrant fruit—was rich and seasoned, like wisdom wafting through the air.

I had only arrived in Manhattan a few days earlier, moving into a one-bedroom apartment about a block away from the hospital. On the plane flight in from St. Louis, the pilot took a detour because of airspace congestion, he told us, flying into LaGuardia from the south, not the usual flight pattern. As we passed over the World Trade Center and then soared low over the city, I craned my neck to look down at the broad swath of Central Park. The brown buildings on its outskirts were arrayed like divers ready to jump into a pool. Down there, I had imagined, all of the metropolis's unique charms were waiting for me: the old, stained sidewalks; the stealthy characters playing junkyard instruments on subway platforms; the deliverymen hurtling through traffic lights on their rickety ten-speeds, I ♥ NY plastic bags swinging from the handlebars. The first time I had been to New York was the summer before medical school, when I spent a couple of weeks with my brother and his wife in their tiny one-bedroom apartment across the street from the hospital, where he had just begun his fellowship. I wandered around the city, going on walking tours of Harlem, joyriding on the subway, chatting with bartenders late into the night. Like many visitors to Manhattan, I was swept away. The delicatessens, the dry cleaners, the corner convenience stores and smoke shops. Unlike in Berkeley, people weren't just milling around, enjoying the sun. There was magic in the movement on the streets. So much was happening, and I could watch it all and remain a shadow. That was the wonderful paradox of Manhattan: you could be surrounded by people and yet be anonymous at the same time. "The United Nations is just down the street," I wrote a friend. "The building they use to broker world disputes, just down the street from me!" New York cast a spell on me that summer that I could neither explain nor resist.

Back on the sidewalk, I felt a light spray from air-conditioning units outside the apartment windows above me. Heavy construction was going on in a lot nearby; large bulldozers were exhuming a deep hole, as if for a tomb, their blades ravenously picking up mouthfuls of yellowish dirt. I passed by an old church and stopped at a fruit stand to buy a nectarine. Then I ambled back to orientation munching on it. A plane flew overhead. Looking up at it streaking across the clear blue sky, sweet juice trickling down my chin and fingers, I couldn't help but think that the abnormal flight path that had brought me here last week was an apt metaphor for my own twisting journey into medicine.

I STOOD ON THE BALCONY in Berkeley and lit a cigarette. My bags were packed, the bills paid, the car loaded. Most of my possessions had been sold, save for some clothes and a few boxes of books, which I forced into the trunk and backseat. After a week of sleepless nights, I had turned in my Ph.D. thesis on quantum dots that morning. I had even found someone to take over my apartment. Now all I had to do was leave.

It was late in the afternoon on Tuesday—August 1995—and the sky over the shimmering San Francisco Bay had turned a smoky orange. Medical school orientation was starting tomorrow. I would be in a Honda Civic somewhere in the Rocky Mountains. After explaining to the dean that I was delayed finishing my physics thesis, she had urged me to at least try to make it to St. Louis by Friday morning for the white-coat ceremony and the recitation of the Hippocratic oath. After speaking with her, I looked it up: ". . . To please no one will I prescribe a deadly drug, nor give advice which may cause his death. Nor will I give a woman a pessary to procure abortion . . ." Arcane stuff. Perhaps,

I wondered, she'd let me write my own oath. Perhaps that could be my first contribution to my medical education.

The air was warm, still, vaguely welcoming. The fraying eucalyptus trees in the backyard gave off a pungent fragrance. Taking a long drag, I felt buzzed, even a bit dizzy. For the first time in months, I was in the moment. But the carefree feeling quickly dissipated as the thought—the same thought that had plagued me for months—reentered my mind, even as I tried hard to resist it: *What the hell are you doing?*

I pulled out of the driveway and headed south toward the Berkeley campus one last time. I passed the International House, Sorority Row, and the dormitory where I had lived freshman year. Ice plant still lined the side of the road, and the landscaping was still immaculate, just as it had been a decade ago. Freshman year, I remembered, I had planned to major in history or political science, but Victor, my randy Russian roommate, had deterred me. He was a double major in math and physics. (And "love," as he liked to put it. He put a mattress in our walk-in closet. Every night, moans from one of his girlfriends titillated me as I fell asleep.) Victor's enthusiasm for his chosen subjects was infectious. He lent me books on abstract algebra. He explained to me the wonderfully nonintuitive ideas of Kurt Gödel, an Austrian logician who proved that all mathematical systems are necessarily incomplete. He told me about Ramanujan, the Indian mathematical prodigy who claimed that the Hindu goddess Namakkal whispered theorems about prime numbers to him in dreams. In freshman chemistry, when I had to memorize the rules for how electrons occupy atomic orbitals, Victor taught me where those rules came from, in a quantum-mechanical language that was both beautiful and inscrutable. The exactness, the inaccessibility, of quantitative science intoxicated me. In the social group I eventually joined, math and physics had prestige, a sort of intellectual exclusivity that was deeply appealing. The spectrum of talent in these subjects was so broad, much broader than in the social sciences or humanities or even the biological sciences, where it seemed that with enough study even the grade-conscious premeds could master the concepts. What separated me from the rest of the pack was what separated Victor from me, and what separated my friend Mike from Victor, and what separated the genius student David Moulton from Mike, and what separated the weird, stinky math professor who ambled around campus mumbling to himself from David Moulton, and probably what separated Einstein from the weird, stinky math professor. The brain function required was so specialized that math and physics seemed to me the truest tests of intelligence. So, by the end of my freshman year, my major had changed to physics, and my intellectual heroes had changed from Churchill and Gandhi to Einstein, Heisenberg, and Feynman, men who changed the world through the power of mathematics.

But by senior year it had become clear to me that theoretical physics, at least at the level I wanted to pursue it, was beyond my capabilities. So, like many of my friends who didn't know what to do with themselves, I took the LSAT and applied to law schools. Trial law had always interested me; in high school I often fantasized about leading a courtroom charge like Atticus Finch in *To Kill a Mockingbird*. Law school, I hoped, would allow me to broach the big questions of ethics, philosophy, and politics that had always interested me. My father, a plant geneticist with a disdain for vagueness and imprecision ("Nonscience is nonsense," he often said), thought it was a bad idea. He didn't need to remind me of his opinion of lawyers. I got into the top schools and even deferred my admission for a year, but in the end I decided to stay at Berkeley for the graduate program in physics. I didn't know what else to do. Though I thought I might like law school, somehow I knew I didn't want to be a lawyer.

One thing I never thought seriously about was becoming a doctor. In fact, for most of my life, medicine was the last thing I wanted to do. My maternal grandfather had been an army doctor in India before he went into private practice. As a boy in India, before we moved to America, I used to watch him at work in his iodine-stained clinic on the ground floor of his palatial flat in an upper-crusty neighborhood of New Delhi. Pitaji's clinic always smelled pungently of medicine, as did he. Through the drawing room window I'd spy him examining patients with boils or sepsis on the mosquito-netted veranda while lizards clung motionlessly to the limestone walls. It was fine, noble work—or so I was told—but it never caught my fancy. To me, even as a boy, medicine was a cookbook craft, with little room for creativity.

My family immigrated to the United States in 1977, when I was eight (we lived in Kentucky for two years, before moving to Southern California). Whenever the subject of lifework came up, I told my parents that I would never become a doctor. Unlike my brother Rajiv, who somehow always knew he wanted a career in medicine, I was more interested in books, literature, philosophy, the big questions of human existence, about which medicine apparently had nothing to say. Even when I experienced a flash of medical curiosity—say, when the pope got sick or a Soviet leader mysteriously disappeared for a few days—it would quickly dissipate or be subsumed by my interest in the politics of the event. I wanted to be a historian or a high-ranking government official or a famous lawyer or actor or a private investigator, something romantic, with character and flair. Medicine was so bourgeois! My father admonished me for being impractical. He wanted me to become a neurosurgeon—one trained at Stanford, no less. To him, that was the apogee of professional attainment. He understood well the privileges of being a doctor. Whenever he was on the phone with the airlines or with the bank, he always identified himself as *Dr.* Jauhar, even though he wasn't a physician. ("It really gets their attention," he'd explain.) My mother, too, wished for me to become a doctor. For her, medicine represented an honorable path to influence, power, and wealth—all the things that had eluded my talented father. But I wanted nothing to do with my parents' dream. In immigrant Indian culture, youthful rebellion is saying no to a career in medicine.

We had left India to advance my father's career as a plant geneticist, but in America my father never achieved the kind of success he felt he deserved—denied, he believed, by a racist university tenure system, which forced him to take postdoctoral positions with no long-term stability and left him embittered and rigid and in a constant state of conflict with professional colleagues. He learned to approach life's conundrums as if they were Aesopian fables. He adopted the habit of distilling life's problems into simple aphorisms dealing with faith, persistence, the value of work—Booker T. Washington stuff. He was always saying things like, "The happiest of people don't necessarily have the best of everything; they just make the most of everything that comes their way." Or he'd say, "Success is to be measured not so much by the position one has reached in life as by the obstacles one has had to overcome." Or, "It is not falling in water but staying there that drowns a man." Or, "Work is worship." Or, "I'm a tremendous believer in luck. I find that the harder I work, the more I have of it." (Or sometimes he'd mangle the adage, as when he'd say, "Don't change horses in the middle of the ocean.") He believed strongly in focus, determination—he'd written a plant genetics textbook in the back bedroom, littered with scientific papers and electron micrographs, while working full-time as a postdoc—and also that the mind is malleable, that satisfaction is a state of mind. He felt an overwhelming urge to keep my brother, Rajiv, my sister, Suneeta, and me from repeating his mistakes.

When I was in middle school in Riverside, California, a medium-size suburb of tract housing and strip malls tucked away in the smog-ridden Inland Empire, my parents invited a veterinarian over to the house for tea. He too had emigrated from India, a lanky man in his forties with a curly mustache, a Nehru jacket, and baggy brown pants that looked like they needed washing. He sat on the ragged couch in our living room loudly munching on my mother's *pakora* fritters. He and my father talked about the evils of Reaganism, but the conversation quickly turned to medicine.

"I always wanted to become a doctor," he said, looking straight at me. "But I could not afford to go to medical school."

"I wanted to be a doctor, too," my father said, pulling up on his fraying brown slacks so that the hair on his shins peeked out over his blue socks. Then he retold a story I had heard many times. My paternal grandfather had died when my father was only thirteen. After his death, the family spiraled into poverty. My father, an able and devoted student, was forced to read his schoolbooks under streetlamps because there was no electricity in the house. For an indigent boy growing up in rural Kanpur, medical school became an impossible dream. My father flirted with the idea when we first came to the United States, but by then he was thirty-seven, with a wife and three young children, and it no longer seemed practical.

"Why did you go to vet school?" I asked our visitor, trying to change the subject.

"Because that is all I could afford," he snapped. "If I could have paid the tuition, I would have preferred medicine."

"I want to be a professor," I announced preemptively. I desired the academic, retiring life of my father.

"He talks like a kid," my father said sadly. "He thinks he is smart, but he is going to land in a ditch."

"Brother, the kids have to make their own mistakes," the veterinarian replied gravely.

"But they should learn from others' mistakes!" my father exclaimed. "You don't have to touch the stove to know that it is hot."

The vet turned to me. He spoke in the stern tone of someone who wasn't used to being challenged. "We are foreigners, you understand? As a doctor, you won't have to depend on anyone."

"They say equal opportunity," my father said disgustedly. "It is an eyewash, a joke."

"You have opportunities that your father and I did not have. You're a smart kid. You do well in school—"

"He says medicine is cookbook," my father interrupted. "He says he wants a challenge."

"He can do research, if that is what pleases him," the vet reminded.

"At least there is some surety in medicine," my mother echoed from the kitchen. She was a typical Indian mother, loving, caring, committed, but small-minded, too, in that only-concerned-with-my-own-backyard way. She had struggled alongside my father, raising the three of us kids, working full-time as a lab tech, making do with much less than she was accustomed to having, sacrificing so my father could write his academic textbooks, which sold a few dozen copies a year. (She always said that nothing good or substantial would come of writing books.) We lived hand to mouth in a house sparsely furnished with lawn furniture, kitsch, little tchotchkes and cheap knickknacks my parents picked up from garage sales. My parents took us everywhere with them, not because we were an extraordinarily close-knit family, but because we couldn't afford a babysitter. There was a time after my father lost his job that we were forced to live on my mother's lab technician salary of $11,000 a year. We couldn't tell anyone; we had to keep up appearances that my father was still working. "We have to live in society," my mother would explain.

"You will get a good job as a doctor," my mother said, bringing in a platter of sweets. "You will get *izzat*, respect. When you walk into the room, people will stand. At the university you may get nothing for your hard work."

"They never let you rise," my father said, shaking his head. "They preach human rights. They talk democracy. What human rights! Where are the human rights in this country? It doesn't matter if you are a citizen or not a citizen; it is the color of your skin. They will always hire a white American if they can. You have to be three times as good as them to get the same recognition. If I could start a practice, I would kick them. I would tell them to go to hell."

The irony of all this was that my father hated doctors. He thought they were all crooks. (He always said scientists like him, Ph.D.'s, were the *real* doctors.) I had heard the stories growing up: the urologist who told him he had testicular cancer when he had a simple fluid-filled cyst; the dentist who botched a filling and wanted to charge him to get it done over again; the rheumatologist who overtreated him with steroids; the pulmonologist who recommended surgery after a marginally abnormal chest X-ray. Dr. Gokhale, our family doctor, had bungled the stitches I needed after a dirt-biking accident, incorrectly diagnosed my brother with water on the knee, and almost killed my grandmother by giving her a drug for a blood disorder she did not have. My parents had a running joke between them about how much Rajiv was going to charge them for medical care in their old age. The clear if unintended message was that doctors were money-grubbers, distinguished from shopkeepers only by their higher education.

I too resented doctors for their money, their airs. At Indian social functions, the doctors would drive up in their fancy cars as we were getting out of our dilapidated old Buick. Their kids wore the best designer clothes: Le Tigre, Polo, Ocean Pacific, Vans. I hated how they looked down on us, on our shoes from Kmart and our jeans from Sears. One of them invented a rhyme about our shoes: "Buddies, they make your feet feel fine, Buddies, they cost a dollar ninety-nine, Buddies, I'll never show you mine . . ." I hated their spoiled daintiness, their self-appointed privilege. I fancied myself a champion of the underdog.

"Uncle, it is not for me," I said to the vet. I was too ambitious, too stubborn, to pay attention to pragmatic considerations.

"One day you may have regrets," was his reply.

I did give it a chance—once. During college, at my parents' insistence and following Rajiv's suit, I volunteered in the emergency room at Riverside General Hospital over Christmas break. The ER was quiet that first night. The biggest excitement was a teenager who came in with a cockroach stuck in her ear. She screamed as a doctor took the insect out, piece by piece.

I spent most of the shift in a back room, reading a book on quantum philosophy called *Wholeness and the Implicate Order*. At 9:30 p.m., when I was getting ready to leave, a call came in from paramedics. "Stick around," a doctor told me. "Things are about to get interesting." Within minutes a young man was wheeled in on a stretcher after crashing his VW Bug into an eighteen-wheeler. As he screamed horribly, the ER staff went to work on him, cutting off his clothes, immobilizing his head, wiping away blood. Someone inserted a catheter through the tip of his penis, which began draining red urine. Someone else prepared to insert a tube into his bleeding chest. That was enough for me. I quickly packed up and left, vowing never to return. Such excitement, I informed my parents, was not for me.

I STOPPED MY LOADED-UP HONDA at the traffic light at Bancroft and Telegraph. The food carts were still out; Berkeley would obviously carry on without me. Freshman year, a chemistry professor had told me that some people believed the world begins and ends at this intersection, and in a sense it had for me. Snaking up the hill behind me was Cyclotron Road, where E. O. Lawrence had built the world's first atom smasher and where I had spent the past five years doing my graduate studies on quantum dots. The research had been published in the most important physics journals. But after a while, the research didn't matter to me anymore.

On my right was Sproul Plaza, where I had spent many afternoons sitting on the steps of the student union playing chess with a demented old man who took my pieces with strange exuberance (and sometimes cheated), while the hippies played guitar or the evangelists and other cranks hollered inflammatory oratory in the background. One of the evangelists got kicked off campus for uttering a vulgar epithet—a controversial action on a campus that had given birth to the free speech movement—but he eventually came back. Berkeley had a way of doing that, pulling you back in.

As I waited at the stoplight, my eyes wandered over to the Carlton Hotel, a single-room-occupancy dwelling where my girlfriend Lisa had lived. She was from Los Angeles, and we had met my junior year in the dorms, when she was still a freshman. When I was in graduate school, we had had a standing date for lunch at least once a week at the little Chinese place on the north side of campus. I looked over at the stone bench near the dried-up fountain where she first told me about her illness: lupus. I stared at the spot, reliving the moment; sadness washed over me once again. I pictured her in her white sweater, looking delicate and pale, her skin the color of milk, with me holding her tightly and whispering that one day she was going to be cured and that I

ESCAPE17

would see her through it. She cried hard that day, and so did I. For her
and for myself.

The disease aged her, sapped her of strength, inflamed her joints,
sullied her unblemished complexion. Her hair thinned; her fingers became swollen, like sausages. The membranes around her lungs became
inflamed and protein started spilling into her urine. For weeks she
could hardly get out of bed. And the worst part was that there was no
cure! At first I didn't believe it. There were entire libraries devoted to
medicine, with hundreds, even thousands, of journals. Surely the answer had to be in one of them.

I brought to my girlfriend's disease the kind of can-do optimism
that is typical of graduate students, a belief that if I looked hard
enough, I would find a solution. The concept of chronic illness was
completely foreign to me. Disease came and went; it killed you or you
got better. Perhaps there were better doctors somewhere—with better
knowledge, better command of the medical literature—that could help
her. I called top researchers. I read medical textbooks. I pored over
Lupus Foundation of America newsletters cover to cover. I asked my
brother, then a new intern, to inquire about emerging therapies. I spent
lonely evenings staring into drugstore windows, wondering if the answer could be found inside the panoply of vitamin bottles. I went to
support group meetings, often without Lisa. One night in San Francisco, a scientist from UCSF delivered a lecture on the frontiers of research into lupus. He was a short man with an imperious air, and I
found him pompous and a bit pedantic, but when I looked around the
dimly lit auditorium, all eyes were fixed unwaveringly on him. The
woman with large discolorations on her face sitting next to me was in
an almost meditative trance. Clearly everybody there was awaiting a
cure, hoping for deliverance.

When I drove back across the Bay Bridge to Berkeley that night, I
gave the idea of going to medical school serious thought for the first
time. My physics research had slowed to a crawl. I was spending most
of my time in the lab tweaking a malfunctioning laser or trying to fix a
broken vacuum pump, not collecting publishable data. Quantum dots,

I feared, were never going to make much of an impact on people's lives. Practical considerations of this kind had never been important, but now, in the shadow of physical illness, only the usefulness of medicine seemed to matter. Physics had been a way to set myself apart. Now, its exclusivity had become its main liability.

My thoughts remained unformed while I tried to muster the courage to discuss them with my family. What would my parents say? Would my father think I was being farsighted or irresolute? Would he think of me as a quitter?

I first talked to my parents about my intentions a few weeks later on a family trip to San Diego, where Rajiv was in his second year of residency at UCSD Medical Center. Rajiv was two and a half years older than I, and as with most brothers of roughly equal age, ours was a complicated relationship. Growing up, he was my playmate, rival, and exemplar. There are faded pictures of us as children, dressed in school uniforms, hugging each other in the smoky air of Old Delhi. In America, we were latchkey kids. When we got home from school, Rajiv would fix me a snack—usually a bowl of cornflakes with a heap of sugar—and we'd sit in front of the TV and watch cartoons. As we got older, we got more competitive, especially in sports. We'd go to public tennis courts in the summer or on weekends and play from morning till night, often evenly splitting our matches. In high school, I edged him out for the final spot on the local team going to the California Interscholastic Federation tennis tournament, but my father forced me to give up my spot because Rajiv was a senior and it was his last opportunity to play CIF. When Rajiv went to college at UC Riverside, only a few blocks from our high school, our relationship changed once again, and he became more of a guardian over me, always inquiring about the minutest details of my life at his old school, closely monitoring and supporting my attempts to break into "the Hill" and other popular social groups. Though I had always done better in school than he, Rajiv possessed an easygoing charm that made people instantly comfortable and won him friends and popularity. If he was a politician, I was a political consultant.

Now I was a graduate student with misgivings and he was a doctor with a degree from the University of Chicago. My parents and I were sitting in Rajiv's sunlit living room, just a stone's throw from Solana Beach, when my father asked me how my research was going. When was I going to start collecting data? I told him that I didn't know.

"But you've been setting up your experiment for over a year," my father said, leaning forward on the black leather couch, the breast pockets of his short-sleeved cotton shirt thick with pens. Even though he had never really supported my decision to go to graduate school, now that I was there he wanted to see me finish up and get on with my life. "You have to learn to focus. I have done a Ph.D. so I know—"

"All right."

"You can't stay in graduate school forever. You have to look for a job, start a family—"

"Okay!" I shouted. I got up and went to the bathroom, where I splashed cold water on my face and coughed into a towel. Then I went back to the living room, where my parents were sitting quietly. My father was leafing through papers in his ever-present briefcase, which was resting on his lap. I sat down on the love seat. "I'm thinking about applying to medical school," I announced.

My mother, dressed in a conventional flower-patterned sari, looked at me quizzically. She turned to my father, who was expressionless. "You can't go to medical school now," she declared.

"Why not?" I replied. I had it all figured out. Over the next two years I could finish up my thesis and take the prerequisites. By the time I matriculated, I would be only twenty-six.

"And then four years of medical school, then three years of residency, maybe even a fellowship. Look at your brother. Do you think you can work like him?" Judging from her tone, she did not.

"It's only a few years," I snapped. Unlike in India, life in America wasn't set in stone once you turned twenty-one.

"I always wanted you to be a doctor," my mother said. "Remember? It was always my dream that both my sons become doctors. But that time has passed."

Her last remark was particularly cutting. It saddened me to think about how many years and how many opportunities had slipped away. My father appeared deep in thought. "What are you thinking?" I demanded.

After a long pause, he said: "Don't change horses in the middle of the stream. Who knows if you will even like medicine?"

That night, we went to the Old Town district to have dinner with my brother and some of his colleagues from the hospital. We sat outside on a cobblestone square illuminated by gaslights, drinking margaritas out of salt-crusted martini glasses while a mariachi band serenaded my father with "Happy Birthday." At one point Rajiv's beeper went off. He stood up and went off to answer the page. My father and mother beamed proudly.

They had always favored my brother, their firstborn, and Rajiv demanded it, too. He knew the privileges of being the eldest son in a traditional Indian family and guarded them closely, like a trust fund. Watching him that night, I thought of all those times I had pitied him studying organic chemistry or preparing for the MCAT while I read novels or blasted Rush records on our turntable. *Why do you begrudge him his happiness?* I asked myself. *He earned it.* I remembered the summer I visited him in Chicago. He was a third-year medical student and would usually leave the apartment for the hospital before six in the morning. I'd sleep till noon, get up, eat lunch, read the newspaper, do some sightseeing if it wasn't too hot, and usually end up roaming through bookstores in Hyde Park. Rajiv would trudge in at 6:00 or 6:30 p.m., always looking a mess but claiming he felt great. Now where was he, and where was I?

His colleagues asked me about my research, but I couldn't bring myself to say much about it. Now that I had lost my enthusiasm, I couldn't imagine anyone else finding it interesting. So I asked them about residency, hospital life. They were working hard but it was obvious that no one had any regrets. Like my brother, they seemed to have embraced their training as a sort of boot camp, a necessary hardship on the way to a fulfilling career. One of them boasted that he had recently diagnosed a case of malaria by examining a smear of a patient's blood under a microscope. Someone else told me that he was in the process of applying for a hematology-oncology fellowship. Listening to them, I felt envious. They possessed everything that I was lacking: passion, confidence, a sense of purpose. Graduate school had left me feeling lonely, marginalized, like an interloper in the real world.

Riding home that night, I was surer than ever that I wanted to become a doctor. Choosing to do so now was as much of a rebellion as dismissing it had been years ago.

The next day Rajiv took me to the hospital. Walking through the teal double doors of the intensive care unit was like entering a sanctuary, scrubbed and sanitized. I had never been in an ICU before. Residents were moving quickly, purposefully, dressed in light blue scrub uniforms and fanny packs. Rajiv took me from room to room, telling me about each case. We passed a young man on a ventilator. A middle-aged couple was sitting quietly at his bedside. "He'll be gone by the afternoon," Rajiv whispered casually. We walked on as he continued talking. After a few paces, I stopped. "What did you mean back there?"

"Where?" Rajiv said.

"Back there. You said that guy was going somewhere. Where is he going?"

"To the morgue!" Rajiv replied. "He has AIDS. He's circling the drain."

I searched his face, bewildered by his lack of feeling. At one time he had been so sentimental. He had wept when I left for college, and again when he went off to medical school. Now he seemed so different, so hardened, like the sort of person who might pick up a ringing phone and shout, "Talk to me!"

"You've changed," I said, not even trying to hide my disappointment.

"So you'll be a different kind of doctor," he shrugged. "Once you get out of the ivory tower." We continued walking while I seethed quietly.

When I got back to Berkeley, I met with a campus psychologist, a balding, bespectacled man who specialized in career counseling. He asked me to take a career interest inventory test. A few days later I went back to discuss the results with him.

"Well, Mr. Jauhar, the test indicates that you have little interest in medical science." The occupations I seemed best suited for were lawyer, college professor, human resources director, and flight attendant.

When I told him I had already decided to apply to medical school, he asked me why. Judging from his tone, he didn't think it was a good idea. If I wanted to do biomedical research, had I considered seeking a postdoctoral fellowship after I finished my physics Ph.D.? If my reasons were primarily pragmatic (the hope of a high salary), what about options requiring less training, like management consulting, investment banking, or business school?

I was yearning for something I couldn't quite put my finger on. "I just want to get out of the ivory tower," I blurted out, and of all the possible reasons that had gone through my mind, that one probably best explained my motivation. I had begun to despise academia. I had been enmeshed in the world of esoteric ideas, and where had it gotten me? The lupus support group meetings had reinforced my belief that the work I was doing was going to have little impact on people's lives. Physics was an enterprise of reflection, ideas. Medicine was an endeavor of prescription, of action. Becoming a doctor, I hoped, would bring me back into the real world. It would make me into a man.

CHAPTER TWO

phase transition

Not like the brazen giant of Greek fame
With conquering limbs astride from land to land;
Here at our sea-washed, sunset gates shall stand
A mighty woman with a torch, whose flame
Is the imprisoned lightning, and her name
Mother of Exiles.

—EMMA LAZARUS, "THE NEW COLOSSUS," 1883

O rientation week passed rather quickly. I spent much of Tuesday in a subterranean classroom near the hospital being trained in advanced cardiac life support. I sat next to a new intern whose biggest worry seemed to be the upcoming urine drug test. In the morning we learned the protocol for treating ventricular fibrillation: "Shock, shock, shock . . . epinephrine, shock . . . lidocaine, shock . . ." In the afternoon I practiced CPR on an inflatable doll, placing the oxygen mask over her mouth and extending her neck slightly to get an adequate seal. I learned how to put a laryngoscope together—straight blade, curved blade—and then use it to insert an endotracheal tube. "Visualize the vocal cords," the instructor commanded. "They look like pieces of cauliflower." I rotated and cocked my wrist to get a better view. "Okay, you just broke your patient's teeth," the instructor barked. Using the heel of both hands, I compressed the mannequin's chest approximately two inches, hearing it click loudly. "Faster, harder, deeper!" the instructor bellowed. "You're not getting enough blood to her brain!" It was embarrassing, acting out like that around a roomful of strangers, most of whom were breezily nonchalant about the whole exercise, but I knew that soon enough I was going to be called upon to do the real thing.

I met a fellow intern waiting in line to get a hospital ID card. Vijay was a lanky Indian fellow who had spent his junior year of college at Oxford, studying biochemistry and "British bitter." He had gone on to study at Cornell, the medical school affiliated with New York Hospital, so he already knew the place well. He had a placid, diffident manner I found instantly likable.

"They say the only mistake you can make is not asking for help," he said skeptically, "but do you think any doctor really wants to be called in the middle of the night?"

I nodded. I had no problem asking for help, I replied. But some things people couldn't help you with.

"It's strange that all week they've hardly mentioned the patients," he went on. "These are the people we're going to be learning on. It's like they're already invisible."

The usual anxiety among incoming interns was compounded in my case by the fact that I had skipped my fourth year of medical school. In my first year in St. Louis, I was told I had the option of "short-tracking," finishing medical school in three years instead of four. The fourth year was mostly electives, and many students spent a considerable portion of it learning how to do scientific research, which I had already done in graduate school. Whether much clinical development took place during the fourth year was a matter of some debate. One of the deans, a jovial pediatrician, told me he viewed it as a year of consolidation: becoming comfortable with what you knew and, more important, what you did not. He said that any "clinical deficiencies" would disappear by the end of internship, and that in any case, none of the Ph.D.'s he knew who short-tracked felt disadvantaged after five years. But this did little to allay my worries. I was eager to get on with my career, but five years seemed like a long time to wait to feel competent.

That week, when I wasn't in class, I ambled around the city by my-self. I went to a street fair on the Upper East Side, where peddlers were pushing cheap trinkets and fresh-squeezed lemonade. In a crowd on the sidewalk, I tried to spot disease. That old man sitting on the bench, eyes closed, T-shirt creeping up on a distended abdomen, legs like tree trunks, capillary tangles all over his shins, dried blood at the corner of his mouth. What did he have? Must be alcoholic cirrhosis!

There had never been any doubt in my mind that I was going to come to New York for residency. People had warned me that the city, with its Darwinian pace, was a hard place to be a doctor, but I didn't care. Somehow I knew even in medical school that in my journey out of the ivory tower, New York City, with its grit, its urbanity, its swirl of humanity, was where I had to be. New York bred ambition, short fuses, a kind of go-to mind-set. Even the on-ramps to the freeways were impossibly short. Amid the litter and dirty brick and rusted embank-ments and peeling paint was a sturdiness no other city possessed. It was a strength I desperately wanted to acquire.

Plus, I was hoping that in a city of eight million people, I'd be lucky enough to meet someone to fall in love with.

At the end of orientation week, all of the new interns were invited to a cocktail reception at the faculty club, a wood-paneled place with festive green carpeting under a massive, ornate chandelier. Hanging on the walls were distinguished portraits of white-coated titans from the medical school's past. Most of the class was there, the men dressed in navy blue blazers and the women in fashionable summer dresses, milling around, displaying an attitude of tremendous earnestness. I was wearing khaki pants and a spotted yellow tie I had just purchased at Brooks Brothers. Some of the orientation speakers, mostly stiff, gray-haired senior physicians, were there, too. I spied Dr. Wood, the resi-dency director. At orientation he had come off a bit uptight, but now, drink in hand, he looked much more relaxed. Standing in a corner, it felt like there was a padlock on the tip of my tongue. I downed a glass of Chardonnay, then another, then another. Pretty soon I was feeling warm and comfortable.

Someone tapped me on the shoulder. It was Rashmi, an Indian woman who had been a student in a physics-for-premeds class I had taught at Berkeley. Rashmi had luxuriant black hair, a sweet, soulful voice, and an almost regal bearing. She hugged me and told me she had seen my name on the list of new interns but couldn't believe it was really me. Somehow we had managed to miss each other all week. "What are you doing here?" she asked, incredulous.

"I'm not sure," I replied uneasily. We both laughed.

As we were chatting, two members of the current class of interns, a year ahead of us, walked in and stood off in a corner, nibbling on appetizers. They had on surgical scrubs; their hair was greasy, matted down. Black stethoscopes cradled their necks. It looked like they were coming off a night on call and had crashed the party for the free food before going home to collapse.

In twelve months, I was going to be one of them. I searched their faces, looking for some clue about the journey I was about to embark on. All week, dutifully completing the tasks of orientation, I had hardly reflected on what was coming up. Now my thoughts started racing. This place was about as far away as I could imagine from graduate school in Berkeley, hiking on Mount Tamalpais, playing basketball in Codornices Park, riding my scooter through the fog-shrouded hills, roaming aimlessly through cafés, smoking pot with my best friend, Farhad, and then getting onto his Yamaha motorcycle and zipping into town for a late night meal at Fat Slice or Top Dog. My life had been slow and leisurely. Lab time had been my own time; I rarely got to work before 11:00 a.m. I had come and gone as I pleased.

You don't know these people, I thought. *You can never know them; they will never know you. They are basically the driven premeds you disdained at Berkeley. They're not curious about you, about things. They want to be here! I wish there were one person I could point to and say, he's like me, she's like me, she feels the way I do, he has the same misgivings.*

Loosened up by the alcohol, I turned to Rashmi. "Do you ever have any regrets about going into medicine?" I immediately rued the question, which was met with silence.

"No," Rashmi replied. "It's pretty much all I ever wanted to do."

Evidently, motivation for a career in medicine was assumed if you were standing in that room. It made me feel even more alone.

After the reception, I walked up First Avenue. Though the neighborhood had a reputation for being gentrified, it was funky by St. Louis standards, with a vibrant bar scene. Already I had a favorite: the Hi-Life, a kind of old-style speakeasy with a brightly lit two-foot-tall neon martini glass on its Prohibition-era storefront. Inside, it was decorated with dark wood paneling, spacious booths with vinyl seats that stuck to your legs, antique lamps, slow-moving ceiling fans, and waitresses with attitude. It was like the bar where I imagined C. C. Baxter had spent New Year's Eve in Billy Wilder's movie *The Apartment*.

Tiny candles were flickering on the faded wooden bar. I sat down and Shannon, the bartender, poured me a martini. If the Hi-Life was the perfect Manhattan bar, Shannon was the perfect bartender: sassy, sexy, with a ribald sense of humor. Over the past week, she had become something of a muse.

I told her about the hospital mixer. "I really have to stop questioning my commitment to a medical career in public," I said.

She was standing on rubber grating at the middle of the bar, wearing black pants and a denim blue oxford shirt, polishing a glass. "If they can't handle it, too bad for them," she said. "You don't have to be like everyone else."

"Yes I do," I said. "I really have to make this work." I did not want to hobble myself with doubt once again. I told her about a recent conversation I had had with my father, in which I admitted to ambivalence about starting internship. "Well begun is half done," my father had admonished. He told me about a recent experiment conducted by his plant geneticist colleagues. They had created a cross between a tomato and a potato: a "potomato." Shannon giggled expectantly, waiting for the punch line. "They thought it would make tomatoes on top and tubers on the bottom," my father said sadly, "but it took too much energy and did nothing."

Drunk now, I went for a walk on the East River esplanade. A storm was threatening. Lonely silhouetted figures traipsed across the bridge over the roadway, where the vehicles were emitting a cacophony of horns and beeps. On the footpath, the Victorian street lanterns glowed ominously. A cargo boat was tied to a pier; the wooden dock was creaking as the boat rolled in the waves. Off in the distance, the Queensboro Bridge unfurled over the river like a steel bracelet. I looked up at the hospital, which was mounted on concrete stilts above the FDR Drive. It was eerily lit in the moonlight, the Gothic spire of one of its buildings jutting straight into the sky. With its massive array of windows, it looked like a house of cards. What dramas were unfolding up there? I wondered. I imagined a group of doctors conferring about issues of life and death. How was I ever going to operate in that world?

I felt like an actor about to take on a role he was unequipped to play. My parents had invested so much hope in my brother and me, all their dreams of success, so any failure of mine would be theirs, too, a failure of many layers, slowly accreting over twenty-nine years. They had always regarded me as their brilliant son, but I had never been put to the test—at least not a test like the one I was about to take. There was so much to be afraid of: running a code; being on call; encountering my own spotty knowledge over and over again. I didn't have what my brother had to pull him through: a jovial, laissez-faire manner, a hail-fellow-well-met good cheer that won him friends and support. I'd probably appear defensive and humorless by comparison.

I feared I was about to lose something, but I couldn't pinpoint what it was. Freedom? Contemplativeness? Innocence about the workings of the human body? Was I going to start feeling less sexual, seeing disrobed bodies day in, day out? "I don't know any doctors who stop wanting to get laid," Rajiv had assured me.

In physics, the grandest of transformations is called a *phase transition,* as when ice melts into water. The physical properties of the transition are novel, not a simple superposition of the starting and ending states. This was the condition in which I now found myself. Part of me wanted to complete the transition, to flow like water, but mostly I

wanted to return to being a square and solid ice cube, where I was secure, where I knew the rules.

I had been preparing for this moment since that visit to San Diego.
I had steeled myself for it, running up hills to the point of nausea, brav-
ing the freezing cold without adequate clothing, anything to toughen
me physically for the challenges that lay ahead. And here I was, about
to begin but still unsure of what I sought. I gazed southward. In the
distance I saw the lights of Alphabet City and the smokestacks of
Brooklyn, and beyond that, Ellis Island and New York Harbor, where
immigrants had sailed through the centuries. New York had always
embraced people trying to reinvent themselves. Why not me?

CHAPTER THREE

medical school

Secure a hand saw and open the chest wall.

—GROSS ANATOMY DISSECTION MANUAL, PAGE ONE

By the time I completed the three-day drive from Berkeley to St. Louis, zipping through vast, hilly vistas browned by the intense heat, past signs that read BE PREPARED TO STOP and EMERGENCY PULL-OFF (were the warnings directed at me?), all the while blasting Dylan and the Dead till I had memorized every lyric, every guitar riff, I had missed all of medical school orientation, including the white-coat ceremony. My classmates must have thought me a freak wandering into the auditorium during closing remarks on Friday afternoon wearing shorts and a T-shirt, black as coal after baking for three days in the Great Plains sun.

I stayed a few days in the medical school dormitory, then transferred to a studio apartment in a high-rise about half a mile from campus in the Central West End, a quaint neighborhood with coffee shops and eclectic restaurants, the closest thing to Berkeley in St. Louis. My first night there, miserably camped on the carpet in virtual darkness trying to memorize the cranial nerves with the aid of a tiny lamp I had brought with me, I phoned Rajiv in New York and told him that I wanted to quit. He laughed hysterically and told me to stick with it. "A lot can change in a few months," he said.

My thoughts were already dominated by the towering hospital off the highway, not by the medical school building half a block away. In my lowest moments that first year, when information was being sprayed at me as if through a fire hose, the hospital came to represent my emancipation from the classroom. My classmates embraced the curriculum, discussing it excitedly in the cafeteria or at parties on the weekends, which only deepened my sense of alienation. Their attitude seemed immature to me. I prided myself on having seen more of the world—even though it had been a rarefied sphere I had wanted to escape. In the formaldehyde-ridden anatomy lab, the humor was dark. When we were dissecting the heart, my partner took the organ, rested it precariously on our embalmed cadaver's forearm, and said, "This guy really likes to wear his heart on his sleeve." But despite the occasional light moments and the protection from any real responsibility that the classroom afforded, I almost immediately grew impatient with the coursework. I had been a student all my life; it was all I had ever been. The lecture hall didn't present any fundamentally new challenges. The hospital, on the other hand, represented the real world, the world I had lost touch with during my years in academia. To succeed there was going to require skills I wasn't sure I even possessed: communication, observation, empathy. What if I went blank interviewing a patient? What if I broke out in nervous laughter? It seemed there were so many opportunities for disaster.

As first-year medical students, we were required to take a course called Introduction to Clinical Medicine. Once a week, we attended a desultory lecture on history-taking and physical diagnosis—where we learned, among other things, the oft-quoted clinical aphorism that about 80 percent of medical diagnoses are made (correctly) on the basis of a patient's history. Afterward, we headed off to the wards of the hospital to practice on patients. I was in a group with four other students. Our instructor was a gangly, awkwardly mannered hematology fellow in his early thirties who, like many doctors I would encounter in the coming years, was clearly ambivalent about the value of the skills he was teaching. Of course, he dutifully taught us the mechanics of medical interviewing and physical examination—palpating for lymphadenopathy, performing a comprehensive neurological exam, and the like—and he uttered homilies about their importance. But the emphasis at our weekly sessions was on normal findings—the "soft-nontender-nondistended-abdomen-with-no-organomegaly" shorthand we would become accustomed to scribbling in patients' charts in the coming years. To the fellow, it seemed, the course was a platform for teaching a new language, not a tool of discovery. Once, in response to a question, he scoffed that it would take two days to perform the physical exam described in our textbook. Even as he taught physical diagnosis, he seemed to be dismissing it as a waste of time.

My first encounter with a patient that year did not go well. There I was in my stiff khakis and bulging white coat, standing at the bedside of an elderly man who was watching television. His gray, curly hair ended at the base of a protuberant forehead, and he had deep creases around his eyes. I asked him if he would be willing to talk with me for a few minutes. Without turning away from the TV, he readily agreed, even offering me a chair. He seemed glad for my company.

Aside from his unwillingness to look me in the eye, he was pleasant and cooperative. I glanced at my note cards detailing the "review of systems." Any depression or anxiety? I asked. No, he replied. Any problems with hearing? "What?" he said, and I laughed politely. Any ringing in the ears? No. Any problems with smell or taste? No. Any vision problems? "What do you mean?" "Flashing lights, double vision, that sort of thing," I replied. "Not since I went blind," he said. Again I laughed, but this time it was no joke. He was totally blind; I hadn't noticed.

Second year was busier than the first, with exams covering entire textbooks of material. The daily routine was stultifying: study, eat, study, eat, sleep. The tests were long and depleting; you wanted to put your heart and soul into them, but there was only so much you could do before feeling sick. In graduate school I had never learned to memorize. You could always look things up; even final exams were often open-book. But now I couldn't rely on logic and reasoning; I had to commit huge swaths of material to memory.

It was during second year, buried in books and still unsure about whether I even wanted to be a doctor, that I first thought seriously about quitting medical school and doing something completely different. One option I considered was becoming a reporter. Journalism had always been a passion of mine, one that my father, a news junkie, had unwittingly fostered. On Sunday mornings, the voice of David Brinkley was as familiar as my mother's urging us to come to the table for her potato *paranthas*. In middle school, my father and I would go to the UC Riverside library to read *The New York Times* or books and newsmagazines on politics and foreign policy, especially nuclear arms control, which was a special interest of mine. For my thirteenth birthday, my father gave me a book of famous front pages from the *Los Angeles Times*: "Peace," "Walk on Moon," "Nixon Quits." Later, we always watched *Nightline* together after the rest of the family went to bed. Though he always encouraged his children to keep up with the events of the world, my father made it clear that journalism and writing were never to be considered career options because they offered no security. "Nonscience is nonsense," he often said.

At the end of graduate school, I had come across a flyer for a science journalism fellowship sponsored by the American Association for the Advancement of Science. On a whim, I applied, and, to my amazement, was one of 13 people selected out of a pool of about 250 applicants, all doctors and scientists with advanced graduate degrees. I was placed for the summer—the summer before starting medical school—at the Washington, D.C., bureau of *Time* magazine.

The summer at *Time* was perhaps the most exciting of my life. My first week there, I was sent to the U.S. Capitol to get a quote from Bob Dole about the working poor. He spent most of the day on the Senate floor, so my plan was to accost him when he went to the bathroom. When I got my chance, I froze, mumbling what must have been gibberish as he strode past me on the marble floor. Later that afternoon, dejected that I had failed my first journalism assignment, I ran into Dole's press secretary and asked for an interview with the senator. He was in the midst of dismissing me when the senator walked up. "This is

Sandeep Jauhar," Dole announced. "He's working on a story about the working poor. Set up a phone interview with him tomorrow morning." I was speechless. The next day, I got my quote. I had been promised five minutes, but Dole and I ended up talking for fifteen.

At the end of the summer, before getting a flight back to Berkeley to finish my Ph.D. thesis and pack up to drive to St. Louis, I asked Dan Goodgame, the *Time* bureau chief, for some names of journalists I could call on in the future. He mentioned a few editors he knew at reputable newspapers: *The Tampa Tribune-Times*, *The Miami Herald*, the *San Jose Mercury News*. "Yes, but what about *The New York Times*?" I said. My presumptuousness must have amused Dan, but sure enough, he had a contact there, too.

One afternoon in medical school, then, I called the office of Gerald Boyd, a senior editor at the *Times*. When his secretary answered, I introduced myself, mentioned Dan's name, said I was calling from St. Louis, and asked if I could speak with Mr. Boyd about journalism opportunities. Before I knew it, he was on the phone. I'm sure he thought I was a journalist because he started asking me about the *St. Louis Post-Dispatch*. I explained that I was not a reporter but a medical student interested in writing about science for the *Times*. He brusquely told me to set up a meeting with him the next time I came to New York.

When I got off the phone, I did what any aspiring journalist might do. I picked up the phone, dialed American Airlines, and booked a flight to New York. Then I called up Boyd's assistant and asked her to set up a meeting. "Who are you again?" she asked.

I told her that I was a medical student.

"And Mr. Boyd wants to meet with you?" she said.

In New York a few days later, I took a taxi to the newspaper's headquarters on Times Square. The security guard called up to Boyd's office, but there seemed to be some confusion about the purpose of my visit, so I waited in the lobby for half an hour before finally receiving a pass and directions to the third floor. Starry-eyed, I walked through the newsroom where the Pentagon Papers had been published, where Sydney Schanberg had written about the killing fields of the Khmer Rouge, where James Reston and Tom Wicker had tapped out the editorials I'd read as a kid. Boyd's assistant showed me into his office and went to get him. On the walls were pictures of him with politicians and dignitaries, including an autographed photograph with a former president. I wondered if perhaps I had overreached.

When he marched in, a tall man with the build of a football player, any hopes I had had of a relaxed conversation were immediately dashed. "I have five minutes," he barked, sitting down. "What do you want?"

"Well, sir—" I stammered, and then I went on to explain my situation.

"Show me your clips," he said impatiently.

"Well, sir—you see, unfortunately, I don't have any clips." I explained how at *Time* magazine interns didn't usually get the opportunity to write stories. He asked to see my reported pieces. I didn't have any of those either. But I did have some story ideas. I took out some loose-leaf sheets from my backpack.

He looked at me like I was crazy. "You can't work here!"

A wave of heat washed over my face. "Why not?"

"You're not qualified." He said it like it was the most obvious thing in the world.

"Well, do you have any internships?"

"You're not even qualified for an internship. Our interns usually have several years of newspaper experience."

He picked up the phone. "Tell Libby to come in here." We sat together in awkward silence. After a couple of minutes, a small woman with curly hair and a friendly face entered. It was Elisabeth Rosenthal, a medical writer. "Libby, this is"—he had obviously forgotten my name—"a medical student who wants to be a journalist. Please talk to him." Then he got up and left.

Libby Rosenthal and I talked for about half an hour. She told me about her own twisting career journey, going to medical school and finishing a residency in internal medicine before becoming a full-time reporter. "If you want to write for a newspaper," she said encouragingly, "try the one in St. Louis." She told me to send her my clips and to keep in touch.

Back in St. Louis, I got an internship at the *Post-Dispatch*. Twice a week, when second-year classes were done, I took Highway 40 to a run-down section of downtown and parked in the paper's weed-strewn parking lot. I wrote stories about wasps, fires, and wild turkeys in Forest Park, and I mailed them to Libby. Though I learned some valuable skills, like writing on deadline—rarely did I get more than four hours to report and write a story—the assignments I received, mostly overflow from the city beat, didn't much interest me. My mentor at the paper told me that I'd have to write stories like these for years before getting to do what I really wanted. So by the time the internship was finished, I had set aside the idea of becoming a journalist, resolved to focus once again on medical school.

The hospital off the freeway still beckoned. By the end of second year, I was obsessing about the clinical clerkships coming up, when I would get my first sustained exposure to hospital medicine. I yearned for work, not more scholarship, and I fervently hoped that third year, which had us rotating through all the major medical specialties, would provide fulfillment. There were three months devoted to adult internal medicine, three to surgery, two to obstetrics-gynecology, one to pediatrics, one to psychiatry, and one to neurology, leaving one month for vacation. Whenever I complained about second year to Rajiv, he assured me that things would change drastically once I got to the wards. He said that most of what I was learning in class was useless in clinical practice. He said that the preclinical years were simply a rite of passage. He told me to adopt the medical student mantra: P = MD. It was through practice that one learned what a doctor should do and be.

WHEN I FINALLY MADE IT to third year, I had narrowed my choice of specialty to internal medicine or psychiatry. Since I was planning on short-tracking, I had to make a decision quickly if I was going to send out residency applications in the fall. Though psychiatry had always appealed to me because of the creativity of its ideas, it quickly became obvious that nurturing my interest at medical school was going to require a thick skin. Many professors openly expressed disdain for psychiatry and psychiatrists. My mentor, a young gastroenterologist with perpetually startled eyes, told me that psychiatry residents came in two types: those from the bottom of the class who could not compete for more prestigious residencies, and those from the top of the class who were mentally ill. "Do internal medicine," he advised. "It will close the fewest doors." Rajiv agreed, calling psychiatry "mental masturbation." After all the effort I had expended to finish a Ph.D. in physics, I couldn't imagine choosing another career that didn't meet with my family's approval.

Of all the medical specialties I had been exposed to, internal medicine seemed the most grounded in the fundamental physiology I had learned in class. In some ways, internal medicine was like physics: rigorous, intellectually prestigious, vast (encompassing ten different subspecialties: cardiology, pulmonology, gastroenterology, nephrology, hematology-oncology, endocrinology, rheumatology, allergy-immunology, infectious diseases, and geriatrics). There was something deeply attractive about a field that was so immense and varied. (And popular, too: roughly a third of my class was applying for an internal medicine residency.) But as with everything in my life, I had doubts. Internal medicine was indeed complex, but it seemed to require rote, algorithmic reasoning. Where was the beauty, the creativity? Seventeen thousand medical school graduates every year—roughly a third of them future internists—and all of us trained to treat patients the same way. What was the difference between an internist and the mechanic in La Crosse who diagnosed that whirring sound in my car engine? He used a stethoscope, too. Wasn't this the cookbook medicine I had always disdained?

One night at the beginning of my first internal medicine clerkship of third year, a resident, a stocky, cocksure man, admitted a patient from the emergency room. "See if you can figure him out," he said to me on his way out of the hospital the next morning.

The patient couldn't tell me what was wrong, and neither could his eighty-year-old mother. "He's been lying on the sofa for weeks," she complained when I went to see him. "He just won't get up." Sloth was a sin, but was it a reason to be admitted to the hospital?

They had been living together in a house in East St. Louis. He was fifty-six and single, working mostly odd jobs until recently, when he started spending his days on the couch, watching television. According to his mother, he seemed sleepy most of the time. He forgot appointments and left chores unfinished. When confronted, he became irritable and withdrawn.

She suspected he was using drugs, but he never left the house long enough to buy any. Sometimes he seemed to be responding to visual hallucinations. She begged him to see a doctor, but he wouldn't go. When he stopped bathing, she called 911.

Though it was my first third year clinical rotation, even I could tell that this wasn't the usual midsummer lethargy. He was lying in bed, almost expressionless. His movements were slow and listless. When he spoke, he slurred his words.

He denied using drugs and said he didn't have any previous medical problems. He vaguely recalled taking a medication, but given his current state, he couldn't remember what it was. I asked his mother to bring in the bottle.

Meanwhile, I asked him a few standard questions. He knew where he was and the year, but not the month or the president. I asked him to count backwards from one hundred by seven, a test of attentiveness, but he stopped at ninety-three. I asked him to spell "world" backwards, but he started and stopped at "w." The mental status tests I had learned in class were useless on a patient with such poor mental status.

The differential diagnosis of his delirium was almost impossibly long. Some of the usual suspects had already been ruled out. He wasn't intoxicated or hypoglycemic. A CAT scan of his brain revealed no stroke, tumor, or bleeding. Seizures could explain the lethargy and confusion, but his mother had never seen him shake.

Of all the diagnostic possibilities, infections were probably the most serious. AIDS could cause a kind of premature dementia, but he didn't have the usual risk factors. Lyme disease was unlikely; *Ixodes* ticks weren't endemic to St. Louis. What about meningitis, I thought, or, worse, syphilis? Untreated syphilis could infect the spinal cord and brain, causing severe nerve damage and dementia. Syphilis was one of the "great masqueraders," along with tuberculosis and lupus, diseases with such protean manifestations that they could almost never be excluded with certainty. In fact, syphilis was enjoying a resurgence in urban areas like St. Louis. The only way to rule it out was to do a spinal tap.

With help from another resident, I had the man sit on the side of his bed, leaning forward onto a table. I scrubbed his lower back with antiseptic soap and then injected local anesthetic into the tissue between the third and fourth vertebrae. It was my first spinal tap, and I gingerly pushed the needle and trocar through the soft tissue, worrying that I was going to pierce the spinal cord. My hands shook in a fine tremor; beads of perspiration wet my brow. I advanced the needle in micron-size increments. It must have taken ten minutes to go an inch. When the needle finally perforated the sac around the spinal column, clear fluid bubbled back through the hub. The resident congratulated me on a "champagne tap," free of blood. We sent the fluid off to the laboratory.

Later that evening, test results started coming back. Blood tests for kidney and liver disease were negative. The spinal fluid was clean, ruling out an infection. But when the level of thyroid-stimulating hormone came back, it was off the scale. My patient had the worst case of hypothyroidism the doctors had ever seen.

The next day, his mother brought in a brown bag. Inside it was an empty prescription bottle. Sure enough, it was for thyroid hormone; he had been taking the medicine at home but had stopped six months earlier after it ran out, slowly sinking into an amnesiac delirium that made him forget he needed it, a lapse that almost cost him his life. Hypothyroid coma has a 20 percent mortality rate even if diagnosed and treated appropriately.

As in physics, everything fit together nicely. His condition had been a puzzle, but through logic and judicious testing, I had solved it. I felt proud of myself.

The next morning I ran into my resident and told him I had made the diagnosis. "Let me guess," he said. "Hypothyroidism."

"How did you know?" I asked in disbelief.

"I tapped on his knee," he replied; the tap had elicited the slow reflex that is a classic sign of the disease. I had been taught this clinical pearl in class, but as with most of what I learned during the first two years of medical school, I had forgotten it. The lapse had caused my patient to undergo a painful procedure he probably didn't need.

I often felt intimidated by the clinical acumen of my internal medicine superiors. On morning rounds, their eyes would turn to me and my throat would tighten and my mind seize, like an engine low on oil. I admired their snappy, confident style. I wasn't sure how much I had in common with them, but fundamentally I knew I wanted to be like them. One afternoon, I watched a resident struggle to reinsert a breathing tube into a morbidly obese man with severe emphysema who, in a fit of delirium, had yanked it out. The patient was choking, grabbing his neck with one hand as he fought off the resident with the other. A pulmonologist suddenly appeared. He strode up to the bedside, pulled out a metal laryngoscope from his coat pocket, violently pulled the man's head back and inserted a new breathing tube in one seemingly continuous motion. The whole thing took less than thirty seconds. "Carry on," he said, strutting out of the room in a theatrical flourish. I must have looked awestruck. "That's Hoffman," the resident said. "He likes to intubate people." I remembered him from a lecture he had given on respiratory physiology. In the lecture hall he seemed pedantic and disorganized, his handouts poorly written and pedagogically unsound, but in the hospital he was *the man*, powerful and in command. I envied his confidence, his swaggering style. It was what I yearned for in my new profession.

So, in the end, I decided on internal medicine. In internal medicine, there was more to know, more to do, more potential to help people, and more potential to impress. It was, it seemed, doctoring in its essence.

Medical school graduation fell on my parents' thirty-third wedding anniversary, an unplanned but perfect gift. They beamed with pride as I strode into the auditorium in my cap and flowing blue gown. The commencement address was delivered by Dean Dowton, a pediatrician who spoke eloquently about his early dreams of becoming a doctor while growing up in the outback of Australia. "From that limited horizon," he said, "I knew nothing of the world at large, let alone the world of medicine." His words resonated with me. Not so long ago, ensconced in academia in a college town overloaded with knowledge and ambition, I had felt the same way.

"Here today," he went on, "we watch the best and brightest transit from an environment which is familiar to one which is new and exciting, even if a little anxiety-provoking. The world these new physicians enter will be one of contrasts: savoring success on the one hand, demanding duty on the other; exalted expectation, followed by endless effort. Are you, new medical graduates, entering a world beyond reach, away from the rest of society?"

He went on to talk about what could be done to bridge the gap between the world of medicine and the world at large. "There are tangible things we all can do to make certain medicine is not a world beyond. You, parents and partners, will be a window through which these new doctors will look into the real world. You will serve this role many times over. We need those who care about us to provide a mirror for our actions as we step out into the brave new world." To me, his comments seemed ironic at the very least. From the ivory tower of the university, the world of medicine and the real world had seemed one and the same. That was why I had decided to become a doctor in the first place. But evidently for someone who had spent enough time in the world of medicine, it was its own ivory tower, removed from the world at large.

He directed his final remarks to us graduates. "Don't be afraid to say 'I don't know.' It gets easier every time you do it. Never be afraid to admit you don't know something, most especially to your patients, but in doing so make a commitment to do your best to find out. No matter the tongue-lashing you might take from a Socratic superior, don't be tempted to hide your ignorance—it is an addiction far too rampant in medicine of all ilks today."

In closing, he offered this thought: "Keep a simple value system. Work out what things in life you care about, the beliefs you hold near and dear, and stick to them. You are about to go through a most tumultuous time. What are you willing to accept? What are you willing to fight for?" I wrote it down in my Palm Pilot: *Figure out a value system.* Arriving in New York a month later, I still didn't have a system down, but I did have some vague ideas about the kind of doctor I hoped to become.

bogus doctor

Buy a long stethoscope.

—ADVICE FROM A MEDICAL SCHOOL PROFESSOR

I spent the first morning of internship running errands. I picked
up a pager from the telecommunications office and a stack of
light brown scrubs and short white coats from the hospital laun-
dry. Unlike other teaching hospitals in Manhattan, at New York Hospital only attending physicians and clinical fellows were allowed to wear
long coats. This had provoked some grousing during orientation, as
my classmates seemed eager to show off their new status as physicians, but it didn't bother me. I didn't feel like much of a doctor yet.

Back in my apartment, I tried one on. In medical school I had always felt proud of my short white coat, walking home through the Central West End with my stethoscope jutting out of the waist pocket. Now,
as I put on a white coat for the first time as a doctor, a sense of pride
washed over me once again. Despite any misgivings I had about medicine, the uniform conferred authority, cachet, membership in an exclu-
sive guild. I stuffed the pockets with useful paraphernalia: a *Pocket
Pharmacopeia*, a *Sanford Guide to Antimicrobial Therapy*, a *Facts and Formu-
las*, a *Washington Manual of Medical Therapeutics*, a small notebook, my
Palm Pilot, a few pens, a stethoscope, a reflex hammer, a tuning fork, a
penlight, a small ruler, a pair of EKG calipers, and a handful of alcohol
swabs. I could have added more, but my shoulders were starting to sag.

I checked myself out in the mirror. I still looked like a medical student, not a resident, much less a doctor. I poked a Washington University School of Medicine pin through a lapel. I clipped my photo ID onto the chest pocket. Someone had once told me that when you become an intern, nurses treat you better because now you can write orders. But I certainly didn't feel any different.

Earlier that morning, at 9:00 a.m. in the wood-paneled clinic conference room, Dr. John Bele, a short man with a penchant for pink shirts, yellow ties, and loafers, had distributed orientation packets and quickly gone over the broad outlines of the rotation. As Dr. Wood had promised, there was to be no call. Unlike our colleagues in the main hospital building across the street, we were going to have weekends off because the clinic was closed. Most days we'd be finished by five or six o'clock, he said, except Tuesdays, when there was evening practice. Teaching conferences were held every day at noon in the main hospital. Lunch was usually provided. Grand Rounds were on Thursday mornings; attendance was mandatory.

He had passed out an exam testing our knowledge of primary care. When we were done with it, we could leave; none of us had patients scheduled that first morning. The test questions were straightforward, having more to do with ethics and doctor-patient relations than management of specific clinical conditions. Even as I was taking the test, I wondered how I was doing in comparison to the others. Some habits from medical school die hard.

After lunch, I walked back to the clinic. The air was thick and still. On the sidewalk, blooming tulips rose out of the gated tree plots like hands coming out of a grave. I took off my coat and swung it over my shoulder. Its contents spilled all over the sidewalk.

The clinic was divided into color-coded sections, though the carpet was one long, continuous gray. For the afternoon, I had been assigned to the Red Area. My room was a crowded space with a computer, a small desk, two chairs, and a sink. In the bookcase were a few outdated textbooks. Next to the sink was a box for used needles. From the orientation packet I fished out the temporary password I had been given—

"bogus doctor"—and typed it into the computer. Four patients were scheduled to see me that afternoon. One, Jimmie Washington, had already checked in. According to her chart, she was a seventy-one-year-old resident of Harlem who had had a radical mastectomy for a breast tumor that turned out to be benign. Over the years, she had suffered from various intestinal ailments, including chronic diarrhea, but an extensive workup had revealed nothing abnormal. Before going out to the waiting area, I phoned her gastroenterologist to inquire about the results of her most recent colonoscopy. "She's fine," he declared, sounding amused. But what did her colonoscopy show? "She's fine!" he repeated.

In the waiting room, patients were buzzing around the front desk, which, with its tall mahogany counter flanked by tall ferns, resembled a fortress. Washington was supposed to be an elderly black woman, but there were several out there. Which one was she? I felt shy about calling out her name. I made a first pass, pretending to be going somewhere, and then doubled back after identifying two potential candidates. I tapped one of them on the shoulder. "Ms. Washington?" I said, the words catching in my throat.

A woman bolted out of a nearby chair like a private at boot camp. "That's *Dr.* Washington!" she cried. She was a statuesque woman, wearing bright yellow bell-bottoms, a pink floral sweater, and a leopard-skin-print top. Her broad face was adorned with big hanging hoop earrings, large tinted glasses, and a thick smear of rouge. Her hair was tightly spun into a glazed Jheri curl. She looked like a character out of a 1970s blaxploitation film.

She bent down stiffly to pick up her cloth bag. "About time," she grumbled loudly. "I can't be waitin' all day."

I felt heat rise up to my face. "Please come with me, ma'am . . . I mean, Doctor," I stammered.

"Hmmph! I been a doctor for fifty years," she announced, following me. By now other patients were looking on. "Dr. Washington does not want to wait!"

In my room, she hung up her scarf on the door hook and dropped her bag on a chair. With her in it, the room felt even more cramped and confining.

"What kind of doctor are you?" I asked gently.

"Ob-stitian gan-cology," she replied, mangling the words.

"Oh, so you deliver babies. Where do you practice?"

"In Harlem," she said, her voice again rising. "Hmmph! I been de-liverin' babies for fifty years. I been a doctor since before you was born."

I looked over her chart. I asked her why she had had a radical mas-tectomy. The modified procedure, in which the chest-wall muscles are left largely intact, had been shown to be just as effective for treating breast cancer. "They wasn't sure it was cancer," she recalled. "They said, 'Jimmie, what you want to do?' and I said, 'You get rid of it, I don't need it!' My friends, they wanted to hold on to their titty, but then they died and lost their titty anyhow. No, uh-uh, I don't need that!"

And how had she been feeling? "I still be coughin' some. My leg is swoll, too. What the hell wrong with my foot? It done hurt so bad, I can't even put a blanket on it. Sometimes I get short-winded. I gots di-arrhea, too. That's why I came up here for."

"I see . . . And how's the diarrhea?"

"It ain't as bad as it was, but it still *baaad*!"

The diarrhea was intermittent, occurring no more than a few times a week, and was of a normal color. I asked her if she had eaten any-thing unusual recently. "What you mean?" she asked suspiciously.

"Anything out of the ordinary. Like from a restaurant."

"I can't afford no restaurant!" she replied, exasperated.

I pulled a fresh sheet of paper onto the brown vinyl examination table and asked her to sit on it. I started to wrap a blood pressure cuff around her left arm, the side of the mastectomy, but she stopped me and told me to put the cuff on the other side. I didn't know why, but I complied with her request. I quickly inflated the cuff. Then I let the pressure out slowly, listening with my stethoscope at the bend of her arm. One-twenty over eighty. Normal. I put two fingers on her wrist and counted her pulse. Then I counted her breaths, pretending to still count her pulse so as not to make her self-conscious and change her breathing pattern, just as I had been taught in medical school. All vital signs were normal.

An ophthalmoscope was attached to the wall. I tried looking into her eyes, pressing my face against hers—eye to eye, cheek to cheek—but her eyeballs jiggled and I couldn't get an adequate view. Close up, the topography of her face was rough, scalloped, pitted, like a lunar landscape. There were a few thick gray hairs growing out of her chin. She smelled of cheap perfume and hair oil, but the odor was inoffensive, even slightly pleasant. Her warm breath smelled nice, too, like she had just chewed mint gum. It occurred to me that she might have made herself up just for my benefit.

I twisted a plastic guard onto my otoscope and looked into her ears. They were waxy but I could still make out the gray eardrums, and as best I could tell, they looked normal. The right side of her chest had been almost totally replaced by scar tissue. I pressed my fingertips on it, and on her neck and armpits, too, feeling for any abnormal lymph nodes, but there were none. I placed my stethoscope on her back, then on her chest, listening to the patter of her heartbeat. It was hypnotic, and as I listened to it, my mind wandered to Berkeley and Lisa and my laser table and the balcony up at Lawrence Berkeley Labs and the International House and my parents, and all this happened in an instant, and then she squirmed and I wondered how long I had been daydreaming, and had she noticed?

When I was done with the exam, I helped her off the table and back into the chair. Then it occurred to me; I had forgotten something: the rectal exam. Was it really necessary? Her most recent colonoscopy had been normal; even her gastroenterologist had said she was fine. But what if my preceptor asked about it? I didn't want to appear like someone who avoided doing rectal exams. "I'm sorry, ma'am, but I think we will need to do a rectal exam," I said fearfully. "Whatever you say, Doctor," she replied, shrugging. Clearly my uniform had conferred an authority upon me that my experience did not warrant. That, or else this lady really liked going to the doctor.

I stepped outside as she undressed. I hated rectals. Just thinking about inserting my finger in someone's rectum made me nauseated. In medical school I had never been able to do one without gagging. Once, a GI fellow had performed a rectal exam on my moribund patient while I was still in the room. I remembered how incredulous I felt when he started gesturing at me with his stool-smeared finger! Some people were so comfortable with the human body. No wonder they became doctors.

When I went back in, she was lying on the table, buck naked. Evidently I had forgotten to give her a gown. I reached into a drawer and pulled one out, and she put it on. I laid out the materials I was going to use on the counter next to the sink. Stool developer (I unscrewed the top so I wouldn't contaminate the bottle). Guaiac card. Lubricating gel. I handed her a wad of Kleenex for afterward, something a paid volunteer in medical school had told me was a considerate gesture most doctors forgot.

How to do this? I could have her bend over, but that seemed unseemly, so I asked her to lie on her side, facing the wall. I put on latex gloves and smeared gel on my index finger. Suddenly it felt heavy. Stepping behind her, I paused respectfully. She looked over her shoulder. "Go ahead, help y'self," she said.

Her generous buttocks, lined with wrinkly stretch marks like water tracks on a dirt road, swallowed up my hand. A fetid odor rose up to my nostrils. I pressed on the spongy wall of her rectum, feeling for masses. Even if one had been there, I probably wouldn't have known because I had never felt a rectal mass before. Holding my breath, I removed my finger and smeared brown film onto the card. I applied a few drops of developer on the stool but the color didn't change, meaning there was no blood. I felt relieved; nothing more to do. I stripped off my gloves, trying hard not to look at them. Then it started. My tongue curled up and my eyes started watering. A dry heave welled up in my chest and I felt my legs start to go. I took a deep breath and tried to think of something, anything—dead kittens!—but I heaved and a tear rolled down my cheek. I closed my eyes, and for a moment both she and I were breathing fast. I vigorously shook my head, trying to rid it of the brown, feculent visual. It was all I could do to chuck the gloves into the waste bin before I vomited.

I left Ms. Washington and went to see my preceptor, Dr. Lane, who was talking on the phone in her office. She motioned for me to take a seat under the many framed certificates that adorned the walls. When I described the case, she agreed with my plan, which was basically to use antidiarrheals on an as-needed basis. Back in my room, I gave Ms. Washington a prescription and a follow-up appointment in three months. "Make it two," she said, retouching her makeup with the aid of a compact mirror. "Okay, two," I said, changing the appointment. Then she gathered up her things, meticulously tied her scarf, slung her bag over her shoulder, and left.

My first patient, I thought. An "ob-gyn" who could have been invented by Melvin Van Peebles! New York was full of these people, larger-than-life characters who seemed to have walked off the celluloid. It was one of the reasons I had wanted to come here. *At the very least*, I told myself, *this is going to be an interesting year.*

THAT WEEKEND, I had an invitation to an exhibition of Indian art at the apartment of an acquaintance on the Upper East Side. I asked my classmate Vijay if he wanted to come along, and he gladly said yes. We met in the lobby of my apartment building next to the hospital and walked to the party. It was a warm Saturday night. The leaves of the flowering pear trees were shimmering, as if decorated with tiny Christmas lights. A rich floral bouquet wafted from sidewalk fruit stands. Pretty, fresh-faced women in stylish summer dresses were strolling around the neighborhood in tight-knit groups. Old men were sitting on benches in front of shuttered storefronts spouting off about the Mets or perhaps their medications. Walking along side streets, we encountered young people on brownstone stoops giggling, cuddling, smoking marijuana. The buildings were pale, staggered, seemingly endless. All the movement, the lights, etched tiny scratches in my brain. Just living in New York, I thought, could be a full-time job.

The door was open when we arrived at the party. I poured a drink for myself in the kitchen and maneuvered my way through the packed crowd to the living room, where a red-sari-clad woman in a painting was standing on a balcony similar to the one at my grandfather's flat in New Delhi. Her hand covered her mouth in an enigmatic expression of shock or perhaps boredom. "What do you think she's thinking?" I asked the woman standing next to me, who was also staring at the painting. "I think she's unhappy with her marriage," the woman replied without missing a beat. Intrigued, I introduced myself and we started talking. Sonia Sharma was a third-year medical student at George Washington University in Washington, D.C., who was spending the summer doing a cardiology elective at St. Luke's-Roosevelt Hospital Center on the Upper West Side. She was pretty, flirtatiously mirthful, with olive-colored skin, flowing dark brown hair, and dimples that deepened into beautiful trenches when she smiled, which was often. She was wearing a light blue J. Crew dress and brown platform sandals. After chatting for a while, she invited Vijay and me to join her and her sister at a nightclub after the party.

At ten o'clock, Vijay and I paid Shannon a visit at the Hi-Life. As I was telling her about the nice Indian girl I'd just met, I realized I had forgotten to get Sonia's mobile phone number. Now, I was going to have to find her in a packed Manhattan nightclub on a Saturday night. Though it was getting late, Vijay and I took a cab to midtown, near Times Square. After waiting endlessly in a line that weaved halfway around the block and then answering some impertinent questions from the burly bouncer—yes, we were doctors, how did he know?—we got into the club. Miraculously, it seemed, wandering through the smoky haze, we found Sonia and her sister. They seemed glad to see us, and for a couple of hours we smoked cigarettes and shouted at each other over the deafening drumbeat. The alcohol, the hip-hop, the buzz—I felt more free and relaxed than I had in a long time, even a bit reckless; it was like I was in graduate school again. We stayed until the club closed at 2:00 a.m. When we parted, Sonia and I exchanged numbers. *Groovy girl*, I thought, riding home. *Too bad she's a medical student.* I was hoping to date someone Indian, but I was pretty sure I didn't want to marry a doctor.

THE CLINIC MONTH WENT BY QUICKLY. With controlled hours and no call, the rotation was fairly easy, leaving me to wonder whether it wouldn't have been better to be thrown into the fire of inpatient medicine earlier. I fell into a comfortable routine, running along the East River in the morning, which helped relieve stress. Since I didn't have to be in clinic until nine o'clock, some mornings I would turn on the television and watch the CNBC talking heads intone pedantically about how the Internet was going to change the face of business. "Does it justify the stratospheric stock prices?" someone would invariably ask, and the response was almost stereotyped, half smile, expression of tired resignation: "Only time will tell."

New York patients had an edge, a roughness, an unsavoriness that kept me on my toes. There was the gay man who'd gotten into a fight on the subway and sprained his shoulder; the alcoholic who wanted to get drunk but compromised and sniffed cocaine instead; the old ladies who had more wrinkles on their legs than on their faces. One afternoon, a middle-aged woman came to me with a surprise. The severe lower back and leg pain and numbness that had plagued her for months, making it impossible for her to even sit in a chair, had all but disappeared. She informed me that she had canceled her back surgery scheduled for later in the month.

But all was not well. Her neck and shoulder, only mildly bothersome previously, now ached as if in a vise. Her left arm was almost entirely numb, except for shooting pains when she flexed her neck. Though a recent MRI had been normal, I was pretty sure she had pinched a nerve in her neck, probably from a herniated disc.

I asked her to close her eyes and gently stroked her left arm. She felt nothing. I stroked a little harder. Still nothing. The sensation in her right arm was normal, but her left arm, even when I scratched it with my nails, was completely numb.

But this didn't make sense. Though her sensory deficit was profound, she had walked in clutching her handbag. And her muscle strength and reflexes were normal and equal in both arms. When I noticed that her closed eyelids fluttered gently whenever I touched her left arm, I could draw only one conclusion: she was lying.

The following week, I attended a lunchtime conference where a bespectacled forensic psychiatrist spoke to us about malingering. "Deception by patients is common," he said, and doctors, because of fear of confrontation or a desire to give patients the benefit of the doubt, often don't pick up on it. Sometimes it is obvious, as when a patient with a back injury cannot go to work but can keep up with his bowling league. Other times the deception is so complete that the lying patient can outfox even the most astute clinician.

Years later, I learned that the lying can assume different guises. One is called *malingering*: the intentional production of false or grossly exaggerated physical or psychiatric symptoms motivated by the desire to avoid work, evade prosecution, obtain drugs, and so on. Another, spurred by the need to play the role of a sick person, is termed *factitious disorder*. When patients lie to themselves, convincing themselves that they are sick when they are not, the condition is called *somatization disorder*.

Whatever the cause, deception by patients is rarely straightforward or simple. Patients may omit details, deliberately or not, or they may fabricate them. They may feign symptoms that do not exist (*simulation*), or intentionally hide symptoms that do (*dissimulation*). They may even tamper with data or laboratory substances.

Malingering patients signal their deception in a variety of ways, the speaker told us that afternoon. They may give hesitant answers or make vague or irrelevant statements. They may express exaggerated confidence in their doctor's ability. Like my patient, they may feel compelled to perform suspiciously poorly on testing.

The most valuable tools for detecting deception are being aware that one might be lied to, asking open-ended questions, and prolonging the medical interview. But, he added, doctors must also know their medicine—for example, that deficits like inability to feel pain or judge temperature often occur together because these sensations are carried by the same nerves.

Very little guidance is provided to doctors for handling malingering patients. Some advocate confronting them. Others feel that this strategy can alienate patients and instead prefer a more sympathetic approach, treating the deception as a symptom. But in the end, the psychiatrist said, the problem was generally confusing and the management of it unsatisfying.

FOR MUCH OF THE OUTPATIENT ROTATION, my classmate Ali had been saying that all of us should get together for drinks, so early one evening toward the end of the month, we met at an alehouse near the hospital. It was a typical Irish pub, with low wooden ceilings, murky lighting, and dartboards. Except for Emily, our entire outpatient group showed up: Cynthia, a pretty, troubled brunette with an asthenic build and pale complexion who was as ambivalent about medicine as I; Vijay, who had accompanied me on the night I met Sonia; Ali, a stocky Persian with a broad face, big brown eyes, and a ski-jump nose—he was all head; Alphonse, a quiet, unassuming man from the Caribbean; and Rachel, a knockout blonde with a Mary Tyler Moore hairdo who always seemed to be wearing a scowl on her face. (She bugged me; something about her smelled of money and high society.) We pulled two tables together and ordered pitchers of beer. At first we were formal with each other, but after a drink or two, everybody started to loosen up.

"Isn't it weird not to be graded after so many years?" someone said as we munched on popcorn. There were murmurs of agreement. We had all become so reward-dependent.

We laughed about our mishaps over the month. Cynthia said she still hadn't figured out how to work the computer system. Just last week she had ordered blood tests for a patient that somehow never got transmitted to the lab, so for forty-five minutes the lab kept sending the patient back to her office, asking her to reorder the tests. Ali emitted a loud, uninhibited cackle not unlike the laugh of a hyena.

Rachel said the clinic experience had convinced her to subspecialize. She recounted how one morning she had seen a patient whose voice was hoarse. She had no idea what was wrong with him, but her preceptor, on a routine flyby, immediately diagnosed goiter, an enlargement of the thyroid gland. "You have to know too much to do primary care," she said. "I just want to focus on something I can be good at."

"It's strange," Ali said. "Sometimes it feels like I'm wearing someone else's clothes and I can't wait to get home to put mine back on." We all nodded. We all felt the same way.

"Does anyone here think we're really helping patients?" Cynthia asked skeptically. "I mean, I can't convince myself that what we're doing is making that much of a difference."

"I don't know," I answered, surprised to find myself defending the profession. "Look at lawyers. What do they contribute?"

Afterward, around eight o'clock in the evening, I walked alone to Central Park. Someone had once told me that when he was a kid visiting New York, he thought the avenues were like tunnels. When I crossed Park Avenue, I saw what he meant. In the distance the apartment houses, rising majestically, seemed to reach out to each other, as if collapsing under the weight of their own grandeur.

I sat down by a tree near the park entrance. A stooped man wearing a blue overcoat and a bowler was feeding nuts to squirrels, beckoning them with, "Come, come, come, little boy." A tiny mouse was chasing its own tail in the grass, going round and round, tirelessly, ceaselessly; a crowd had gathered to watch it. I looked up at the magnificent buildings on Fifth Avenue with their balustraded terraces and molded façades, each a small world in itself, reaching up to the sky.

In the grass I perused a handbook on critical care cardiology Rajiv had loaned me. In internship your next hurdle is always the biggest, and yet this evening, that really seemed to be the case. The cardiac care unit at New York Hospital was the epitome of pressurized, high-intensity medicine. For all intents and purposes, my residency was going to begin on Monday: overnight call, emergencies, all the craziness and hullabaloo of inpatient medicine. Residents in the CCU wore cotton scrubs like a badge of honor. The very term told me that I was finally going to get my hands dirty.

I thought back to my one and only experience in the CCU, in my first clinical clerkship in internal medicine at the beginning of my third year in medical school. I was working with a star resident of the internal medicine program at St. Louis. David was confident, competent, quick. He thrived under pressure.

One afternoon, my team was called to the CCU. A patient, James Abbott, had just been admitted with excruciating chest pain that had started a few hours earlier. He was in his early fifties, extensively tattooed, just the sort of tough I wouldn't want to meet alone in a parking lot at night—but right then he was whimpering. He kept stroking his sternum up and down, as if trying to rub the pain away. It was obvious that he was having a heart attack. He had all the classic risk factors: hypertension, high cholesterol, a history of cigarette smoking. His electrocardiogram and blood tests showed characteristic signs of low blood flow to the heart muscle. I don't recall our examining him, but for this most common type of cardiac emergency, there is little diagnostic role for the physical exam.

A few hours later, we were paged back to the CCU. Abbott was now writhing in pain, and his blood pressure was dropping. David had a nurse get an electrocardiogram. He ordered an intern to prepare to insert a catheter into Abbott's radial artery. Then he asked for an intubation tray. "Check his blood pressure," he told me.

I had measured blood pressure only a few times, mostly in my classmates. I carefully wrapped the cuff around Abbott's left arm and inflated it. Then I let the pressure out slowly, listening with my stethoscope at the bend of his arm. "One hundred over sixty," I called out.

"Check the other arm," David said. By then he was scrubbing Abbott's arm with iodine soap. More people arrived, attracted by the commotion. I wrapped the cuff around the right arm and quickly inflated it, but when I let out the pressure, I heard nothing. *Must be doing something wrong*, I thought. I tried again while people jostled me, with the same result. *Must be the noise*, I shrugged, and I let it go. For a moment I thought to ask David to check the pressure himself, but he was busy doing more important things.

The next morning David caught me before rounds. His face was pale. "That guy had an aortic dissection," he said. A CAT scan had revealed a corkscrew-like tear from the abdominal aorta all the way back to the heart. "The night resident picked it up," he said. "He noticed there was a pulse deficit between the arms. No pressure on the right."

I listened in silence. A pulse deficit is a classic sign of aortic dissection, but in the hubbub of the previous afternoon, I had somehow ignored it. I thought about telling David about the blood pressure measurement I had taken, but I didn't. Abbott's dissection was by now far advanced, and surgeons who had been consulted said he would not survive an operation. He died eight hours later.

For weeks I couldn't get over the idea that I was somehow responsible for Abbott's death. If we had caught the dissection the previous day, was there a chance he could have been saved? I eventually managed to convince myself that the death wasn't entirely my fault. But that didn't make me any less afraid of cardiac patients.

I closed the cardiology book and got up. A leaf fluttered to the ground, its shadow flitting to meet it. The memory of Mr. Abbott had left me feeling nervous, blunting the good feeling I had had when I entered the park. I sprinted home to get in some more reading.

on call

"When I die," said dear and whimsical old Doctor Pycroft, "I shall have a bell hung on my head-stone, with an inscription asking the compassionate passer-by to ring it long and loud. And I shan't get up."

—REGINALD L. HINE, *CONFESSIONS OF AN UNCOMMON ATTORNEY*, 1946

Mrs. Piniella is dead." The words came to me in a dream, resonating in my head like a Gregorian chant.

"Mrs. Piniella is dead." Those words again; what did they mean? Who was Mrs. Piniella? Why was she dead?

My eyes opened to find a ghastly face peering at me. I recoiled, as if from a jolt, emitting a short, muted howl. The gargoyle moved in closer, too fast for my eyes to accommodate.

"Wake up, Doctor," the nurse said. "Mrs. Piniella is dead." Her face, silhouetted eerily by the corridor light, was now just inches from mine. I stared at it, uncomprehending.

"That means you have to pronounce her," came a gentle voice from across the call room. It was Steve Coles, the resident who was supervising me in the CCU. The exchange must have woken him, too. "Just go and examine her and write a quick note," he said.

I closed my eyes, trying to return to my dream.

"Doctor, wake up," the nurse pleaded, shaking me gently the way my mother used to on middle-school mornings. She was short and stocky, with a broad Filipino mug and a mop of ink black hair. Her stale breath warmed my face.

"Okay, I'm coming," I said. I turned over onto my stomach. The thudding in my chest reverberated across the tiny mattress. This was a different kind of fatigue than I had ever experienced, a tiredness mixed with unnatural excitation that went straight into the bones. I heard the door close.

A few minutes later I was drifting back to sleep when Steve's voice jarred me awake. "Just write a quick note," he called out. "And make sure you call the family."

I pulled myself out of the cot and stumbled in the dark to the bathroom. Leaning over the sink, I splashed cold water into my eyes. Though I had been asleep for only half an hour, my mouth felt dirty, so I rinsed it with some hospital mouthwash. Then I turned off the light and tiptoed back through the call room. Slinging on my white coat, I opened the door. Light flooded in from the hallway; I exited and shut the door quickly.

I passed through the conference room, which was littered with printouts, X-rays, and the detritus of the previous evening's meal. Faded scrubs and stained white coats were draped over the backs of chairs. Candy wrappers and empty potato chip bags had accumulated in the space between the computers. I plodded to the nursing station. Five in the morning is a strange time to be awake, the nexus between night and day, when everything moves slower and trying to speed it up seems almost obscene. Suddenly I stopped, fumbling through my coat pockets. I was carrying laminated cards for Normal Lab Values, Cholesterol Guidelines, Framingham Risk Assessment, Pediatric Growth Charts—everything, it seemed, but the one thing I needed most: Death Pronouncement. How was I going to do this? I had never declared someone dead before. It wasn't taught in medical school, and they hadn't gone over it during orientation. Steve undoubtedly knew what to do, but he was sleeping, and I didn't want to wake him up. All day I had hovered around him like a shy toddler around a parent on his first day of preschool. I didn't want him to think that I could do nothing on my own.

The nurse who had woken me looked up from her beauty magazine and pointed her head in the direction of the room. "How'd she die?" I asked. The nurse shrugged her shoulders. "She just died," she answered flatly.

Without alarms, the room was eerily quiet. Taking a deep breath, I went in. Nancy, a fellow intern, had signed out that Mrs. Piniella was probably going to pass away tonight. For most of the day she had displayed "agonal" breathing—loud gulps of air followed by prolonged periods of apnea, or no breathing—a pattern that frequently heralds death. I inched up to her body. "Mrs. Piniella," I whispered. I removed the bedsheet. Corpses had always made me feel queasy. In anatomy lab I had mostly watched as others dissected. Her eyes were closed, her mouth slightly open, her nostrils flaring a bit, a snakelike plastic tube hanging out of one of them. Her arms were grossly swollen and had a pale bluish tinge. I gently pushed on her chest. "Mrs. Piniella." She did not move, but then I had never seen her move. I pinched her hand. I rubbed my knuckles on her breastbone, trying to elicit some response. There was none.

I racked my brain, trying to remember what to do to verify a patient's death. I vaguely recalled that you had to establish the demise of three major organ systems: the brain, the heart, and the lungs. I shined a penlight at her pupils. They were fixed and dilated. I shook her and called out her name. No response. I applied my stethoscope to her chest. It was deathly quiet. I put two fingertips on her carotid artery, and for a moment I thought I felt a pulse—could she have a pulse without a heartbeat?—until I realized that it was probably just my own, transmitted through my fingertips.

I draped the sheet back over her face. "Yes, she's dead," I told the nurse outside, as if the whole exercise had been some sort of test.

"You have to write a note, Doctor, and put an order in the computer."

"Order for what?"

"The order that she is dead."

The order that she is dead?? My lips curled up into a grin, inviting the nurse to laugh with me at the absurdity of her request, but she just continued to stare at me blank-faced.

"All right," I finally said.

I sat down and jotted a brief note. "Called by nurse to pronounce death at 5:10 a.m. Patient had no spontaneous respirations. On exam: no breath sounds, no heartbeat, no pulse. Assessment: Death. Plan: No resuscitation, as patient was DNR."

I entered an order into the computer. Unlike most orders, this one was just one simple click. I filled out the death certificate. Under "cause of death," I wrote "cardiac arrest." Under "due to or as a consequence of," I wrote "heart failure." "Was an autopsy performed?" I checked "no." I wasn't about to call the family at this hour to ask for one. The nurse looked over my shoulder.

"You have to change the time of death, Doctor."

I looked up. "Why?"

"Because I put four o'clock in my note, and there cannot be a discrepancy." Sure enough, she had written "4 a.m." on the previous page.

"But when did she die?" I asked, puzzled.

"About an hour ago, Doctor," the nurse declared, a bit flustered. "I did not want to wake you. You looked tired."

It was too early to argue, so I wrote another note. The computer wouldn't let me backdate the order, so I left it the way it was.

Back in the call room, Steve was lying awake. "Did you pronounce her?" he asked.

"Yes," I replied.

"Everything okay?"

"Yes, no problems."

"Did you call the family?"

"Uh, no."

"And the attending?"

I knew I had forgotten something. I went back outside and made the calls. Mrs. Piniella's niece seemed relieved when I delivered the news that her aunt had died. The attending physician sounded annoyed for being woken.

It was too late to go back to bed—I didn't think I'd be able to wake up again—so I took a seat in the conference room and looked over the whiteboard. It was divided into a grid, with each square representing a patient's room. Within each square were tiny unfilled boxes denoting tasks that still had to be completed: "CBC Q4," "blood cultures x2," "wean vent." In my mind, I went over the past twenty-four hours, my first day in the CCU. When I arrived yesterday morning at six-thirty, I was met by Amanda and Nancy, my fellow interns in the CCU. Amanda was a soft-spoken woman with large, quiet brown eyes who had gone to Yale as an undergraduate and then to medical school in the South, which left her with a winsome mix of southern drawl and clipped New England patois. As I would soon discover, she always came in early to preround and finish her daily progress notes before the attending physician arrived. Her unassuming, intelligent manner was very appealing. Nancy was a good-looking blonde with a rather severe visage and matching personality who reminded me of the nurse Hot Lips Houlihan from the television show *M*A*S*H*. She had gone to medical school here at Cornell with Vijay, who had warned me that she was competitive, even a bit cutthroat.

Amanda and Nancy had come in early to receive sign-out from the departing intern. They had already divided up the fourteen patients, taking five each and giving me four. "So there's an advantage to coming in late," I quipped. Nancy forced a smile and handed me a stack of sheets. "You'll need these for rounds," she said curtly.

The CCU was a rectangle, with most of the rooms arrayed along a long wall running parallel to the East River. There was a central bay with a nursing station and a medication room. At the front entrance were a clerk's desk and a pneumatic tube system for ferrying specimens to the laboratory in the basement. At least once an hour one could hear the *hut-hut-hut* of a test tube containing a blood sample being whisked away for analysis. Sleek and modern, constantly buzzing, the CCU occupied a world apart from the rest of the hospital, which by comparison was relatively staid. Staff were constantly walking through, wheeling machines. Alarms rang incessantly. Consultants were always around, scribbling notes. That first morning, the nurses were in the middle of their change-of-shift routine. "Bed Two is still constipated," a nurse announced. "She hasn't had a bowel movement for me in three days. Bed Four got agitated again last night, requiring Xanax, which he's still getting PRN. Seven is status-post a 250 cc bolus of normal saline because he was running tachycardic most of the night. Twelve was suctioned once: large, yellow . . ."

I hurried to see my patients before attending rounds began at eight o'clock. The first of them, Paolo Fellini, was a well-to-do businessman who had been enjoying his retirement for years when he was felled by a massive heart attack. Over the ensuing weeks, he had suffered numerous complications, including respiratory failure requiring a ventilator, blood infections requiring broad-spectrum antibiotics, and a stroke, which incarcerated him in a sort of dementia that left him unable to recognize even his grandchildren, whose get-well cards were pasted all over the walls. On his bedside table was a picture of him standing on a boat, smiling broadly, looking every bit the Connecticut waterman he once was, a stark contrast to the man who lay before me. He was now wearing a diaper—judging by the fetid odor, it was filled with stool—and a hospital gown that was more off his body than on. His mouth was open: a thick crust coated his lips and tongue. His legs were twisted into an unnatural position, a result, no doubt, of his stroke. On his arms were large purplish bruises where attempts had been made to draw blood, and several tears in his paper-thin skin were still oozing. A plastic tracheotomy tube jutted out of his throat, connecting to a blue baffled hose that originated from a spigot in the wall. A bag was attached to his bed railing, filled with Coca Cola–colored urine. At the bedside were a teal blue IV monitor, several oxygen canisters, a ventilation bag, and a bundle of purple tubes which snaked across the floor and fed into inflatable cuffs on his legs. A bag of milky tube feeds and several bags of clear medicated fluids were hanging on a metal hook suspended from the ceiling. Above his head, connected to a flexible metal crane, was a small television, which was off.

When I got near him, his eyes jiggled apprehensively in their sockets. "Good morning," I said. "I'm Dr. Jauhar." His breath faintly smelled of old rice. "What is your name?" He did not respond. "Do you know where you are?" I reached for my stethoscope. On the monitor, his heartbeat quickened and his breathing became more rapid and shallow. The ventilator started wailing. For all the talk of coma, he clearly sensed my presence.

His ribs poked out of his bony chest like spokes on a wheel. So rippled was the topography of his chest that I could not find a flat place to put my stethoscope. I finally wedged it between two ribs. "I'm not going to hurt you," I said as he grimaced horribly. I had read that patients who make it out of intensive care units often liken the experience to combat. Many suffer chronic anxiety and depression; others develop post-traumatic stress disorder. Drugs like morphine and fentanyl are used not just for pain relief but to keep patients from remembering their suffering.

I tried sitting him up so I could listen to his lungs, but he resisted. I tried pushing him gently onto his side but he would not budge. Tears streamed down his sunken cheeks. I looked around for a nurse to assist me but no one was available. His lungs made deep, guttural groans, like a foghorn, so clogged were they with fluid and muck. I placed my hand on his abdomen and pressed gently. He opened his mouth, as if to emit a blood-curdling howl, but because of the tube in his throat, there was no sound. "I'm sorry, sir," I kept saying.

Outside the room, I jotted down a few notes. It was already seven forty-five. The encounter had taken almost fifteen minutes. I was going to have to scramble to finish seeing the rest of my patients before eight o'clock.

I hustled to the bedside of Camille Panizzo, an eighteen-year-old with a rare blood disorder requiring frequent blood transfusions. Over the years, the excess iron from the transfused blood had accumulated in her vital organs, including her heart, which had enlarged and thickened, leading to congestive heart failure. In the CCU she had had numerous runs of ventricular tachycardia, a potentially life-threatening heart arrhythmia. Electrophysiologists were considering implanting a defibrillator in her chest to shock her heart in case it stopped, but in the interim they had decided to treat her with intravenous lidocaine, an anesthetic that suppresses arrhythmias. The infusion had worked—the ventricular tachycardia had subsided—but now she was deeply somnolent, a side effect of the drug.

When I arrived, she could barely open her eyes. She had delicate, appealing features—blond, curly hair, high cheekbones, and a narrow nose. Her jaundiced skin was the color of polenta, probably because of all the iron in her liver. Her eyelids only fluttered when I introduced myself, but I could still make out that she had green eyes, and that they were beautiful. Her mother, also blond and pretty, like a middle-aged flight attendant, was sitting by the window. She asked me if a decision had been made about a defibrillator. I told her that it was my first day but that I would check on it and get back to her. "They have to do something about this medication," she said wearily. "I can't stand to see her like this."

The mood next door could not have been more different. Ramón Ojeda, a middle-aged taxi driver, had had angioplasty, where a tiny balloon and a coil of wire called a *stent* was used to open a severely blocked coronary artery. Now, just a day later, he was sitting up in bed, admiring a magnificent view of the sun-soaked East River and the Queensboro Bridge. He was going to be transferred to a regular floor today. When I informed him of this, he feigned disappointment. "Look at me here," he said, arms outstretched. "I'm king of the world!"

Across the hall, my last patient, Irving Waldheim, was lying on a cardiac recliner, staring at a wall. Waldheim was a wizened man in his late sixties with a shock of wild, professorial hair and gray bushy eyebrows. His skin was pallid and shiny, with a residue of perspiration. Like Mr. Fellini, my first patient, he had suffered numerous complications during his monthlong stay in the CCU, the latest being unremitting fevers of unknown origin. The workup, including numerous blood cultures and CAT scans looking for occult infections, had been negative. Now his doctors were saying that, ironically, the antibiotics he was on might be causing the fevers.

The room was dark, one of four in the CCU without windows. Next to the wall was a plastic bucket filled with foamy secretions. On the bed was a quilt knitted with a verse from the Twenty-third Psalm: "The Lord is my shepherd. I shall not want. He maketh me to lie down in green pastures." I asked Mr. Waldheim some questions but he did not respond. Since I was running late, I didn't press. I was about to leave when his son, who was just coming in, asked me if his father could be moved to a room with a view. "I think some light would do him good," he said. I told him that I would check with the other doctors.

When I finally made it back to the conference room, the team had already assembled at the long table, their white coats draped over the backs of the vinyl chairs. "Jauhar's brother," someone said as I took a seat. The attending physician, Jonathan Carmen, nodded to acknowledge me. Dr. Carmen was in his late thirties, muscular and square-jawed, with a balding pate and an almost menacing visage. My brother, who knew him well, had described him as smart, savvy, your basic tough kid from Brooklyn who'd made it up the hospital ranks through hustle and hard work. I didn't know how much of his story was myth and how much fact, but it was appealing nevertheless, and I had been looking forward to meeting him. "I've heard a lot about you," Carmen said, looking me over intensely. "Thank you," I replied stupidly.

One of the senior residents turned to me. He was tall, with glasses, short brown hair, and handsome features. "I'm Steve," he said, extending his hand. "We'll be taking call together."

Carmen quickly went through the logistics of the rotation. There were three intern-resident teams, so call was every third night. Rounds were long, he warned, "so keep your presentations on point. Start with the chief complaint. And don't just tell me what the patient said. Sometimes I'll hear the chief complaint is, 'It's cold in here.' " He drew out each syllable in a high-pitched nasal sneer, like Jackie Gleason on *The Honeymooners*, and we all laughed. "That may be the chief complaint, but that's not the reason the patient is in the hospital."

On rounds, we huddled around a metal rack bulging with charts, Carmen and the fellow in the center, then the interns, then the residents, who hovered on the periphery, periodically breaking away to answer pages. Outside each room, arms folded in postures of serious purposefulness, everyone listened intently as Amanda, Nancy, or I read off vital signs, medications, ventilator settings, fluid intake, urine output, nutritional data, and lab results from the flow sheets. Carmen and the cardiology fellow interrupted frequently to fill us in on details or to ask questions or to make clarifying comments. One of our patients was a nephrologist with kidney failure who wept inconsolably when we went to see him. It wasn't clear what was wrong, except everything. There was a music school teacher who woke up with chest tightness and went to work, only to go to the ER in the evening and be told that he was having a heart attack. A young man with an artificial heart valve had continued to use heroin and now was hospitalized with another valve infection. "When's the surgery?" he asked defiantly, and Carmen brusquely told him that it was up to the surgeons. When a resident brought up the issue of drug withdrawal, Carmen said, "Just give him what he needs. Let's not worry about detoxing him here."

There was a pecking order to examining the patients. Carmen got first dibs, then the fellow, then the resident on call (today it was Steve), then the intern on call (me), then the remaining residents, and, finally, Amanda and Nancy. Carmen usually placed his stethoscope on a patient's chest, but rarely did he perform a complete physical exam. He acted more like a facilitator who knew what was there but was trying to direct us to discover it for ourselves.

I quickly discovered that Carmen loved to teach, and he favored the Socratic method. In true form, interns were first in line to get "pimped" (or interrogated), residents second, the fellow third. Knowing a question was eventually coming my way left me feeling anxious, like sitting on an electrified grid and waiting to be shocked.

The first question came about halfway through rounds, when Carmen handed me an EKG. "Can you read this for us, Dr. Jauhar?" he said. My heart started thumping; a giddy sensation coursed through my belly and lower body. Then I stared at the EKG and couldn't believe my luck. It was something I had reviewed in Central Park the previous week.

"I see P waves that are not followed by a QRS complex, which tells me that there is some kind of block," I started off. This (as I would soon discover) was classic roundsmanship, pretending to figure out in real time what you already knew. "The PR interval is getting prolonged before each dropped complex."

"So what's the diagnosis?"

"Type I, second-degree block."

"Right: Wenckebach," Carmen said, referring to the cardiologist who had discovered it. "Good." The team walked on in silence. When no one was looking, Amanda smiled at me and gave me a thumbs-up.

At the bedside, Carmen showed us how to interpret the pressure tracings on a telemetry monitor, explaining how certain cardiac conditions give rise to certain waveforms. The terms were familiar from medical school, but I understood only a small fraction of what he was saying. By the time he was finished, I had scribbled down five things I needed to read about: transvenous pacemakers, dilated cardiomyopathy, systemic vascular resistance, thermodilution, and the Fick equation. I reproached myself for not reading more during the outpatient month.

Outside the closed door of Mr. Waldheim's room, I asked if he could be moved to a room with windows. "He's circling the drain!" one of the residents blurted out.

"It wasn't my idea," I replied defensively. "His son was asking."

"I have no objections," Carmen said, cutting off the conversation. "Just check with the nurse manager."

When we got back to the conference room, someone flipped off the lights and we assembled in front of a digital workstation. Carmen pulled up the first X-ray. "Dr. Jauhar," he barked. I jumped. "Can you read this for us?"

I stared at the image, trying to make out the serpentine shadows running across the screen. Chest X-rays were not my forte. In medical school we had been taught a systematic way of reading them but I had forgotten it.

"The bones look normal," I said, trying to buy time.

"What else?" Carmen said sharply.

"It looks like he has fluid in the lungs."

"What are these?"

Two pendulous shadows draped the screen. "Breasts?" I replied. There were snickers.

"Correct. This is Camille, your patient. But don't look at the lungs yet; just read the X-ray systematically."

This was precisely what I had forgotten how to do.

"What's the first thing you do when you read an X-ray?" Carmen asked rhetorically.

I sat quietly, staring helplessly at the screen.

"You ask yourself, 'Is it a good-quality film?' Assess the radiographic penetration. Look at the spine. You should just barely see the intervertebral spaces. See them too well and it's overpenetrated. Not at all and it's underpenetrated." He paused. "Okay, what else?"

I did not reply, inviting in the sharks. "You count the ribs," Nancy volunteered. A bolt of anger shot through me. How dare she show me up!

"Right, you want to assess the quality of inspiration. You should be able to count at least ten ribs. So, Dr. Jauhar, count the ribs."

I pointed to the first rib. "That's the second rib," Carmen said. "See how it comes straight out? The first rib is C-shaped." I pointed uncertainly to another line. "That's the clavicle," Carmen said impatiently. He took my finger and placed it on a white marking on the screen. "That's the first rib."

I counted them from top to bottom; there were ten.

"What else?" By now he was answering his own questions. "You said it already. Look at the lung fields."

"They look wet," I stammered.

"You should get into a habit of calling things by their correct name. She has diffuse interstitial edema. As you alluded to before, there is pulmonary vascular congestion. See how the costophrenic angles are blunted; these are bilateral pleural effusions. These tiny markings are Kerley B lines. The cardiac silhouette is big. Of course, this is a portable film so you can't really say if the heart is enlarged, but we know it is."

An acorn was pressing into the center of my brain. My throat was tight and my mind had ground to a halt. If not for my seat back, I felt that I would fall backward.

"You have to read these things systematically or you'll miss something," Carmen said, his tone softening a bit. "But you know this already."

The cardiology fellow pulled up the next film and someone else took the hot seat. In the dark room, my face burned with embarrassment. I couldn't recall ever feeling so publicly humiliated, and on my first day in the CCU, too.

Later that morning, I was inputting orders into a computer when Rajiv stopped by the conference room. Even in his cotton scrubs and day-old beard, he looked debonair. He asked me how rounds went. I told him about the X-ray debacle. "Don't take things so seriously," he said. "That's why it's a three-year program." I nodded indifferently and got back to my work.

IT WAS NOW five-thirty in the morning, and I was done pronouncing Mrs. Piniella dead. Amanda and Nancy would be coming in soon to preround, so I printed the flow sheets for the day and started writing skeletons of my daily progress notes, to be filled in later as the blood tests and other data came in. An Indian man had been admitted by Steve during the night to rule out myocardial infarction, so I went to see him. A nurse was sitting quietly at the computer in his room, in-putting data. The patient, an elderly man with the quiet dignity of those who had endured and fought the British occupation, was sitting up in a chair. "It was the strangest thing, Doctor," he said, breathing a bit fast but otherwise looking comfortable. "Last night I did not know where I was."

"Did you know that you were in the hospital?" I asked.

"No."

"What did you think when you saw the nurses?"

He looked away, straining to remember. "Well, then I gradually came to know it. But it had never happened to me before like this. This sense of not knowing the place."

"Were you short of breath?"

"No," he replied. "Just confused. But it never happened before."

I nodded, having already seen a few cases of ICU psychosis. "That happens here sometimes," I said.

"Oh, okay." He looked relieved.

"Was your wife here with you?"

"No, she came later."

"Tell her to visit more frequently." He said he would do that.

At six-thirty Amanda and Nancy arrived. Amanda brought break-fast for me—a toasted bagel with cream cheese and coffee (it was cus-tomary at New York Hospital for the on-call intern to bring in breakfast for the post-call intern). We sat at the conference table while I reviewed overnight events. I told Nancy about Mrs. Piniella; she thanked me for filling out all the death forms. Then the three of us went out to pre-round. Nurses kept asking me to do things, seemingly oblivious to the fact that I was post-call, so I tried my best to avoid them. On rounds, Dr. Carmen mostly left me alone. Periodically I'd nod off and yank my-self awake, momentarily disoriented. Trying to stave off sleep was like trying to pull open a screen door in a hurricane. It took every last ounce of energy.

We rounded quickly, and I was essentially done with my work

by late morning. Before leaving, I stopped by to say goodbye to Mr. Waldheim. Per his son's request, he had been moved to a room with windows. I walked in to find him sitting in a chair, admiring the Queensboro Bridge. He gave me a thumbs-up, and his message was clear: all he wanted was a room with a view.

At noon, when rounds were finished and progress notes were done and orders had been written and consultants had been called, Steve and I walked out together. I could hardly believe it: my first call night was finally over. Only 140 more to go during residency. The thought might have depressed me, but I was giddy at the prospect of going home after thirty hours on and having a free day. I had heard about the brutally utilitarian post-call routine of one of the senior residents. When she would get home, she'd pop a couple of pills of Valium and go straight to her bedroom, locking the door, often sleeping for sixteen hours until the next morning. It didn't matter if the baby wanted to play, or if her husband wanted to talk, or there were errands to be done. She was totally focused on getting her sleep. But not me; I was going to stay up; leisure time was too precious to squander on sleep. I was going to check stocks or maybe go for a run. I was going to watch the talking heads on CNBC. I was going to order lunch from Chickenfest. I was going to call my mother. I was going to write in my journal. I was going to read the newspaper. I was going to read magazines. I was going to read . . . well, anything but medicine.

We walked by the information desk in the lobby. An administrator had called me during rounds to tell me that I had forgotten to sign the death certificate. She had been waiting for me, and scolded me for taking my time to come down. I just smiled and apologized and signed my name. The night was over and I wasn't going to let anything bother me.

Steve led me out an emergency exit and into a courtyard. The day was bright and sunny. In a daze, I walked to the main thoroughfare. "Thank you," I said to Steve when we got to my corner. "I couldn't have gotten through the night without you." He smiled and patted me

on the back and told me to get some sleep. I walked the two blocks
back to my apartment, my shadow cutting the sidewalk ahead of me.
The summer sun reflected off the smudges on my glasses, breaking
into tiny speckles, like puddles on a crater-filled road. In the living
room, I sat down on the couch, turned on the television, and collapsed.
When I woke up, it was after dark.

road trip

The doctor has paid for the power with suffering.

—MELVIN KONNER, *BECOMING A DOCTOR*, 1987

orning was the busiest time in the CCU, when patients were wheeled off for catheterization and other procedures. One of the most common reasons for admission was to rule out myocardial infarction. Residents called it a ROMI (pronounced "roamie"), and this was the bread and butter of the CCU, often requiring a trip to the catheterization lab. There was always a long line of gurneys by the front desk, like airplanes on a runway waiting to take off.

After rounds I usually hovered around Steve, my resident, like a groupie. He was a lanky man, over six feet tall, with long arms that dropped down below his knees. He told me that he was planning on getting a job in a small town after he graduated. In small towns, he said, internists were doing a lot more than their counterparts in big cities: stress tests, flexible sigmoidoscopies, even implanting pacemakers. "Once you get out of the city, it's a whole new world." He had briefly considered becoming a "hospitalist," a new breed of internist that exclusively took care of hospitalized patients, but he had decided against it. He said he believed that primary care medicine would provide ample intellectual rewards. Like Steve, at one time I too had worried about being challenged in medicine. Now my fears were very different.

One morning, Steve taught me a mnemonic for organizing the problems in my daily progress notes: RICHMAN (respiratory, infectious, cardiovascular, hematological, metabolic, alimentary [or gastrointestinal], and neurological). Another time, he taught me how to insert an arterial line. I put on a sterile gown while he threw a sterile sheet over the patient. Then he tore open a procedure kit and spilled its contents onto the drape. His long fingers started moving rapidly, opening packages of needles, drawing up saline flushes, arranging the instruments we were going to use with the meticulousness of a sushi chef. After he was done, he taped the patient's right arm to a bedside table so it wouldn't move. Then I cleaned it with antiseptic soap. With a needle I stabbed a small vial of lidocaine he held up in the air, drawing some of the medicine into a syringe. I injected a tiny bleb into the patient's arm to numb it up. "Go deeper," Steve advised, and I did. Then I took a longer "finder" needle and poked it through the skin, trying to locate the artery. The patient winced.

"Go in at more of an angle," Steve suggested. "Okay, pull back a little bit, I think you went through the artery. A bit more. Pull back. Pull back." A burst of maroon filled the barrel. "Okay, perfect. Now take off the syringe. No, leave the needle where it is—" but I had already pulled it out of the artery. "That's okay, just put the syringe back on and try again."

I tried again, but this time with no luck. "Go in at the same angle," Steve said, making a jabbing motion with his hand, but I was unable to draw back any blood. "Okay, sharpen the angle . . . sharpen . . . sharpen . . ." With each attempt, the patient groaned, and I started to sweat. I was reminded of a patient I had tortured as a third-year medical student trying to get an arterial blood gas. Dean Dowton had told us to come up with a code of ethics in his commencement address; my first rule was that I was only going to allow myself three attempts at a procedure before asking someone more experienced to take over. But now I found myself wanting to try again and again.

"Let me give it a shot," Steve finally said. I was hoping he'd miss, at least once, but he hit the artery on his first attempt. When he removed the syringe, blood spurted out the hub of the needle, splattering red dollops onto the table and the tile floor.

"Okay, hand me the wire," he said. My hands were shaking so badly that the wire, which resembled a guitar string, kept flopping about wildly. Perspiration was trickling down my face. He inserted the wire through the bore of the needle and into the artery. Then he pulled out the needle, leaving the wire inside the vessel. With a scalpel, he made a deep nick in the arm, and forced a stiff plastic catheter, a dilator, through the soft tissue to create a track for the catheter that was going to follow. The patient groaned but did not move. Blood started gushing. Steve slipped the catheter over the wire and tried pushing it into the artery, but it buckled. He tried again but it still wouldn't go. I looked on nervously as the wire protruded unnaturally out of the man's forearm, like a nail askew in a thick plank. "It's probably bent," Steve said. He turned to the nurse who was with us and politely asked her to bring him another wire. Then, with his finger pressed on the wound, he casually turned to me, like a man waiting for a train. "Never let go of the wire," he said, and I nodded nervously. I couldn't believe that even at that moment, Steve was still trying to teach me something.

The nurse returned with a new wire and Steve quickly inserted it into the artery. The catheter passed over it easily. He pulled out the wire and connected the catheter to a manometer. Soon a blood-pressure waveform was prominently displayed on the monitor above the bed. "Okay, sew it in," Steve said. While I made stitches, he gathered up the needles, discarding them into a sharps box, threw away the procedure tray, and stripped off his gown. "Congratulations," he said. "You just put in your first arterial line."

"You did it," I replied, not wanting to be patronized.

"Yes, but you'll do it next time," he said encouragingly. "See one, do one, teach one."

That night I wrote in my diary:

Next to Steve, I feel lame, effete, like a shell of a resident. He has a feel for the hospital that I don't have. They say I'll develop it, but I cannot imagine a time when he was as confused as me.

I know I can learn a lot from him. He is truly a wonder to behold. The only thing I would fault him on is his tendency to denigrate patients in conversations with other doctors. But that's hardly unique to him.

ONE AFTERNOON IN THE CCU a few days later, an Australian man was returned to his room after an electrophysiology procedure. Within an hour his blood pressure plummeted. His eyes darted back and forth, like a scared child's, even as he insisted that he was fine. The consensus among doctors in the room was that he was in cardiac tamponade, where fluid rapidly accumulates in the sac around the heart, hindering its ability to fill with blood. The only effective treatment is to drain the fluid. "Page your brother!" someone shouted to me.

When Rajiv came barreling through the double doors, I breathlessly told him that I had paged him 911. "Don't ever fucking do that," he barked, marching past me. In the room, a technician was performing an echocardiogram, which confirmed that a massive amount of blood had accumulated in the pericardial sac, compressing the heart with every beat. Suddenly Rajiv was in a sterile gown, and I was being asked to step outside. A nurse threw a blanket over the patient. Rajiv tore open a pericardiocentesis kit. Everyone, including attending physicians, watched raptly as he drew lidocaine into a syringe. He seemed to relish the attention, chatting comfortably with the nurse who was assisting him. "Can you move the table over, please?" he asked politely. This was not the brother I knew from childhood, the one who was easily intimidated, who feared dirt-biking in the hills behind our house. I had always been the fearless one, doing cross-outs and tabletops while he adopted a more conservative style. Now I was the one perched on top of the Islander Hill on my Univega bicycle, fearfully looking down.

Rajiv had always been good with his hands, much better than me.

Growing up, he had been the tinkerer and I had been the thinker. It was disheartening to realize how useless my skills were now.

The patient had stopped moving under the drape. He was either being extremely cooperative or was sinking into cardiogenic shock. Rajiv stood on a step stool. After numbing the skin below the breastbone, he pierced it with a six-inch-long needle, directing the tip, with the aid of ultrasound, toward the left shoulder, directly at the heart. I stepped away; I couldn't watch. I could hardly believe what was happening. Wasn't there someone better equipped to do this than my older brother?

I had always been in Rajiv's shadow, and never more so than in the CCU. Dr. Carmen and the others expected me to do well because of Rajiv. I couldn't just worry about myself; I had to worry about his reputation, too. "I don't want to mess this up for you," I had told him the night before starting the rotation. "You can't," he replied confidently.

A few minutes later, while I was sitting at a computer checking labs, the mood of the crowd suddenly changed. People started filing away. When I went back into the room, the drape was off, the patient had regained his color, and his blood pressure was almost normal. Bloody fluid was draining into a plastic bag. I found Rajiv chatting with some fellows by the nursing station. People were walking up and patting him on the back. When he saw me, he snapped his fingers loudly. "Did you see it?"

"I missed the last part," I replied.

"Well, it was fucking awesome!"

"How did you know where to go with the needle?"

"I didn't. I just pushed and prayed." Then he broke into a cackle that usually meant he was pulling your leg, but you could never be sure.

I stared at him, incredulous. In twenty-nine years, I had never wanted to be like my brother more than at that moment. He was so calm, cool, and collected. He seemed to view hospital dramas as some sort of Vedantic play in which he was merely another actor.

"It's an amazing feeling," Rajiv said. "Here this guy goes from being in shock to actually talking."

"What did he say to you?"

"Ah, that was the best part. He apologized."

"Apologized?"

"Yeah, the first thing he said when he woke up was, 'I'm sorry for not being a good patient.' "

"What did you say?"

"I said, 'Shut the fuck up.' " Then he broke into another full-throated cackle.

As he was walking away, he stopped. "Don't ever page me 911. I thought something bad had happened." I started to say something: "Wasn't this—?" He cut me off. "You know what I mean. Like with the family. Like something had happened to Dad."

MRS. WILLIAMS NEEDED A CAT SCAN. She was on a stretcher, in a tangle of wires and tubes, a woman of about seventy with thinning gray hair and a churchgoing face. A nurse was giving me instructions for the road trip. "Just keep the monitor on her at all times," she barked, like a quarterback calling out a play. She picked up a section of clear plastic tubing. "This is your arterial line. And this here is your central venous pressure. I'm going to disconnect it; you don't need it. This is the heparin. This is the nitroglycerin." She pointed to the bulky yellow monitor at the foot of the bed. "The yellow line is your oxygen saturation. That's your heartbeat and that's your blood pressure." She reached underneath the stretcher, where a green metal canister was lying on its side. "That's your oxygen. It should last about thirty minutes."

She paused to take a deep breath. "This is your code box," she said, holding up a sealed gray box that looked like a mechanic's tool kit. Inside it were drugs—epinephrine, atropine, lidocaine—that I had never used. "Just break it open if you need it. Of course, if she arrests, you're going to use the paddles." I nodded; I had never used defibrillator paddles before. "You charge it like this, see." She turned the knob back and forth quickly. "One hundred joules, two hundred joules, three hundred joules, see." My face must have betrayed terror because the nurse offered an almost sympathetic smile. "Don't worry," she said. "If you need to, you can always call a code."

The middle-of-the-night road trip is an intern rite of passage. Steve and the other residents had done it, and there was no reason to think that I couldn't do it, too.

A young black man in dreadlocks and lime green scrubs showed up. He was my escort. Without a word, he grabbed hold of the back of the stretcher with one hand and a metal IV pole with the other and maneuvered it to the double doors. Then he punched a plate on the wall, the doors flung open, and we were off.

Coming out of the CCU, with me holding on to a side rail, we tried turning left, but the stretcher went crashing into the far wall. "Oh my!" Mrs. Williams exclaimed. She had few teeth, hollow cheeks, and kind of gummed her words when she spoke. I didn't know much about her, except that she had been admitted to the CCU with chest pains. That was pretty much all Amanda had signed out.

We rolled the stretcher down the checkerboard-tile floor, toward the freight elevator.

Even at this late hour, I could see white-coated men sitting on stools in the satellite pharmacy, sorting pills. Their presence was both creepy and oddly reassuring. More banging, but we managed to steer the stretcher onto the corrugated metal floor of the freight elevator. With each bump I checked to make sure the IVs were still connected. An EKG sticker had come off her chest, dangling uselessly on a wire, making the heartbeat tracing temporarily go flatline before I pressed it back on. We rode up to the sixth floor in silence, except for the reassuring *blip-blip-blip* from the monitor.

Coming out of the elevator, we made a left and rolled up a ramp and down a hallway, past the pediatric oncology wing. Suddenly we were in an old part of the hospital. The corridors were lined with beat-up chairs and rusting file cabinets below peeling paint. We stopped at an intersection. I looked up from the monitor nervously. "I hope you know where you're going, because I don't." My escort's flat, somber expression did not change. "I've only been here two weeks," I tried to explain.

Without a word, he turned left. A couple of turns later, we entered a darkened hallway. It had a faintly chemical smell, like that of a darkroom. "This is it," he mumbled, disappearing into a room. From the corridor I could see a doughnut-shaped CT scanner sitting on a metal gantry that looked like it could use a good scrubbing. After a couple of minutes, the escort came out and started walking back in the direction of the main hospital. "Hey!" I called out. "Where are you going?"

"Call me when you're done," he said without turning around.

"What's your number?" I shouted, but he was already gone.

A burly technician with tattooed arms came out of the room. "Okay, Doc, bring her in," he said.

I rolled the stretcher up to the radiology table. Mrs. Williams was now even more tangled up in wires and tubes. Her rumpled gown was slipping off her shoulders, exposing her breasts. The pulse oximeter had long since come off her finger. One of her IV lines had somehow made its way between the side rails. I disconnected it, looped it back over the railing, and quickly reattached it before any of the medicated fluid dripped onto the floor. The technician pumped on a pedal below the stretcher, raising it to the same level as the scanner. Then I pulled on a latch and lowered the side rail. "Give me your hand, Mrs. Williams," I said, reaching across the gantry.

"Hold on, Doc," the tech said. "We've got to give this line some slack or her IV is going to come right out." He pulled the metal pole in closer, but it didn't look like the tubing was going to be long enough. He stared at it for a few seconds. "Can we stop the drip?" he asked.

"Sure," I replied automatically. Which drug couldn't be stopped for just a few minutes?

I disconnected the line and reached again for Mrs. Williams's hand. "Doc, she's going to need some help." He went and got a white sheet. "Okay, pull her onto her side." As her face pressed up between the rails, he quickly tucked the sheet under her body and rolled her onto her back. Then we grabbed the sheet on each side and slid her over onto the scanner table.

"This is only going to take five minutes," I said, patting her on the hand. The tech and I went into the tiny control room. "Don't you want to be able to see the monitor?" he asked me, taking a seat at the console. "Yes, of course," I said. I ran in and turned it around.

Digital images of my patient's head soon appeared on a computer screen. "What is the scan for?" the tech inquired, adjusting a knob. After a pause, I said, "I'm not sure." In all the excitement, I had forgotten to ask.

The first images looked okay. Now it was time for higher-resolution cuts.

"She's got to lie real still for this next scan," the tech said.

I peeked into the room. Mrs. Williams's head was still in the scanner. "Try not to move, ma'am. We're almost done."

She groaned loudly. "I don't feels so good. Oh Lordy, I don't feels good."

"What's the matter?" I asked.

"My chest is hurtin'," she said.

Just my luck. Only one more pass through the scanner and now she was having chest pain? "That's okay," I said. "Just try to keep still."

She shifted her weight uncomfortably. "But I'm getting these pains in my heart."

"We'll take care of it once the scan is finished. You don't want to have to come back here, do you?"

She didn't answer.

"So please just lie still for a couple of minutes so we can finish up." I was focused on completing the scan, whatever the indication for it was.

"Let's do it," I said, returning to the control room.

"You sure, Doc?" the tech replied skeptically.

"Yes, I'm sure," I snapped. The tracings were fine; her heartbeat was regular. Tasks were piling up back in the CCU. I did not want to have to bring her back.

Midway through the final scan, she started moaning. "Oh Lord, oh my!" "Thirty seconds," the tech said, his eyes peeled to the screen. The mumbling got louder and her feet started shifting from side to side. "Oh Jesus, help me!" she groaned. "All right, Doc," he said, punching off a lit button. "I think we got what we needed."

We pulled Mrs. Williams back onto the stretcher. "Oh Lord, oh Jesus, get me out of here!" she wailed. I clenched my teeth to keep from laughing. For a moment the whole situation seemed rather comical. What was I doing here in the middle of the night, in this abandoned corner of the hospital, with this tattooed technician and this helpless old lady? The whole road trip had been so nerve-racking. I was just glad that it was over.

I quickly reconnected the IV line and turned the machine back on. *Beep . . . beep . . . beep.* I turned the machine off and tried again. More beeps and a red light started to flash. I tried silencing the alarm but it kept ringing. The rotors started whirring in my head. The IV had been delivering nitroglycerin. *Nitroglycerin is used to treat angina.* I turned the machine off and tried again. *Angina means decreased blood flow to the heart.* I punched the buttons on the front panel. *Decreased blood flow can cause chest pain.* I squeezed the bag, trying to get the drip restarted, but all I got were more flashing lights. Then it hit me square in the gut: *My patient was having a heart attack!*

Her moans and the alarms mixed into a dissonant instrumental. I spun toward the tech. "Do you have any nitroglycerin?" He looked at me like I was a lunatic. I flipped open the code box the nurse had given me. There were vials of lidocaine, epinephrine, atropine, saline. No nitroglycerin. *Dammit,* I screamed in my head. Steve had told me to carry a bottle with me at all times, but I had ignored the advice.

Now I was in a full-blown panic. "I have to get her back to the unit," I cried. "Can you call Transport?"

"I already did," the tech replied, nonplussed. "But he said it would take a few minutes."

"I can't wait. Can you help me bring her back?"

He looked at me helplessly. "I can't leave, Doc. I'm the only one here and there's another patient on the way."

I grabbed the IV pole and the back of the stretcher and started racing toward the elevator. "Tell Transport to catch up with me," I shouted. I swerved, barreling into a chair, backed up, and tried again. *If she dies, this is going to be your fault!* I screamed in my head. *You'll be fired. Risk management will have to get involved. How did you get yourself into this mess? Why did you insist on finishing the goddamn scan?*

"You're going to be okay, Mrs. Williams," I said, trying to mollify her as she started to shriek. "The nurses are going to give you some medicine and you're going to be just fine."

We got to an intersection. Which way? Earlier we had turned left, so now I had to turn . . . right. Simple calculations were eluding me. For a moment I thought about stopping to call a code. But where was I? It was the middle of the night and I was in the middle of a vacant corridor. How were you supposed to call a code anyway? Who were you supposed to ring? Where were the phones? *God,* I prayed, *if you get me through this, I'll be a better doctor. I'll take things more seriously. Please, just let me get through this night.*

Back at the freight elevator, I struck the button furiously and the doors opened. On the ride down, her cries were deafening. When the doors opened, I saw the escort. He appeared to be waiting for me. "Oh, thank God," I cried. "Help me get her back!" Without a word, he took the back of the stretcher and we raced it back to the CCU. On the way there, I tried to explain what had happened. "I stopped the nitroglycerin drip, and she started having chest pain, but then I couldn't get it restarted." He didn't appear to be listening. This was my mess, and he seemed to want no part in it.

When we rolled into the CCU, three nurses materialized immediately. Evidently the tech had called ahead to tell them I was on the way. "We couldn't get her into the scanner," I said breathlessly. "I stopped her nitroglycerin. I couldn't get it restarted. Maybe there's air in the line. It's her nitroglycerin. She's having chest pain."

"We'll take care of it," the nurse who had sent me out forty-five minutes earlier said calmly. I wasn't prepared for her sympathetic tone, and almost instantaneously tears filled my eyes. I felt guilty, undeserving of her empathy. "I stopped the nitro and she started having angina," I said again. "I didn't know what to do, so I brought her back."

"You did the right thing," the nurse said. "We'll take care of her."

I was so on edge that I felt numb. I hovered as the nurses whisked Mrs. Williams back to her room. As they got her into bed, I continued trying to explain my actions from the door. "We finished the scan. I probably shouldn't have disconnected the IV."

"It's okay," the nurse said. She smiled broadly. "Congratulations. You just made your first road trip."

When the nurses restarted the nitroglycerin drip, Mrs. Williams's angina subsided. Before long she was lying in bed comfortably. I was right, there had been a small air bubble in the line, making the machine turn off automatically. For a while I lingered outside the room, peeking through the curtain to check on her. Finally I slipped away. She was in good hands now, much better than mine.

I wanted to run away but there was nowhere to go. Back at the workstation I tried checking labs but I couldn't concentrate. There were still a slew of tasks to complete. Soon Steve was going to start walking around the unit to make sure everything was done, and after that I was going to have to print up flow sheets and start prerounding. I stared at my reflection in a glass door. The veins were popping out on my glistening temples. The image ricocheted off the glass door behind me, trailing off to infinity.

In semiconductor physics, there is the concept of an electron-hole pair. A hole is the absence of an electron. It is not a real particle, though it behaves like one. It is a shadow particle, a phantom, behaving exactly opposite to an electron. Gazing at my reflection, I was struck that in some fundamental way I had become a hole, a shadow of my former self, behaving antithetical to my true nature. I was a thinker, not a doer. This was too much doing for me. I was beginning to appreciate what it was going to take to make me into a doctor—into a man.

first death

The patient, it seems, is not so well sleeping.

The screams echo off the walls.

—THE VELVET UNDERGROUND, "LADY GODIVA'S OPERATION"

A middle-aged woman wearing navy blue slacks and faux pearls emerged from one of the CCU rooms. "Can someone come take a look at my husband?" she hollered. Since I was on call again, that someone was going to have to be me.

"What's the matter?" I said, remaining seated at my computer.

"He's twitching," she said insistently. I looked over at the telemetry monitor. The tracings looked fine. The pulse oximeter was reading 100 percent. Earlier in the day, there had been a cardiac arrest on the tenth floor, six flights up. When I arrived at the code, one of the residents was up on the rolling stretcher, straddling the dying man, riding him like a jockey, thumping on his chest all the way down to the CCU. During the subsequent code, I briefly performed chest compressions but the patient died anyway. Afterward, my scrubs bloodied, I had to go upstairs to the surgical suites to get a new pair. Now it was late in the afternoon. My progress notes weren't written, labs weren't checked, and Amanda and Nancy, my co-interns, were getting ready to sign out. The code had ruined the flow of the day. I didn't have time to respond to every little twitch.

"I'll be there in a minute," I said. I picked up the man's chart. He had been transferred to New York Hospital from a hospital in Brooklyn. The transfer summary, scribbled in chicken scratch by an intern at the other CCU, indicated that Alexander Jusczak, a fifty-five-year-old resident of Coney Island, had been getting ready to go on vacation when he collapsed on the driveway outside his home. His wife found him unconscious and called 911. When paramedics arrived, they performed CPR and inserted a breathing tube into his airway, reviving him briefly. He was taken to a local hospital, where he apparently had had another cardiac arrest (here the details were vague). Cardiac catheterization revealed a total blockage of the left anterior descending coronary—the so-called widow-maker lesion, often afflicting middle-aged men and often fatal. The entire front portion of his heart wasn't moving. Cardiologists inserted a special "balloon pump" to assist the heart and transferred him to New York Hospital, known for its cardiac work, for angioplasty.

No mention was made about whether he had ever regained consciousness.

As I was reading all this, his wife came out again. "Isn't there a doctor who can see my husband?" she cried plaintively. I signaled that I was coming. "Please! He needs help!" I quickly followed her into the room. Her husband was lying naked, unconscious, with catheters in his groin, penis, arms, and neck. His abdomen was mottled and distended. Stubble coated his chubby face. A thin plastic tube filled with green liquid slithered across the bed and up into his nose. At the bedside a special monitor recorded each inflation and deflation of the pump.

"There! Why is he doing that?" she demanded. His left eye winked playfully while his lips quivered. I took out my penlight and shined it into his pupils, but they did not react. I tried shaking him but he did not respond. I placed my hand on his cheek, trying to dampen the fine oscillations, but they persisted.

Her eyes were trained on me. Reflexively, I removed the stethoscope from around my neck and placed the bell on his chest. His lung

sounds were coarse, indistinct. The pump in his chest sounded like a
piston in a car engine. I stared at the monitor. I wasn't sure what to
make of all the data.

His wife broke the silence. "Why is he shaking?"

"I'm not sure but I think he's having a seizure," I replied. I suddenly felt burdened, like I was carrying a secret I had to unload.
"Please wait here. I'll be right back."

The unit was moving at a languorous pace befitting a late Friday
afternoon. Sunlight seeped through the window blinds, reflecting
brightly off the hard counters. This was California weather, and mem-
ories of my previous life came flooding back. Friday nights in Berkeley,
my lab-mates and I would go to the Bison Brewery on Telegraph Avenue and sit around for much of the night sipping wheat beer, playing
pool, talking about physics, philosophy, and politics. The goofy guy
with the depressed girlfriend who was taking Prozac. The bad-boy
physicist from Holland who had a penchant for double espressos and
hand-rolled cigarettes. Fridays had always filled me with such a wonderful sense of expectancy. Now I was just dreading another night
on call.

At the other end of the unit, Rajiv was gabbing with Joe, a first-
year fellow. "I need some help," I called out. Rajiv raised his forefinger
and continued talking. "Now!" I shouted.

Back in his room, Jusczak was still twitching, and momentarily I
felt relieved that Rajiv and Joe were there to see it. The tics were like
petulant scowls, not unlike a Tourette's spasm. Joe immediately asked
Mrs. Jusczak to step outside. "Is it a seizure?" I asked timidly. Joe nodded, tapping on his forehead. "He probably burned some rubber with
the cardiac arrest," he said.

Uncontrolled seizures can damage the brain within minutes; they
must be treated immediately. Joe ordered a nurse to administer fifteen
milligrams of Valium. When she did, the seizures subsided. "How long
has this been going on?" he demanded.

"A few minutes," I replied hesitantly.

I went to check the patient's labs. I scrolled down a computer screen, looking for anything unusual. Then I noticed something highlighted in red. Jusczak's blood sodium concentration was 153, well above normal. High serum sodium can cause neurological impairment. The brain does not like sitting in salty fluid. Like a celery stalk, it will shrink as water diffuses out of it by reverse osmosis. If this happens quickly enough, seizures can result. With nothing else to go on, I concluded that this was probably what had caused the seizures (though it was hard to be sure).

Back in the conference room, Amanda and Nancy were waiting patiently to sign out. "How did we miss it?" I heard Carmen say when Joe told him the sodium level. Joe shrugged and shook his head. "Nobody checked the labs," he replied. Of course, checking Jusczak's labs had been my responsibility, but I had been too busy doing other things. I sat down, saying nothing. Amanda and Nancy started handing off their patients to me. Carmen, who was getting ready to leave for the weekend, told Joe to update him that night.

Most seizures terminate with intravenous sedatives, and Jusczak's did too, for a while. But at midnight they started up again with a vengeance. Now they involved not only Jusczak's face but his hands and feet, too. His eyelids were clenched shut. I tried prying them open but my fingers slipped on his oily skin. His mouth appeared to be emitting silent screams. The telemetry sirens wailed: *ding-ding-ding*. We pushed more Valium, then Ativan, then an intravenous load of Dilantin, an antiepileptic. Again the seizures stopped, but they resumed within minutes with seemingly greater force. Joe told a nurse to give free water through the nasogastric tube to dilute the salty blood. We paged a neurology consultant, who came by and suggested phenobarbital, which worked, but only briefly.

I spent most of the night at Jusczak's bedside with Joe and a nurse. The bright ceiling lamp illuminated his naked body like a spotlight. Sweat drenched my T-shirt; my thighs were sore from standing. Every movement took energy I didn't have. When Joe went out to call an anesthesiologist, I started pushing drugs on my own. I was amazed at how easily my confidence flowed when it became clear that we were fighting a losing battle.

The convulsions seemed to gain in force and amplitude with the passage of the night. Over several hours, the sedative drips were dialed up well beyond the maximum limits in the textbooks. Eventually his whole body was quivering like a bowl of gelatin. We tried everything: glucose and thiamine, useful for hypoglycemic and alcoholic seizures, which he didn't have; Versed, a potent benzodiazepine, which paradoxically seemed to fuel the spasms; a cooling blanket, because there was some evidence suggesting that hypothermia could prevent brain damage after cardiac arrest. It was a reach, but we didn't know what else to do.

An anesthesiologist eventually showed up and put Jusczak on propofol, a milky white anesthetic. The seizures immediately ceased. With the propofol running into his body, they never resumed.

The nurses had put Mrs. Jusczak into an empty patient room. I found her there at four in the morning, sprawled on her stomach, still in her business suit. The room was musty, though with the faintly pleasing odor of perfume. I thought about waking her to give her an update but decided to let her be. Her husband almost certainly had irreversible brain damage at this point, and I did not want to provoke an outburst so early in the morning. I pictured her at his funeral, walking beside his coffin, wearing a black veil. I pictured the pallbearers in their black suits. I shuddered thinking about what had occurred over the past twelve hours.

I lay down in my call room, fatigued beyond words, certainly beyond anything I had ever experienced before. I had stayed up all night only a few times in my life: once in college before a history final, a couple of times in graduate school when I was collecting data, and now seven times over the past three weeks. The thoughts began to flood in, even as I tried hard to hold them back. *Why didn't you check the sodium earlier? Aren't you responsible for what happened?*

The following afternoon, after taking a restless nap, I took out my
diary and the discontent came pouring out:

Do doctors care? I don't know. I don't see a lot of caring. Maybe I myself
don't care, or care selectively, which is hypocrisy, which I despise. No, I don't
see much attention to the psychosocial aspects of medicine. There is lip service, but by and large, no one seems to pay it much mind. Like this morning.
Steve had no interest in holding Camille's mother's hand, in asking her why
she was crying. It was pretty obvious why, but I think she would have appreciated it, if only as a gesture to recognize her pain. I myself didn't make an
effort, not because I was uncomfortable but because there was so much to
do. I thought it best to spend my time doing what needed to be done.

It's almost criminal the callousness with which we treat some of our patients. Remember Mr. Fellini. Poor man; it was almost comical how he cried
out for us to leave him alone, to not hurt him, punish him for his helpless-
ness. This was a man loved by his family, a businessman or banker, perhaps,
one who asserted his will on others, and now he is a helpless child. Nature
did not wire into us the desire to take care of our aged. Maybe that's why
the contempt, the frustration, with gomers. They are heavy, dead evolution-
ary weight. They sap our resources. We don't want to take care of them.
Baby shit doesn't smell. But gomer shit smells the worst.

I should have known that I wouldn't be able to do this. What are we doing, poking and prodding people at two in the morning, drawing blood like
vampires? The 2:00 a.m. blood draw is just an exercise, a way to protect
yourself from being questioned on rounds for neglecting something. This
whole month we never acted on a lab test in the middle of the night. When I
asked Matt about it, he said, "This is what we do here. This is the CCU. Here,
we should be able to get labs every hour if we want to. The techs should just
do our bidding." Implicit in his remarks is the belief that more is better. I am
not convinced.

Sometimes, you have to take a chance, but doctors don't want to take a
chance. Sometimes you have to say, "This is the most likely cause; we're not
going to do a bunch of tests to rule out every possibility. This is a simple
fainting spell, and we're not going to do any further workup." But doctors

aren't willing to go out on a limb like that, take a chance, not cover themselves; hence all the waste, the unnecessary tests.

Maybe Matt will always be a better resident than me, because he cares at some core level to do all the little things that I find burdensome, like making the call to the lab to reproach the tech for a canceled (or delayed) test, or learning stuff like how to read a chest film and which antibiotics to use and when. When Fred, the third-year resident, was telling me today about the difference between heparin and warfarin, it was sad how little I cared. I'm sure that indifference is contributing to my problem, which is not performing. Perhaps at some level I am just lazy.

Today, when I was walking up Second Avenue, I was thinking: so much of medicine is simply supportive. Nothing is definitive; there are so few things we do that cure: some chemotherapy, I'm told, antibiotics, maybe angioplasty. The therapeutic taps don't work; the fluid reaccumulates. The studies to find lung cancer—so what, death is inevitable. And then it's made worse by the futile interventions at the end.

That night I called Rajiv at his apartment. I told him about what had happened to Mr. Jusczak after he left. I didn't want pat consolation, but that was exactly what Rajiv offered, as if I were engaged in some sort of fashionable exercise in self-reproach. He told me that the cardiac arrest had probably lowered Jusczak's seizure threshold. He told me that nothing could have been done to prevent the seizures. He told me to take a more "laissez-faire" approach or I would end up hurting my patients.

"There's just too much going on in the unit," I blurted out. "It's hard to keep track of it all." Rajiv suggested keeping three-by-five note cards. "That's not the solution!" I cried. "I'm not sure all this is for me."

"Shit happens," Rajiv said, by way of ending the conversation. "I know you love to beat yourself up, but don't do it here."

I thought about Jusczak all weekend. His face appeared to me in a dream. I was wandering around a run-down hospital, trying to find him. The corridors were decrepit, and the bathrooms were smeared with urine and feces. People were turning on me, accusing me of things I hadn't done, accusing me of putting them down. It was bizarre. I woke up terrified.

On Monday morning, I went to see Jusczak before rounds. The seizures had stopped, the sedative drips were off; he had settled into a coma. His wife was with him. Her hair was tousled, her makeup streaky; little black speckles dotted the bags under her eyes. She still had on the same suit, except now it was stained. The neurologists had told her over the weekend that her husband's prognosis was dismal. One of them had written in the chart that the chances for any kind of meaningful recovery were essentially nil.

She said, "Good morning." It caught me unprepared, how she was able to engage in such a simple nicety. I returned the greeting and walked up to the bedside to conduct the requisite exam. A strong odor emanated from the body, an unwashed smell. His head was turned unnaturally to the right. His legs and arms were turned inward, a fetal position aptly called *decorticate posturing*, a sign of severe brain damage. He was intubated, exhibiting no spontaneous breathing "over the vent." I shined light into his eyes. Jutting out over his eyelids was a thick layer of clear gelatinous material. I rotated his head from side to side. His eyes moved with the motion of his head. This absence of "doll's eyes"—a primitive reflex—was a sign of a damaged brainstem.

"What do you see?" his wife asked, looking on.

"There is damage, but I'm not sure how much," I lied. The guilt welled up inside me. If only I had checked the sodium when I was supposed to, perhaps this whole tragedy could have been averted. In medical school we had been taught to treat the patient, not the numbers. In this case, the logic seemed to have broken down. In this case, treating the sodium earlier could have been the difference between life and death.

"The neurologist will be coming by soon," I quietly informed Mrs. Jusczak. "I'm sure he will speak with you."

He arrived a few minutes later, a lanky Australian fellow with a brisk, impatient clip and the brainy look befitting someone in his profession. He immediately asked Mrs. Jusczak to step outside. I looked on as he performed his examination. He took a Q-tip and spun a tiny wisp of cotton. Then he lowered an eyelid and lightly brushed the cornea with the cotton, trying to evoke a blink; none came. He tapped on the knees with a hammer; the reflexes were abnormally brisk, further confirmation of brain damage. He took the handle of the hammer and scraped the soles of the feet. The big toes flexed upward—the Babinski sign—confirming that there had been extensive cortical injury. I asked him what the EEG, a brain-wave scan, had shown. "Diffuse slowing," he replied, "but that doesn't really matter. It's been seventy-two hours and he hasn't woken up. That's a very poor prognostic sign."

Outside the room, Mrs. Jusczak stopped me. "He is my best friend, you know," she said. "Don't get me wrong; he isn't perfect. But he is smart. And he is a good father. He did a good job with our son." I asked her where her son was. "At home," she replied, her voice breaking. "He thinks his father has pneumonia." Down the hall, a peal of laughter rang out from the nursing station. Takeout food had just been delivered.

"I know you're busy but he's all I have. He's only one person to you but he's everything to me. He is my whole life." She rested her arms against the countertop. A nurse came scurrying up. "Watch out for my clipboard, hon," she said. "I don't want you to knock it over."

I informed Mrs. Jusczak that I needed to get back to rounds.

Later, a surgeon came by. He was an older man with gray hair, blue scrubs, and a potbelly. "I've been trying to call your office all morning," Mrs. Jusczak told him. He looked at her impatiently. "They tell me he's brain-dead," she quickly added. He looked puzzled, and then his expression softened. Apparently he was unaware of what had happened over the weekend. "Call my office if you want to talk," he said. And then he was gone, too.

I wanted to stay, commiserate, maybe even grieve—after all, he was my first death, too, or at least the first one in which I had played any significant role as a doctor—but I was on call again that night. Soon new patients would be rolling in, the runway would be lined up with stretchers, and I was going to get swamped with the usual tasks. In the afternoon, I heard her crying loudly in his room. "Wake up, wake up, I don't want to live without you." Her cries could be heard in the unit for hours, yet the place just rolled on. The telemetry monitors kept ringing. They had never been able to distinguish between mundane stirrings and real danger, and now, it seemed to me, they could not distinguish between life and death.

Mr. Jusczak was pronounced brain-dead by the neurology team the following morning. That afternoon, his wife ordered him removed from the ventilator. She wept uncontrollably as attendants put his body on a gurney and took him to the morgue. On the death certificate, the cause of death was accurately noted as status epilepticus. No mention was made of the high sodium. When I called Rajiv later that day, he stopped me in the middle of my rant to ask me what the hell I was talking about. He had already forgotten.

heart rhythms

What about the wife and babies if you have them? Leave them! Heavy are the responsibilities to yourself, to the profession and to the public. Your wife will be glad to bear her share of the sacrifices you make.

—SIR WILLIAM OSLER

One night in August, about two months into internship, Sonia and I were strolling past a red firehouse on Seventy-fifth Street when the subject of marriage first came up. The Upper East Side was languid and barren, as denizens had feverishly gotten themselves out of the city to savor the last spell of the summer. After nearly two months basically living in my apartment, Sonia herself was getting ready to return to Washington to start her third year of medical school. I had been thinking that it was just as well. I liked her very much, but frankly, I didn't think the relationship was going to survive if she stayed in New York.

I had had so little to offer in our summer together. Though we managed to go out on dates a couple of times a week, it was almost always on my post-call days, when I was edgy and sleep-deprived. Between fourteen-hour shifts in the hospital and every third night on call, it was all I could do to plop myself on my couch, order dinner delivery, read a few pages of medicine, and watch a few minutes of *Seinfeld* before going to bed. Just last week, Sonia had spent three hundred dollars to get us tickets to a *Mostly Mozart* concert at Lincoln Center, but I had slept through the entire performance. At my apartment, the mail was piling up; the newspaper went unread; clothes needed to be laundered. Most evenings I found myself wanting to be alone to catch up on life. To me, all this spelled a relationship in trouble, but Sonia, ever an optimist, seemed to take the bumps in stride.

She came from a family of physicians, so she seemed to understand much better than I the pressures on a dual-doctor relationship. As the firstborn daughter of two doctors, she had been cloaked in the medical profession her whole life. Her mother had trained as a radiologist but was now a practicing internist. Her father was the director of intensive care units at three hospitals. Her grandfather, like mine, had been a doctor in India. Two out of her three maternal uncles were doctors, and so were their wives. Her aunt was a primary care physician in Ohio, and the aunt's husband a gastroenterologist. Her sister was already in medical school, and most of her high-school-age cousins were preparing to pursue premedical studies. My father yearned to be a doctor; my brother, of course, was training to be an interventional cardiologist. I found it ironic that though I had never wanted to become a doctor, physicians now intimately surrounded me in virtually every sphere of my life.

Under an aluminum canopy outside a Korean deli, she asked me where things with us were heading. Were we going to stay together after she moved to Washington? Were we eventually going to get married? I told her I didn't know. We had only been together a couple of months. I couldn't look much beyond my next rotation, let alone months or years into the future. Plus, I remained ambivalent about the relationship, if not about Sonia. Though I didn't tell her this, marrying a doctor seemed limiting to me in some fundamental way I couldn't quite put my finger on. What would we talk about? I pictured a future sitting at the dinner table discussing arterial blood gases or Medicare reimbursement. Internship was already beginning to confirm my worst fears that medicine was a cookbook craft, bereft of beauty. Wouldn't I get more out of marrying a linguistics professor, or even a lawyer?

At the same time, I knew how lucky I was to have met Sonia, and so soon after coming to New York, too. She was warm and funny, sexy and stylish, upbeat and forgiving. Her mind was somehow able to sample all the possible outcomes of a situation and settle on the most positive one. She had a great sense of humor. When Bruce, my goldfish, was sick, Sonia put him into a plastic yogurt container filled with water and stress-coat liquid, dubbed it the "FICU," and said he was having a "code orange." We shared many of the same interests: literature, dining out, walks in Central Park. Growing up, we both had felt a sense of alienation from our Indian peers, and yet as adults we both wanted to reconnect with our heritage. She was even Punjabi; our mothers had grown up in the same district of northern India, and her family was fairly traditional like mine (which is why, like mine, they were pressuring her to marry and settle down). Of course, we had our differences—if she was Venus, I was more like Saturn—but the relationship seemed to have all the makings of one that could lead to marriage. Yet the doctor issue was holding me back.

My father sensed my ambivalence about the relationship. When my parents came to visit in the late summer, they met Sonia at my apartment. A couple of days later, my father and I went to the Hi-Life to talk about my budding romance over a couple of beers. Sonia had made quite an impression on him. After meeting her, he had described her, only half facetiously, as Sophia Loren with Einstein's brain.

"Your problem is that you want someone from heaven, but you live on earth," my father said, sipping a Budweiser.

"That's not true," I said.

"Then what's the problem?"

"No problem, just stuff I need to think over."

"What kind of stuff?"

"Just stuff."

"Like what?"

"Well, for one thing, she's a medical student," I blurted out. "I don't think I want to marry a doctor."

I expected a scornful response, but my father nodded thoughtfully and said, "I can understand that. How will you find time for each other?"

Of course, my concerns ran much deeper than that, but I decided to let it go. I was glad that for once my father could see my point of view.

When I talked with colleagues, most of them thought that marrying another doctor was a good idea. A friend of my brother's, a gastroenterology fellow, told me: "Marry a doctor. When you get paged away during your anniversary dinner, only another doctor will understand." Dr. Carmen, who was married to an internist, said there were advantages to marrying another doctor. "Julie and I speak the same language," he said one morning when I stopped by his office. "We belong to the same clique. I don't have to go home and say, 'I started a dopamine drip on a patient today. Oh, and by the way, dopamine is a drug we use to . . .'" Amanda, my co-intern in the CCU, who was married to a lawyer, said that being in the same demanding field could be good for our marriage. "You'll always have your work to talk about"— but that was precisely what worried me. Her advice presupposed an equivalent level of commitment to our profession, which I knew wasn't there—at least not yet.

For Sonia, medicine was a cornerstone of her life. She loved reading all about lipid physiology and diabetes. What I was content to memorize, she wanted to dig into more deeply. I was afraid she and her family would eventually see through my façade.

When I spoke with Dr. Carmen, I told him about a recent study I'd read in a medical journal. A group of researchers surveyed over a thousand doctors, comparing the quarter in dual-doctor marriages with the rest in "mixed marriages." Overall, they found that dual-doctor marriages were relatively happy and stable. Compared with other physicians, doctors in dual-doctor marriages reported greater satisfaction in discussing and sharing work interests with their spouses, more involvement in child rearing by both partners, and a higher family income.

The survey also found that dual-doctor marriages were traditional in unexpected ways, particularly in the area of family. Compared with other female doctors, for example, women in dual-doctor marriages spent more time rearing children, more often arranged their work schedules to fulfill family responsibilities, worked fewer hours, and earned less money. That was surprising. I was so used to seeing assertive, independent women in the hospital that it was hard to believe they reverted to traditional roles at home. "Medicine is not a radical profession," Dr. Carmen said. "The women are by and large traditional, and so are the men. They come from good families that stress education and family values. Probably the most radical thing women in this field do is go out and have a career."

Sonia felt like many of the doctors I spoke with. "I would never feel comfortable with a lawyer or a Wall Streeter," she said on that languid summer evening. "For me it's about finding yet another place of common ground. I love that we are in the same field. We can help each other. We can even go into practice together!" Inside, I groaned. I never wanted her to see me practicing medicine. In the hospital I felt constricted, anxious, racked with doubts. I didn't want her to see that side of me.

"So are we going to get married?" Sonia asked me again, as we waited to cross the street.

"Let's see how things go," I replied.

"So I guess in the coming months you'll be deciding whether to rule me in or out," she said with a mischievous glint. It was a reference to my time in the CCU, where we were always ruling out myocardial infarction. It was the kind of comment Sonia was always making: pithy, honest, funny, without a hint of animus. I burst out laughing.

customer service

Medicine, as a general technique of health even more than as a service to the sick or an art of cures, assumes an increasingly important place in the administrative system and the machinery of power.

—MICHEL FOUCAULT, *POWER/KNOWLEDGE: SELECTED INTERVIEWS & OTHER WRITINGS,* 1972–1977

The clock-radio alarm sounded at 5:45. It was still dark outside. Even though Sonia had been in Washington for several weeks now, I still kept to what was now my side of the bed, as if transgressing into her space would mar a sweet memory. I lay in bed for a while, swathed in the covers, drifting in and out of sleep. The month in the CCU had left me with a touch of insomnia, and I had tossed and turned most of the night. So this must be what Rajiv had meant, I thought. In medical school, when I confessed to him that I worried about whether I'd be able to wake up in the morning during internship, he replied rhetorically: "Do you wake up for finals? Then you'll wake up for internship. It's like having a final every single day of your life."

A Neil Young song came on the radio, and for a few minutes I was transported back to parties in the Berkeley Hills, where beer and joints were passed around liberally from one friendship-braceleted hand to the next. Those days held so much promise: living among the giant redwoods, the rooftops peeking out over the dense clouds, everything green and fresh. Now I was living in a concrete jungle, and the thought of going to the hospital across the street and standing on my feet for twelve hours and rounding on patients I hardly knew, and drawing blood and inserting IVs and doing all the other things that were expected of me, filled me with dread. It felt like I was in a boat being pulled along by a powerful current, not knowing where I was heading, only that I was being propelled toward some discovery I might not want to make, but that I needed to confront.

I forced myself out of bed, put on my shorts and sneakers, and went downstairs for a jog. A morning run to relieve stress had become an indispensable part of my day; I knew I'd be useless in the hospital without it. Outside, the air was hazy, as the rising sun diffracted through the early morning fog. The sidewalk in front of the building was the usual minefield of dog turds. People were buying coffee from the cart at the corner. A few green-scrubbed figures were already scurrying toward the hospital. Must be surgical residents, I thought, always the first to get to the wards.

I sprinted down the bike lanes of the promenade. The East River reflected the sunlight like a mirror. Roosevelt Island glittered like a shiny brooch as cargo boats floated by. I was crossing over a peeling overpass when I ran into Alphonse, a fellow intern, who was heading into the hospital in slacks, a button-down Oxford shirt, and tie. I had first met Alphonse during the outpatient month in July. Tall and muscular, intense and soft-spoken, he had a strong Caribbean accent and an elusive, tranquil island air about him. His hair was thick and curly, and his short mustache looked like it had been painted on. "Just coming back from your run?" he said, grinning impishly. I nodded, trying to hide my embarrassment. Most mornings Alphonse arrived on the 10-North ward, our current assignment, nearly an hour before I did.

By the time I went in, it was almost six-thirty. In medical school, I had strolled proudly into the hospital in my short white coat. Now, I marched in at an anxious clip, head down, as though to duck the long day that stretched before me. I thought of how my father used to walk me to the school bus stop in New Delhi when I was a boy. We usually left home at dawn. My fingers would ache as his warm, sweaty palm tightly squeezed them as we crossed the busy road, trying to avoid the slow traffic and bullock carts and roaming white Sindhi cows. At the bus stop, or sometimes in the park on the way there, he'd force-feed me an overripe banana. On this morning, nostalgia for that time, for my father, came flooding back. It was on mornings like these, when I yearned for the day to have ended already, that I missed having some- one there to hold my hand, to force-feed me breakfast, to pull me for- ward, to watch my back.

I hurried past the dour security guard, past the library and the café, which were closed, and into a marble lobby. This was the Green- berg Pavilion of New York Hospital. For all the drama I always imag- ined going on in here, right now it was placid, almost like a museum, displaying gilt-framed portraits of hospital benefactors instead of mas- terpieces. In a corner was a small piano, and hanging nearby was a no- tice addressed to hospital employees:

Welcome all customers in a friendly manner. Make eye contact and smile. Create positive first impressions. Treat everyone with respect. If possible, exceed your patient's expectations.

Next to the notice was a typed testimonial from a patient:

"You take the time to listen, answer questions, and make patients feel, no matter what, that they are your number one priority."

I shook my head, as if to block a thought, and rode the elevator to the tenth floor. Ward 10-North was one of only three general medical wards in a hospital sectioned mostly into subspecialty units. Here, the patients, often underinsured, some homeless or with criminal back- grounds, were treated for bread-and-butter disorders: AIDS, pneumo- nia, congestive heart failure, and the like. 10-North was the place in the hospital where you were most likely to find security guards carrying revolvers or orderlies conducting 1:1 surveillance watches (while sitting in the hallway outside the wayward patient's room reading *People* magazine). It was ward medicine in all its unfiltered mess.

The physical plant, however, like the rest of the pavilion, was gleaming and new. At the end of a long, brightly lit corridor were tall windows looking out onto the sloping steel girders of the Triborough Bridge. The staff workstation had a fax machine, a copier, a chart rack, several desktop computers, a shelf with about thirty different requisition forms, and a whiteboard with the names of the forty-odd patients, color-coded by intern/resident team. It was here that doctors, nurses, and social workers took refuge, writing orders, checking labs, pressing on their eyeballs while on hold on the phone. Sometimes a patient or family member would lean over to ask a question, but even that was frowned upon.

The routine on 10-North was call every fourth night, with a cap of six admissions per night per intern (the overflow went to more senior residents), except on Saturdays, when you were expected to admit patients all night long. At 10:00 p.m., chief residents came around for "cookie rounds" to discuss the day's admissions over a box of Entenmann's. (They always brought an assortment of goodies but never the thing you desired most after sixteen hours on your feet: fluid.) Overnight, you were responsible for your own patients (those you'd admitted in previous days), plus the patients you admitted that night, plus all the other patients who had been signed out to you for the evening. "Cross-coverage" was definitely the hardest part of being on call. You had to make critical decisions about patients you barely knew. Sign-outs were often inadequate (sometimes just names and lists of medical problems) as interns and residents rushed to get out of the hospital after their own long shifts. The nurses could call you for anything, and they often did: fever spikes requiring blood cultures, respiratory distress requiring an arterial blood gas, insomnia requiring sedatives. It helped to have a short "differential," a list of diagnostic possibilities, for the cardinal symptoms—chest pain, abdominal pain, shortness of breath—committed to memory. The next day, post-call, you could go home after your notes were done and you had taken care of any unfinished business from the night before—including signing out all your patients to other doctors. It was supposed to be done by midmorning, but it almost never was. Around noon, other residents would start offering their help. "What're you still doing here?" they'd say, as if they had just noticed you. "What can I do to get you out?" The key was to finish your work quickly, or you could easily stay past three o'clock. The longer you stayed, the less efficient you became, the more time it took to write notes or call consultants, and once you hit the wall, any chance of getting out in a timely fashion was pretty much shot.

I arrived on the floor at six forty-five to find Rohit, a second-year resident, sitting at the nursing station. He was a short Indian man with a bright, open face and a broad, insincere smile. He looked like someone I might have avoided at my parents' kirtans (prayer meetings) when I was growing up.

"You're late," he said, checking his digital watch. "We have to pick up night-float admissions at seven o'clock."

"Yes, I know," I said, hovering in the corridor.

"All right, hurry up and see your patients," he snapped, turning back to the computer. "You've got fifteen minutes."

I went down the hall to the first room, which was filled with the stale effluvium of sleep. Michael Harrison was a typical patient on 10-North, an emaciated black man of about seventy who was on dialysis for end-stage kidney and heart failure. His neck was sinewy, his arms pencil-thin. His temples were bony, yet full at the forehead, imparting an intellectual look. Short wispy hairs were growing out of his chin. His skin looked like it was frosted with ice, probably a sign of kidney failure. It was obvious that he had once been handsome.

I said good morning. He opened his eyes slowly, nodded, and then closed them again. It was early; he wanted to sleep.

I asked him how he was feeling. "Okay," he mumbled. I pulled down the blanket that was covering his body. A catheter filled with dark, reddish brown urine the color of beer passed through the end of his shriveled penis. I pressed gently on his edematous legs, leaving tiny craters with my fingertips. "You're going to get more dialysis today," I said. He opened his eyes. "Not today, I ain't goin'," he said, shaking his head. "They took me upstairs yesterday and they left me on the machine two hours longer. They said three hours and then they did five. They said I be back in three hours but I ain't come back."

"Well, maybe they needed to take out more fluid," I said.

"No, that ain't what it was," he replied, shaking his head. "They was just foolin' around. In that dialysis room, all they do is drink beer."

"I find that hard to believe." Mr. Harrison was always making such claims.

"Yeah they do. I think so, at least. Probably smoke pot, too. I told one of the aides there, 'I'm goin' to speak to your manager.' He didn't care. He just laughed."

He coughed, and then cleared his throat loudly. His head moved searchingly from side to side. I picked up a box of tissues and offered him one, but he had already raised the bedsheet to his lips and wiped his tongue of the phlegm. It was thick and green and coagulated, with a pinkish tinge, and it stuck to the sheet like a thick gob of glue. I swiped a handful of tissues and wiped the sputum off the bedspread, trying to avoid looking at it.

"Nobody cares," he continued philosophically. "Nobody wants to bother with you when you're like this. They go on past you, they don't care. They say, 'I'll be back,' but no one come back. I need pills, but they don't care. Yesterday they gave me nothing to eat."

"Why? Did you have a test?"

"No."

"So why didn't they bring you a tray?"

"I don't know," he replied, exasperated. "They overlooked it."

I glanced at my watch. It was ten minutes to seven. "I'll come by to see you later," I said.

"Can you turn me over?"

"I can't do it right now," I replied automatically. "I'll tell the nurse to come in."

"You can't just turn me over? The nurse said she couldn't do it; she didn't have the time." I looked over my list. Rohit was surely going to give me a hard time if I didn't at least get my patients' vital signs before rounds.

"All right," I said, putting down my sheet. "I'll turn you over." I lowered the bed rail. His body lay crumpled on the bedsheets. I reached around him, wedging my hand under his moist armpit, and scooted him up in the bed so that his head reached the pillow. Then, with my other arm, I reached under him and spun him onto his side.

"That's better," he said. "If you ain't been through this, you don't know what it's like. The nurses tell me I ain't allowed to sleep on my stomach. It's the regulations, somepin' about it's against the law. But I can sleep on my stomach if I want to. It's my body."

I nodded impatiently.

"All peoples are human," he continued, like a man who had seen his share in the world. "It don't matter if you white or black or a foreigner like you. It don't matter. We all human. Everybody deserve to be treated right. Not like this. You ask them, 'Can you turn me over?' and they say, 'Go to sleep; just go to sleep.' I say, 'I can't go to sleep. My butt be hurtin', how am I supposed to sleep?' "

I shifted on my feet. I had to get out of the room.

"What day is it?" he asked.

"September 8," I replied.

His eyes glimmered. "It's my birthday."

"Oh," I said, pleasantly surprised. "How old are you?"

"Six . . . nine."

"Sixty-nine?"

"No, six . . . plus . . . nine." He smiled devilishly. "I'm fifteen years old."

Outside, I jotted down a few notes. The encounter had taken almost fifteen minutes. At the rate I was going, I'd have to start coming in at five o'clock to preround. I immediately dismissed the thought. Why ever go home?

At the nursing station, Alphonse and Rohit were waiting for me. "Did you know that it's Mr. Harrison's birthday?" I said. "Nice," Rohit replied, turning away. "Tell the nurses to give him something."

We walked down the long hallway to the stairs. Up ahead were the resident call rooms. Through a window, off in the distance, I could see a smokestack, a few skyscrapers, and the Triborough Bridge. Every morning I would spend a few moments staring out at the bridge, watching real life go on. It reminded me of the Bay Bridge in San Francisco, and looking at it reminded me of my old life. The view was both sad and something that I relished.

We headed downstairs to the conference room to pick up our admissions. Rohit took the scuffed gray steps two at a time as Alphonse and I followed. We exited the stairwell on the fifth floor and took a shortcut through the oncology unit. The atmosphere here was quieter, more sedate. The ward smelled of disinfectant, unlike 10-North, which always had a musty odor. We marched through double doors, entering a carpeted back hallway where a fax machine had printed out the admission list by ward and resident team. We picked up a sheet.

In the conference room, the night-float residents were presenting cases as the ward teams, arranged in small groups, took notes. "This is a lady that's a soft admit because she's a VIP," said a resident. "This guy's a two-pack-per-day smoker for thirty-five years and we're putting him up in a two-thousand-dollars-a-night hotel room," said another. In one group, a team giggled as a resident explained how he was trying to arrange a CAT scan for a morbidly obese patient by transferring him to the Bronx Zoo, where they had a scanner for elephants and other large animals. Cynthia, a classmate, came over to say hello. "Rumor has it you don't preround," she whispered. I was stunned; who had been talking? "I preround," I protested. "Just not on every patient."

After picking up our admissions, we hurried back to the floor. Precariously resting our coffee cups on the wooden banister outside each room, we made rounds. Since Alphonse had managed to preround on all his patients, he had a lot more to say than me.

One of his patients was Peter DiGeorge, whose room had the rank odor of morning breath. "He has that HIV look," Rohit said out of earshot. When I asked him what that meant, he just looked at me and shrugged, as if it required no further explanation. At the bedside was a wooden table with drawers, and on the far side of the room were light pink curtains framing windows overlooking the central atrium. DiGeorge had been admitted to the hospital because of tiny blood clots that were seeding his skin. He had a broad nose, a high, arched forehead, and a beard that looked like a patch of ragweed. In deportment and appearance, he resembled a boxer dog. Two gold teeth jutted out of his mouth like fangs. His goatee, complemented by his arch eyebrows, gave him a sinister look. He was wearing large aviator glasses that partially obscured crusted lesions around his eyes. When he opened his mouth, I could see it was coated with large white plaques of *Candida fungus*, an opportunistic infection often seen in AIDS patients. Rohit exposed his legs, which looked like the surface of a blueberry muffin. The bluish spots culminated in a large round one above the right ankle, which was about a centimeter wide, with red and black crust, exuding pus. With his bare hands, Rohit pushed on the sides of it, and DiGeorge winced. Rohit had taken a Polaroid of the lesion yesterday to present at morning report with Dr. Wood. When DiGeorge had asked for a copy, Rohit had promised to make him one, but we never did. "We're going to continue your antibiotics," Rohit told him. "Nothing new today."

Our next patient was a tiny man who had lost both his legs in a car accident several years earlier. Despite his devastating disability, he was fairly spry. Above his bed, which had a special mattress to prevent bedsores, was a pulley contraption, which he immediately grabbed with his unusually muscular arms to help himself up. As he leaned forward, holding on to the metal handlebars, Rohit pointed out a pressure ulcer on his upper buttocks, which looked infected. On his abdomen was a stapled wound from a recent gallbladder operation. Again with his bare hands, Rohit pressed on it, trying to see if it was tender, which it wasn't. The patient pointed to a tiny bulge under the skin of his abdomen. "What is this?" he asked.

Rohit rubbed over it with his fingers. "Maybe a gallstone."

"But they took my gallbladder out."

Rohit shrugged. "Call Surgery and have them take a look at it," he told Alphonse. Then he tapped on the man's stumps and walked out, Alphonse and I following in step.

In the hallway, I looked over at Alphonse and made a face. The thought of all the resistant microbes in the room—perhaps even on my skin—was making me queasy, and I was disgusted by the fact that Rohit hadn't washed his hands. "Wash your hands, dude," I said before we moved on. Rohit gave me a withering look. "Oh, I guess I forgot," he said.

My team had several Russian-speaking patients. They always insisted on talking through interpreters, but there was never anyone around who spoke Russian. On rounds, we managed to get by with a few miscellaneous words, like *balit*, rubbing our chests or abdomens or pointing to our temples to inquire about pain. We often promised to come back to talk to these patients, but we rarely did. By the time an interpreter showed up, you were done with your notes and had already written orders and made a plan for the day, without any verbal input from the patient.

We went to see my night-float admission. Agnes Lahey was an obese woman of about seventy with a large broad face and a mouth that was missing several teeth. She was wearing dark, horn-rimmed glasses, a steel bracelet, and several rings, even though jewelry was supposed to be put away by the nurses for safekeeping. She had the overweight, sweaty look of a trailer-park queen.

Rohit had described her as a "social admit," a "frequent flyer," and, in fact, this was her eleventh hospital visit, including visits to the ER, in the past six months. Social admissions were a significant percentage on 10-North. The hospital, we were told, nearly always lost money on these patients. "Utilization reviewers"—hospital spies, basically—would continually check with us to make sure we were getting these patients out in a timely manner.

Lahey met all the demographic criteria for the type of patient who is often a social admit. She was elderly, a widow, with a long list of chronic medical problems, including diabetes, hypertension, arthritis, perhaps even a touch of dementia. She was a retired hospital cook whose husband had died in a "personal fight" about ten years ago. Now she was living with her daughter and granddaughter in a small apartment on Seventy-seventh Street. A social worker had written that in the summertime, Lahey frequently came to the hospital complaining of heatstroke. The hospital had even bought her an air conditioner to prevent repeated visits to the ER.

When I asked her why she was in the hospital, she said that she slipped while walking with a cane in her house and fell into her cat's litter box. "I went to three hospitals before I came here," she said. I asked which ones. "One was St. Charles . . . or St. George . . . or some such saint. Another was—" She stopped.

"St. Luke's?" I said.

"No, it was a funny name."

"Presbyterian, Bellevue . . .?"

"No, those are natural names. I think it started with an *S*."

"Southside?" I said.

"Yes, Southside," she replied hesitantly. "Yeah, I think that was the name."

I took my stethoscope out of my coat pocket. "Everyone here keeps saying I want to be here," she said. "But I don't want to be here. I hurt my hip falling down and now I can't walk. I hear what people say. They say, 'I wish she wouldn't come around so much.' It makes me feel really rotten, real bad. I'm here because I need to be here. I don't get a thrill from it."

I lifted the edge of her diaper to inspect her hip. A rancid, fishy smell wafted into my nostrils. "Years ago, the hospital was very good," she said as I took a step back. "You could call a nurse and ask for this, that, and the other, and you got it. Don't get me wrong, I like it here.

People are more friendly in the hospital than on the outside. I'm just saying that the old hospital was much better. People had more time for you. The food was pretty good, too.

"Look here." She pointed to her IV, which had a half-filled syringe attached to it. "The nurse came in to give me an injection and she just left it here. She said she'd come back but she didn't. She was flushing the IV and then she went off, said she had something else to do. I just noticed it. It's hard to get something, sometimes. They're always doing something, the nurses."

I bent over to listen to her chest. She leaned forward to meet me. "Don't tell the nurse I said anything," she said. "Or else she'll take it out on me."

I nodded, putting the stethoscope back in my ears.

"I don't want to go to a nursing home or a retirement center," she whispered. "If I can't come into the hospital every once in a while, I don't know what I'm going to do."

MORNINGS ON 10-NORTH were a collective phenomenon. It was like the *bhajans* Sonia and I once attended in the West Village, where a few people would start chanting—*"Om namo shivaya, om namo shivaya"*—and then people would start clapping, and the clapping would synchronize, the energy grow, and then you were one, a collective being. Life on the wards was like the plasmons I had studied in condensed matter physics, where individual electrons, moving randomly, coalesced into something greater than the sum of their parts. There was a sort of synchronized buzz. You could almost hear it, the hum. You could see it, the mass of doctors and nurses and social workers and case managers and utilization reviewers becoming one organism, running around doing seemingly random things that were so amazingly coordinated. In the midst of this collective excitation, I kept thinking, *Why am I so lonely?*

Ward life as an intern was a constant juggle of competing tasks. You could be speaking to an attending when a nurse would interrupt and tell you that the blood test you had ordered for that morning somehow got overlooked, and now you had to draw it yourself, and oh, by the way, the patient has kidney failure and the last serum potassium was at a life-threatening level, so you'd better hurry up before the patient has a cardiac arrest. It was hard to develop perspective because everything seemed equally necessary. Ensuring that the radiology department received the requisition slip seemed as important as the scan itself—perhaps even more important because it was your job to ensure that the slip was faxed and received, not sitting in a corner somewhere. Tasks got reduced to their most elemental quality: done/not done. The rhythm of the day was digitized into tiny boxes, to be filled in at every hour.

Having so much to do was bad enough, but not knowing why you were doing what you were doing was terrifying. Why was I ordering a tagged red-blood-cell scan? That CAT scan: Should it be done with or without dye, and with high-resolution cuts or not? Why exactly was I calling the Infectious Diseases service (whose famously distempered fellow seemed to relish tearing into diffident interns). I was constantly afraid. When you didn't know what you were doing from moment to moment, it seemed like *anything* could happen.

Patients were needy, their demands overwhelming. Sometimes they'd want you to linger so they could talk, especially the VIPs, who'd tell you about all the hospital fund-raisers they'd chaired or the money they had donated or the philanthropy they had performed, but none of that really mattered, not because I was egalitarian or inured to wealth or power, but because for an intern nothing is more important than finishing up and getting the hell out of the hospital. Sometimes, after a long day, I'd simply walk up to the bedside and place my stethoscope on a patient's chest without any pleasantries or preliminaries. One time I did it when a patient was sitting on a bedside commode, straining to have a bowel movement. "I've been sitting here so long," she said mournfully. "Least the nurse could do is give me toilet paper to wipe." I told the woman that I'd find a nurse for her. "But first—first, could I just listen to your lungs?" I loathed myself for even asking, but it was the end of the day and I didn't want to have to come back to conduct my exam. I had her lean forward on the commode, all the while thinking: *Has it come to this? Have you lost all shame?*

Everyone seemed to know how the place worked except me. "Don't you see I'm waiting for the chart," a transporter would shout while I was on hold with the lab. "I'm sorry," I'd say. "I didn't realize you were waiting." And then she'd turn to a colleague as though I had said the most incredible thing in the world. "He said he didn't see me standing here. Ha!" The colleague would murmur her support. If I asked where my patient was going, it would lead to further rebuke. "Taking him where?! To X-ray!" Not only had I been inconsiderate, I didn't even know which test my patient was having!

People always acted like you were doing something wrong but they wouldn't tell you what it was. Sometimes I'd be sitting by myself in a corner and someone would come up and say, "Pack it in, honey, you can't always be getting in people's way." My brother had warned me to keep the nurses happy. If they liked you, they'd look out for you, keep you from going astray. Without doubt they were powerful, but their power was only in the inverse: they couldn't really make things better for you, but they could certainly make things worse. The ward clerks were generally rude and abrupt. Leafing through their tabloids with their long false fingernails, they would barely look up when you asked them a question, and then only impatiently. The ecology on the wards was hostile; interactions were hard-bitten, fast-paced; conversations were brief, clipped, urgent, spoken at a volume and frequency I wasn't used to or comfortable with. I kept waiting for a sense of hardiness, a sort of occupational pugilism, to develop, but it never did.

It seemed like the only people I wasn't scared of were my patients. They were as much at a loss in this place as I was.

AT SIX-THIRTY ONE EVENING on 10-North, I had finished my notes, checked labs, ordered medications and morning blood draws, updated the medication sheets, and held several conferences with anxious families. I had tickets to the U.S. Open that night and was hoping to get out to Flushing Meadow in time to catch one of the stadium court matches. The ward was quiet; most of the other residents had already left. I was getting ready to page Alphonse to sign out when a patient walked up to the workstation pushing an IV pole. Stocky, middle-aged, Mr. Diaz wore a drab, light blue hospital gown that looked like it was about two sizes too small. The intense scowl on his face might have alerted me as to what was going to happen next, even before he started shouting.

"Where is my fucking pain medicine?" he blared.

The ward clerk swiveled around in his chair. He was a big, burly man with a shiny globe of a head, who was nicknamed Mr. T. "Who is this man's nurse?" he boomed.

She emerged from the medication room: thin, grim-faced, with short brown hair tied in an imperious bun. She asked Mr. Diaz what the problem was.

His eyes darted furiously. "Where is my Percocet?!"

The nurse replied that it wasn't due for another hour.

"My legs are burning. I got AIDS neuropathy! I was supposed to get my Percocet at four o'clock!"

"That's not what the doctor wrote," the nurse shot back. She turned to me, as if trying to enlist support. "I've been trying to explain to him: the order is for every six hours with no rescues. I can't give him anything until someone changes the order."

I was happy to do it, but before I could say anything, Mr. Diaz's face turned an unhealthy maroon.

"That is not my fucking problem," he roared. "Give me my pills!"

"Get them yourself," the nurse retorted, walking away. That seemed like the wrong thing to say at that moment.

Mr. Diaz bent over and hoisted the IV pole over his head. Fluid was still running into his arm as he charged at the nurse.

"Watch your back!" Mr. T shouted. The nurse sprinted around to where I was sitting.

"Give me my pills!" Mr. Diaz said, still holding the pole over his head, pointing it at us like a javelin. We remained frozen in place. One of the nurses continued her charting.

I had always sympathized with people who lost control. It used to happen to me all the time when I was a kid, getting into fisticuffs with other children on the playground or with my brother, who with his shrinking disposition would always run away when I became enraged. One time, I boxed his ears so hard the ear canal bled. I remembered how compassion from my parents had always defused my anger. And now, as I gingerly walked over to Mr. Diaz, I believed the same approach would work on him.

I stopped about ten feet away from him. Mr. T shot out of his chair. "Get back now," he commanded.

"Sir, please put the pole down," I said gently. "We'll give you your pills." I was ready to fly if he charged at me, but something told me that wouldn't happen.

"I know you're in pain." I inched a little closer, emboldened by his quiet attention. "Just try to relax. I'll change the order."

Still brandishing the pole above his head, Mr. Diaz looked me up and down curiously. His face seemed to smooth out a bit, even as his gown still clung wetly to his chest. Then he turned back to the nurse. The sight of her appeared to enrage him again. "You think you can treat people like dogs," he snarled. "I ask you for pills, you don't come. I ask you for water, you say I'm asking too much." He turned back to me. "When you want something, they don't come. When you don't want them, they're on top of you."

I nodded sympathetically. From what I had seen of 10-North, his comment didn't seem that far off the mark. The nurses were taking care of too many patients per shift to pay sufficient attention to any one person.

"What are you smiling at?" Mr. Diaz blared at the nurse. "You think this is funny? I got the virus! I've been in pain all afternoon!" He was gesticulating violently again, spittle spraying from his lips. "I'm a veteran. I served my country!" He took a half step and flung the pole at the workstation. He did it almost halfheartedly, as if it was an inevitable consequence of the stakes he had set. The pole wobbled and dove into the tile floor, clattering loudly, yanking out his IV. Blood started trickling down his arm and dripping onto the tile floor. He leaned against a wall and let himself down. No one moved.

"Anyone come near me, they're going to get AIDS," he said, choking back sobs. We watched him quietly. A sort of calm descended on the ward, like after a suicide bombing.

Security officers soon arrived. Their mere presence, with their quiet authority, seemed to relax him. "All I wanted was my medicine," he said, watching the officers put on gowns, gloves, and plastic face shields. "She could have just gave me my medicine."

The officers roughly stood him up and frog-marched him back to bed. A nurse followed with a syringe filled with sedative. Once they disappeared, a quiet buzz returned to the ward. Mr. T went back to answering the phone. Nurses arrived for the change of shift. "Never a dull moment," someone said.

A little while later, I went to see him. A nurse was tending to him as a security guard kept watch. He was sprawled on his bed, out cold. His arms and legs were tied to the bed rails and over his midsection was a restraint that looked like a cloth corset. Beads of perspiration glistened on his balding head, like dew on morning grass. His pupils responded sluggishly to my penlight, a consequence, I assumed, of the massive dosage of sedative he had just received. Punching buttons on his IV monitor, the nurse said: "This is the sort of crap we have to deal with every day."

I nodded. Though I was sympathetic to Mr. Diaz's suffering, I was annoyed that the episode had disrupted my plans for the evening. "He was out of hand," I told the nurse.

The next day, I heard Mr. Diaz was sorry, but when his doctors found out about his outburst, they dismissed him from their clinic. He apparently had a history of threatening behavior and was already "on probation."

Over the next few days, intrigued by what had happened, I asked my colleagues about their own brushes with menacing patients. At least half claimed to have been verbally or physically abused by a patient within the past year. Many were innocuous encounters of the sort I would have been inclined to ignore: ranting by a paranoid schizophrenic, a wild punch from a withdrawing alcoholic. But a few were of a more serious nature. A nurse told me that a patient had tried to break a window in his room with an IV pole. When asked why, the patient said he needed to go to the bathroom, but that the nurse had waited too long to help him. A doctor in the emergency room, a short, balding man with a gruff, thuggish demeanor, recalled the time a CEO with chest pain had shouted maniacally at him, then swung at him and threatened to have him fired. "I call it the McDonald's mentality," he said. "At McDonald's, it's first come, first served, but it can't be that way in the ER. I've heard people say, 'That guy's only had chest pain for two hours. I've had back pain for six months.' "

And this was just in my hospital, a relatively staid institution on the Upper East Side. When I looked in the medical literature, I was shocked by what I read. An ear, nose, and throat specialist in Michigan had been shot and killed by a patient who faulted the doctor for making him dizzy. A plastic surgeon in Washington was killed after performing a face-lift. A psychiatrist in Miami was shot and killed on a hospital psychiatric ward. On average, I learned, one American physician is killed by a patient every year. And many more are victims of assaults.

According to a report I found, health care workers are assaulted more frequently than any other professional group. Psychiatrists and social service workers ranked fourth in the likelihood of being killed on the job, behind taxi drivers, convenience store clerks, and police officers. Some experts estimated that up to 40 percent of psychiatrists had been assaulted by their patients. More than half, according to one study, continued treating their assailants.

Of all health care workers, nurses probably had it the worst. In a survey, two-thirds of 1,200 nurses reported being assaulted by patients at least once in their careers. One-third said they had been assaulted in the last year. In Great Britain, nursing was considered the most dangerous profession—ahead of bar bouncing—with over a third of nurses being attacked on duty. Eighty-one percent of nurses in a survey said the profession was not as safe as it was when they started.

Some hospitals had instituted changes in response to the violence. A hospital in Detroit had put metal detectors into its emergency room, which in the first six months detected thirty-three handguns and more than a thousand knives. In Australia, a hospital created a "violence management team." Made up of a doctor, a senior nurse, and four orderlies, the team received almost three hundred calls in its first four years of operation.

When I told Rajiv about the Diaz incident, he shrugged it off, as if my exaggerated reaction was just further evidence of my naïveté. He told me a story from his own days as a resident. Once, at about three in the morning, he was performing a history and physical on an HIV-positive patient when, without warning, the man became enraged and blocked the exit of the examination room. "I asked him a question, like did he ever do drugs—you know, a standard part of the social history—and he freaked out. He said that no one cared, that doctors always assumed that he was doing drugs. He started shouting that I was a foreigner, how I was following a set protocol, how I was the third person to ask him that question that night, how I didn't care about understanding him."

"So what did you say to him?" I asked. "How did you draw him out?"

"Draw him out?" my brother replied. "Are you kidding? I pushed him out of the way, ran down the hall, and yelled for security."

By this point in my internship, I had already come to appreciate that there was a fundamental disconnect in the hospital. Good relations with patients weren't rewarded; efficiency was, which meant focusing on the work at hand, operating with a kind of remote control, in front of computer screens and nursing charts and requisition forms, and on the phone. Face-to-face time was a relatively insignificant part of the job. The high counters around the staff workstation delineated not just a workspace but a type of kingdom, too. It might as well have been ringed by a moat.

falling down

The great secret of doctors, known only to their wives, but still hidden from the public, is that most things get better by themselves; most things, in fact, are better in the morning.

—LEWIS THOMAS, *THE LIVES OF A CELL: NOTES OF A BIOLOGY WATCHER*, 1974

September was an awful month. Four interns announced they were quitting. Cynthia, a classmate, informed Dr. Wood that she was transferring from internal medicine to psychiatry. The news threw me for a loop because I had been thinking about doing the same thing myself. When we talked about it, it was clear that Cynthia didn't see herself in internal medicine. The work was overwhelming—and Cynthia was quick to get overwhelmed. One morning I found her post-call: greasy face, matted red hair, stethoscope draped lopsidedly around her neck, all signs of a rough night. "Patient crumped last night," she said, referring to a rapid and unexpected clinical deterioration, as I handed her a bagel and coffee. "Then he coded. Before I knew it, he was dead."

She opened the aluminum wrapper and started wiping away some of the cream cheese with a plastic knife. "And you know what?" she added almost parenthetically. "I was kind of hoping he would die. One less note for me to write. That's how I felt. Is that wrong?"

"But you know what?" she went on, not waiting for a reply. "I had to write a note anyway, and fill out a death certificate, and deal with the morgue, and call the attending and the family. So it didn't really save me any time at all."

Days on the wards were blurring into each other, and yet every single day was all too painfully real; you couldn't even find solace in amnesia. Checking vital signs, updating medication lists, inserting IVs, drawing blood, reviewing labs, examining patients, one after the other after the other, like an assembly line. After a while, it was hard to stomach. I was starting to snap, taking out my frustrations on the people least equipped to fight back. One particular exchange I remember:

"Oh good, you're here. I have a bunch of questions about all these medications."

"Yes, ma'am."

"So first of all, the fo-fo—"

"Fosinopril."

"Yes, when do I take that?"

"In the morning."

"Yes, but what time?"

"When you take the rest of your medications."

"When should that be?"

"When you normally take them."

"Yes, but when?"

"With breakfast."

"When should I eat breakfast?"

"Eight in the morning."

"I don't wake up that early."

"Then at nine or whenever you wake up."

"I can wake up at eight if you think I should take my medications then."

"No, nine is fine."

"What about the warfarin?"

"Anytime."

"Well, you said at night."

"Then take it at night."

"Because if you say take it at night, I'm going to take it at night."

"Night is fine!"

"What time at night?" And so it went for each drug, twelve in all.

If internship was supposed to stoke intellectual curiosity, I never saw it. Like me, most of my classmates seemed disengaged, mentally exhausted. With patient rosters of fifteen or more each, we were preoccupied with getting our work done. Anything that got in the way— even a bona fide medical mystery—was more often seen as a bother than a learning opportunity. When faced with challenging cases, we almost reflexively called for an expert consultation so we could move on to the next task, however routine. Many consultations were appropriate, but many simply allowed us to avoid thinking about a hard case, because thinking took time. There was no reward for clinical excellence, only the sound of your own hand patting your back.

I was taking care of a man in his seventies with a peculiar problem: when he was sleeping, he would periodically stop breathing. When he was awake, he was lethargic and disoriented, sometimes psychotic. No one on my team knew what was wrong with him. I still don't.

One day the attending physician, a smart and able man, was on the ward perusing the patient's voluminous chart. "You know what?" he said to me. "One day they're going to talk about this guy like they talked about AIDS patients twenty years ago. He falls outside our paradigm. He's a real mystery."

Then he said: "You know what he needs? A medical student."

I must have looked puzzled. He went on: "He needs someone who can spend time with him. Get a new history, read through this chart, examine him from head to toe, ask questions. He needs someone who's going to make him their project."

I nodded, and then we got on with our work. I was caring for about twelve patients at the time. He, in addition to his teaching and research responsibilities, was seeing patients in clinic. There didn't seem to be any time to grapple with a medical mystery. We both realized we were failing our patient by not devoting adequate attention to his problem, but we were too busy to care enough to do something about it. Rajiv had once told me that if you didn't make a diagnosis within forty-eight hours of a patient's being admitted, it never got made, and for the most part, I had discovered, he was right.

The worst was when you were alone with patients and you realized you knew next to nothing about them. They'd be on bi-level positive airway pressure ventilation or something, and you didn't want to go through the chart to figure out why, but you felt guilty, so you hedged and read a little bit and learned a little bit, and read some more and discovered some more, and you realized how much you learned was dependent on how deeply you were willing to look, and what was pushing you was a sense of duty, but the duty was ill defined and couldn't you just ignore it and go home? You'd get mad at the consultants who came by and casually left their recommendations in barely legible handwriting, focusing on a particular organ system, until you realized that you were no better than they. You also didn't want to take responsibility. There was a constant tug-of-war between desire and duty. Your desire was to get the hell out of the hospital and have a life; your duty was to be a good doctor. You wanted to do the right thing, but doing the right thing took time. Patients were complicated; there was so much information to gather and digest, and even if you collected it all, you probably wouldn't know what to do anyway, so why bother?

If you did everything, you felt overwhelmed. If you didn't, you felt guilty. Like my patient with the bedsore. Should I look at it? He was heavy as a rock, and waiting for a nurse to help me push him on his side was going to take too long, so every morning I'd let it go, rationalizing it by thinking, *What's the point? What am I going to do about a bedsore anyway? The surgeons are already involved*—but I wasn't sure they had looked at it either. Could I really come by every morning and pretend it didn't exist? It was these sorts of compromises that made me feel perpetually guilty. I felt paralyzed by my desire to live a life outside the hospital and to do the right thing inside it; to be the kind of doctor I had hoped to be and also be the kind of intern I was expected to be. It was a Faustian bargain. So I would compensate by writing long off-service notes, hoping someone on the next rotation would address the issues my team had ignored. When I complained to Rajiv, he said, "You can't save everyone," which was just the sort of glib remark he was good at making but that never made me feel better at all.

ON CALL NIGHTS, the ward was like a sleeping village, and you were the night watchman on patrol with your penlight and stethoscope. Senior residents were available for backup, but after 10:00 p.m. they were almost always admitting patients or at home sleeping. You could call them if you needed help, but few of us ever did. Not calling backup, I quickly learned, was considered a sign of strength, and for an intern there was nothing more flattering than to be considered "strong." Once, I made the mistake of calling a third-year resident at her apartment in the middle of the night to ask for help performing a spinal tap. She roared at me on the phone for not taking care of the procedure earlier, before she came on duty at 10:00 p.m. When she arrived on the floor, she quickly saw my patient, told me a tap was unnecessary, and then berated me some more for wasting her time. I never called another resident for the remainder of the year, electing instead to page Rajiv (in the middle of the night, if necessary) when I needed help. If I could get so much flak asking for help managing a potential case of meningitis, I could only imagine the kind of wrath I'd incur calling about atypical chest pain or something equally benign.

On night duty, it wasn't the emergencies that overwhelmed so much as the little things, the minor issues—the insomnia, the constipation, the headaches—that the nurses had to make you aware of in the middle of the night. Even when the nurses didn't call, it was impossible to enter any sort of restful sleep. The expectation of the pager going off was enough to keep you in a state of chronic anxiety. Sometimes I'd pace back and forth in the call room, or just outside in the corridor, looking out the window onto the East River and the points of yellow light dotting the skyscape, wondering what sort of calamity would next be visited on me. If I did fall asleep, I usually woke up with a drenching wetness on the back of my neck. Once, a nurse called to tell me that a young man, nervous about a procedure scheduled for the morning, had had fleeting chest pain. When I saw him, he was visibly nervous but otherwise fine. When I told the nurse that a twinge of chest discomfort in an otherwise healthy young man did not require an extensive workup, she made it clear that if I didn't at least perform an electrocardiogram, she was going to file a complaint. So I went and got a machine and wheeled it to the patient's room, but it was broken, and I went and got another one on a different ward, but it was broken, too, and by the time I performed the EKG forty-five minutes later, the patient was fast asleep and irritated at being woken, and, of course, his EKG was completely normal.

There were set times on call when you could expect a flurry of pages, like when the nurses checked vital signs at 4:00 a.m. That was when they called about fevers. Your response was always the same: blood and urine cultures and a portable chest X-ray to rule out pneumonia—but sometimes you discovered that a patient was already on antibiotics or that blood cultures had been drawn every night for the past week, every single one negative, and then you had to decide whether you really needed to stick him again, but most of the time you did so anyway, not for the patient's sake but for your own, lest someone fault you in the morning for not doing it. That was the sad reality of residency: much of the time you were ordering tests to protect yourself. "The endgame of life is so depressing," I wrote in my diary. "Look at Mr. Fisher. Successful lawyer, Goldberg patient. Now look at him. Sick, febrile, dying of who-knows-what: cancer, TB, sarcoidosis? If you think about it, it could make all of life seem unworthwhile if, in the end, we end up dying in the hospital, awakened at 4:00 a.m. by a stupid intern trying to draw another set of blood cultures."

Sometimes I worried about how I was going to get through another night on call, until I realized that my patients were helping me. Their bodies had homeostatic reserve, the capacity to self-correct, to compensate for my mistakes. In physics, an oscillator quickly returns to its equilibrium position after being displaced, and so it is, I came to believe, with the human body. Most of my patients were going to be fine despite anything I did, and if they were going to die—well, that was probably going to happen despite me, too. Health was like the wilderness: it could only be spoiled by human intervention. "We're not saving patients," Rajiv told me. "We're just stabilizing them so they can save themselves."

I became awed by this concept, but most of my colleagues seemed indifferent to it. We performed our interventions with such confidence, such arrogance, but most of the time there was no way of predicting whether we were doing the right thing, or even a good thing. We'd give potassium for hypokalemia, or diuretics for edema, or nitroglycerin for high blood pressure—and we would overshoot. The diuretics would make our patients dehydrated or the nitroglycerin would lower their blood pressure too much—and then we'd have to give them intravenous fluid or raise their blood pressure with other drugs, and the process would start all over again. Sometimes we would give drugs just to treat the side effects of other drugs. Sometimes we would do illogical things like giving fluid and diuretics at the same time, and no one questioned it, including me. There was too much going on, too much complexity, to start asking questions. I wasn't sure where to begin; I wasn't even sure I knew enough to know what to ask. My energy was low, my enthusiasm flagging, and the system was in automatic drive anyway. The easiest thing to do was to get out of the way.

When the nurses woke you in the middle of the night, you had to be prepared to deal with the unexpected. You knew that energy, clarity, fluent speech were coming; you just didn't know when. One night I was half asleep when I got paged. *Must be blood culture time*, I thought, reaching for the phone. In the dark, the receiver vibrated like an image from a jittery screen projector. When I called the number on my beeper, an urgent voice told me to go to Mrs. MacDougal's room. When I got there, it was as if I had walked in on a play. Mrs. MacDougal was standing precariously in the middle of her private room in a puddle of urine. Bright ceiling lights were beating down on her like stage spotlights. She was an attractive woman, for ninety-one, with a sharp patrician nose and handsome cheekbones like Lauren Bacall's. Her gown was open in the back, exposing her scoliotic torso, which was covered with age spots, like cow patties in a field. A nurse and two orderlies were circling her like muggers. They were trying to get her to go back to bed, but the old woman was insisting on going to the bathroom alone.

"We'll help you go in the bedpan," someone said, grabbing her arm to keep her from falling.

"I want to go to the bathroom!" she shrieked, trying to wriggle free.

"We can't let you walk there."

"I'm not going in the bed!"

"You're going to slip and fall."

"Leave me be!"

I was trying to keep from falling over myself. I tried reasoning with Mrs. MacDougal, but she wouldn't listen to me either. After a couple of minutes of urging, I asked the nurse why we couldn't just let her go to the bathroom.

"She could break her hip," the nurse said indignantly.

"She could, but I don't think she will," I replied.

"I can go by myself!" Mrs. MacDougal cried.

"I know," I said, "but let me walk you anyway." I offered her the crook of my arm and, much to my amazement, this appeal to her lady-like instincts seemed to work. Off we went, with an aide on either side, to the toilet.

An aide went in with her while the rest of us waited outside. "She's sundowning," the nurse said, clearly irritated, referring to a kind of nocturnal delirium often observed in nursing homes. "Before you leave, order restraints."

"Do you think that's necessary?" I asked skeptically.

"What if she sundowns again?"

"Just call me," I replied. People in the hospital were always obsessing about disasters that never occurred. I had seen it myself in the CCU, where nurses would use PRN ("as-needed") sedative orders to keep patients groggy and cooperative through the night.

When Mrs. MacDougal came out, I walked her back to bed. "You're a nice young man," she said.

"Thank you," I replied.

"I like you."

"Well, I like you, too." That was the nicest thing I had heard all week. I was going to show these nurses that a little kindness could go a long way.

The next page came about forty-five minutes later. When I arrived back in the room, the scene was much the same as before, except now Mrs. MacDougal was standing in a slurry of feces. She was yelling some of the vilest obscenities—"Cocksuckers! Motherfuckers!"—that I had ever heard from a nonagenarian's lips. The stench was overpowering. I cupped my hand over my face, but the putrid odor still registered in my olfactory lobes.

"Mrs. MacDougal!" I cried through my fingers. "What are you doing?"

"Who the hell are you?" she screamed hoarsely.

"Dr. Jauhar!" I said, incredulous. "Don't you remember me? You promised you were going to stay in bed."

"I need to go to the bathroom."

I ordered her back to bed immediately.

"You're not my doctor!" she shouted. "Call Silverman. Tell him to get me out of here."

I told her that Dr. Silverman wasn't available.

"Get out of my way," she cried, swinging wildly at me. She slipped and fell into my arms, rubbing brown excrement onto my scrubs. Steadying myself, I felt my right sandal slide a bit. The nurses were looking at me with I-told-you-so satisfaction.

For a moment I fantasized about putting Mrs. MacDougal into a choke hold and dragging her by the neck to bed, elbowing the nurse and orderlies out of the way, hissing, screaming at them to end this godforsaken shitfest. But, of course, that couldn't happen; I had to deal with the situation calmly. "Give her five of Haldol and two of Ativan," I shouted out as I tried to keep her from tipping over.

"Yes, Doctor," the nurse responded sarcastically before going out to get the medicine. The two aides and I managed to force her back to bed. When the nurse returned, she administered two intramuscular injections. Almost immediately, Mrs. MacDougal stopped struggling. Within minutes she was snoring heavily. I felt momentary relief, until the reading from the pulse oximeter started to drop: 99 . . . 98 . . . 97 . . . Pretty soon an oxygen mask was plastered to her face and I was turning a knob counterclockwise on the wall. Ninety-four . . . 93 . . . 92 . . . The brief calm quickly turned into another round of panic. Why had I been so impulsive? Was there an antidote for Haldol? Should I call an ICU consult? Where were the nurses now? For the next couple of hours I remained at her bedside, watching her snort like a pig. I stabbed her wrist with a needle to get an arterial blood gas, which revealed borderline oxygen and carbon dioxide levels. I prayed the drugs would wear off. Why had I allowed myself to be goaded so rashly? In an effort to protect her (or perhaps myself), I was afraid that I had killed her. It was an apt metaphor for my internship thus far.

By the next morning, Mrs. MacDougal had returned to her sweet, great-grandmotherly self. At lunchtime a few days later, nurses, social workers, and people with nondescript titles like "coordinating manager" met to discuss patient "disposition"—who was going to be able to go home, who was going to require long-term care, and so on. Rohit told me to attend on his behalf. At the meeting, everyone seemed to be having a rollicking good time talking about the patients, exchanging gossip about family dynamics, and so on. The subject of Mrs. MacDougal came up. "Dr. Jauhar had a wrestling match with her a few nights ago," a social worker said, and everyone laughed except me. Someone asked where Mrs. MacDougal was going to go once she left the hospital. Her daughter wanted to put her in a nursing home, but she wanted to go back to living independently. "No way that's going to happen," someone said with a certitude I found troubling. Someone asked me for my opinion. I had had so little interaction with her, just one unfortunate incident, that I wasn't sure how to respond. I was wary of saying anything that could send her to a nursing home for the rest of her life. She had been delirious, no doubt, and a danger to herself, but she had also been in an unfamiliar environment with people she thought were trying to hurt her. Surely that had to enter the calculus for predicting future behavior. It was anyone's guess what she would be like in a more familiar environment. Wouldn't putting her into an institution just increase the likelihood of further sundowning? I thought of the Chekhov story "Ward No. 6," and the incarceration of Yefimitch. I did not want to be responsible for institutionalizing another person. I had seen it before on the psychiatry wards. If someone said they were well enough to go home, we would say they lacked insight into their disease and keep them even longer. *Where was Dr. Silverman?* I wondered. We were discussing the future of a stranger over sandwiches and soft drinks. And that was beginning to seem normal.

psychotherapy

Yes, there are two paths you can go by, but in the long run,
There's still time to change the road you're on.

—LED ZEPPELIN, "STAIRWAY TO HEAVEN"

I 'd been working for thirteen hours straight, without even a toilet break. One week ago, as an October chill started to take hold, a gnawing tightness had developed at the base of my neck, extending into my right shoulder and radiating down to my elbow. Now, my eyeballs were stinging, too, as if they had been doused with salt water. Pressure extended from the back of the orbits into my brain and down into my throat, rendering it parched and my voice feeble. I could almost feel my cortex rubbing on the inside of my scalp, producing a kind of tactile white noise, like strips of Velcro being pulled apart. Extreme fatigue heightens physical sensation. It makes time run slower, trapping you in the moment.

I was supposed to meet the resident Josh for dinner to talk about switching to psychiatry, but first I had to drain the fluid out of a young woman's cirrhotic abdomen. I had put off the procedure all day, and even though it was past seven and Rohit and Alphonse had already left, I wanted to get it over with today. I was on call again tomorrow, and Saturday calls were the worst. No cap on admissions, scores of patients to cross-cover. I wouldn't have time for any extra procedures.

I walked over to the stockroom to get vacuum bottles for the drainage. In the large white bins I found the usual assortment of test tubes, catheters, syringes, bandages, gloves, plastic tubing, tape, gauze, dressing-change kits, drainage bags, syringes, scalpels, thoracentesis kits, bone-marrow biopsy kits, triple-lumen catheter kits, lumbar-puncture kits, saline bags, bedpans, cups, straws, socks, mouthwash, needles, diapers, sponge pads, iodine soap, hydrogen peroxide, masks, and bunny boots—but no vacuum bottles. Without vacuum bottles to speed up the drainage, the procedure was going to take forever. I went downstairs to the gastroenterology floor to find some.

Most interns have a favorite procedure. Already, mine was the abdominal paracentesis. I admired its brute-force simplicity. You push a catheter directly through the abdominal wall and into the abdominal cavity to drain accumulated fluid. It's easy and safe. Plus, your patient almost always ends up feeling better.

Wafting through the corridor on 10-North was the sickly sweet smell of *Clostridium difficile* diarrhea. I marveled at how the nurses were able to go about their business, without masks, seemingly oblivious to the stench. The thirty-something woman, HIV-positive, was lying in a room at the end of the hallway. She had unruly black hair and bloodshot eyes, and apart from her protruding abdomen, which looked like it was carrying triplets, she was wispy thin. Her belly had been hurting for weeks, she said, and she had been getting satiated after only a few mouthfuls of food. She had to sashay from side to side when she walked. I set the vacuum bottles down on the floor at her bedside and told her that I had come to drain the fluid. "Okay," she replied flatly. She had gone through this procedure many times before.

I went over to the sink and washed my hands. After toweling off, I tried putting on a pair of gloves, but my hands were still moist and my fingers kept getting stuck in the latex fronds. I tried pulling on the latex but it clung tightly to my skin. I walked back to her bedside, the tips of the gloves hanging uselessly off my fingertips.

Her belly was laced with stretch marks, like thick, wrinkly worms. I pressed just below her navel, a sharp, shallow jab that set the fluid in motion, like water in a pail. There must have been ten liters in there, a consequence of cirrhosis, from hepatitis, AIDS, her insatiable thirst for rum—or all three. I tapped on her abdomen like a drum, using the transmitted sound to map out the location of the fluid. Dull was fluid, hollow was air—and as best as I could tell, the fluid was everywhere.

I scrubbed her belly with iodine soap—she shivered; it was cold—and then injected lidocaine into the skin and soft tissue of the left lower quadrant. The injection formed a mound the size of a fingerprint, which I pressed down to distribute the anesthetic, liberating a tiny spot of blood, which trickled away. I pushed a big 22-gauge needle through the site of the injection, forming a fleshy tract for a plastic catheter, which entered the abdominal cavity quite easily. Almost immediately, warm yellow liquid came bubbling back, soaking my gloved fingers. I attached one end of a piece of tubing to the catheter, plunged the end with the needle into a vacuum bottle, and then sat down to watch the fluid drain. It came out in a steady drizzle, like a leak in a water balloon. "Take it all out," the woman insisted. "I'm only supposed to take out a few liters," I replied. Someone had once told me that it was unsafe to drain more than that at one sitting. I had forgotten why, but I was glad to have a reason to stop so that I could keep my dinner date with Josh.

The bottle filled up quickly. Midway, I got paged. It was Josh. He wanted to know if we were still on. I told him I was running late but that I would meet him at the restaurant as soon as I was finished.

The fluid was really gushing; perhaps the catheter had settled into a high-pressure pocket. I reached for another bottle, but then I realized that I had stupidly left it on the other side of the bed, out of reach. I placed the nearly full bottle on a chair and hopped around the bed to get the unused bottles. I heard a snap, and when I looked back, the tube was whipsawing back and forth on the chair, like a garden hose, spraying lemonade-colored fluid on the floor. For a moment I was paralyzed. What happened? Did she move? Did I not secure the needle? I watched horrified as tiny puddles of HIV-infected fluid settled onto the uneven tile floor. My gloves were still hanging off my fingertips, so I tore them off and stepped around the spill to put on another pair. Then

I grabbed the gushing needle and plunged it into a new vacuum bottle. Even with the fluid safely discharging into the glassy cavern, I continued to grip the needle tightly, my heart pounding in my ears. The young woman stared out at the room, oblivious to the disaster that had just unfolded. *Fool!* I shouted at myself. I had been rushing to get out on time, and now I had created an even bigger problem for myself, a veritable biological hazard. I was going to have to call Housekeeping, write an event note, maybe fill out some sort of incident report. The evening nurses were irritable enough without giving them another reason to be annoyed.

I filled up a second bottle and told my patient that we were done. Even with just two liters out (plus whatever was on the floor), her abdomen was noticeably less distended, and she said she was feeling better. I pulled the catheter out of her belly and threw the tubing and sundry sponges and towels into a red biological waste bag. I took the bottles over to a "soiled utility" room and left them by the sink. Back in her room, I got a roll of paper towels and wiped off the floor and chair, working quickly before anyone arrived. "Thank you," she said as I searched the bedding anxiously for stray needles. "You're welcome," I said curtly.

At the workstation, I told a nurse what had happened. "You could have called me," she said in an exasperated Caribbean twang. "I was sitting right here."

I told her I was sorry, that I hadn't wanted to bother her, and, much to my surprise, she told me to leave. She would call Housekeeping for me.

I sprinted the block back to my apartment, peeled off my scrubs, and jumped into the shower. My skin felt cool and sticky, and even though I was already a half hour late, the urge to wash away the hospital grime was irresistible. Under the warm water, amid the crackle of droplets ricocheting off the porcelain, I thought about Rajiv's latest heroics. Just this week, he had inserted an intra-aortic balloon pump at the bedside into a patient with an acute myocardial infarction, then wheeled him to the cardiac catheterization lab, where he performed angioplasty and saved his life. What a contrast to my own incompetence! I had frozen on a simple abdominal paracentesis. I didn't even have the presence of mind to pinch off the tubing when the fluid was spilling on the floor. *Never rush a procedure!* I had often told myself. But I couldn't even follow my own rules.

Outside, around 8:30 p.m., Second Avenue was ringing like a sharply illuminated, multicolored carnival. Young people were stumbling drunkenly out of bars, smoking cigarettes. Rich kids in suits and evening dresses were stepping into a limo, perhaps on the way to a cotillion. Long, bare, sexy legs dangled off brownstone stoops. I had nearly forgotten there was a world outside the hospital, and it was neatly going on without me.

I thought about what I was going to say to Josh. Was I really going to quit internal medicine like Cynthia? I couldn't help but think that all my work—the sacrifices, the debt, the suffering—would be wasted if I quit now. Yet the thoughts—the second thoughts—kept swirling in my head, like an obsession I could not block. *What are you doing? You don't belong here.* The sacrifices I had made so far were minor compared to what would be required of me in the future—as a resident, or fellow, or attending physician. Medicine was supposed to lead me to a world of responsibility. What did it say about me that I had desired the challenge but couldn't sustain the commitment?

I had struggled to feel interested, competent, but that state of mind had eluded me. Out of desperation, I had tried being more friendly with my supervising residents, hoping to find succor in fraternity, but they preferred to maintain the traditional resident-over-intern hierarchy. No matter what I did or how hard I tried, they always managed to find a weakness. If I thought I had picked up an unusual diagnosis, they would start pressing with questions that would force me to give up my hypothesis. If I thought I had composed a watertight case, they would find an oversight. "Where's the EKG?" Rohit would demand in the middle of a presentation, and when I would pull it out, he'd look it over nonchalantly, hand it back to me, and say, "And the old one?" and then I'd have to stammer an excuse for why I had been unable to find it and feel deflated again. It was hard not to succumb to a culture where missing something gets magnified into personal failure. Even the language of medicine betrayed this attitude. The term *failure* was used to describe not only organs that had ceased to function, but also those that were merely insufficient.

Rohit admonished me for taking too long to write my progress notes. "How am I supposed to write my notes without labs?" I demanded. Test results weren't posted in the computer until late morning.

"Just write 'labs pending.' "

"Then how am I supposed to come up with a plan?"

"That's not your job."

"So what is my job?"

"To write a progress note."

"Why am I writing the note?"

"To document that someone examined the patient."

"That's all?" I said angrily.

"That's all," he replied with brusque finality. "No one reads your notes."

The truth was that I had already stopped writing long notes. I had stopped paying attention to social history, habits, the sorts of things that make a patient into a real person. I was writing down physical exam findings I believed were present, even if I didn't pick up on them myself. I didn't want to make any more concessions. My progress notes belonged to me.

The hardest part was not having someone to commiserate with me. Sonia was in Washington, busy with her own clinical clerkships. When I told her I was living for the weekends, she thought I was referring to her near-weekly visits to Manhattan, which were nice, but what I really meant was that I was living for the days when I wasn't in the hospital, with or without her. The few interns who complained openly only criticized the backbreaking schedule or an unhelpful resident or a rude attending. No one I spoke with, apart from Cynthia, criticized medicine itself or questioned their commitment to the profession. That seemingly was off-limits. My parents found it hard to sympathize, too. They (rightly) viewed the decision to go to medical school as my own choice and internship as a temporary phase, a sort of boot camp on the way to a better career. "Who told you to leave physics?" my father would say when he was fed up with my grievances. "You like to grumble. You like to blow on cold milk." He had never had much patience for "flickering," and nothing was going to change anyway, and wasn't I just a bit too quick to whine and never see the bright side? "Going into medicine was the best thing that could have happened to you," he often said. "You had landed into a ditch. Now at least you have some direction."

When I got to the restaurant, a Hungarian holdover from a previous era, Josh was waiting for me outside. A tall, thin man with a bushy goatee, he always reminded me of a young Vladimir Lenin. He was doing a five-year joint "internal medicine-psychiatry" residency. A few weeks back, Rajiv had suggested that I talk with him about my career issues.

He shook my hand warmly and we went inside. We sat down at a table by a window overlooking a busy street. The waitress brought us bowls of cold cherry soup, and we started talking. Though I had intimated some of my concerns to him over the phone, I took this opportunity to more fully explain my disillusionment. He listened carefully but didn't say much. *This must be what psychiatrists call reflection*, I thought. I felt like a patient sitting on the proverbial couch.

I talked about my interest in psychiatry. Josh asked me what I liked about it, and I told him that, despite the mumbo jumbo, psychiatry at least seemed to be trying to get to the heart of things. While internal medicine dissected, psychiatry synthesized. Internists described disease in a phenomenological way, as a collection of symptoms, as the result of certain chemical excesses or deficits. Psychiatrists, on the other hand, it seemed to me then, were trying to go deeper, into the structure of illness itself. What interested me about psychiatry was what most doctors disparaged: the abstruse theories, the symbolic representations, the weirdness. I had always felt more comfortable with the strange, the grotesque, the questioners of themselves. I often remembered the mentally ill patients I had cared for in medical school. There was Noah Stearns and his dream of traveling "the open road" to California; when the police picked him up, he was wandering around in his hometown, eating weeds. Or Terence Hode, who lost his mind when his wife left him, spending sixteen hours a day watching porn and listening to the Red Hot Chili Peppers. Or Eleanor Wilson, who started telling people that workers at the post office were trying to keep her from "reaching a better life." Although I had always been reluctant to admit it, I enjoyed these patients so much more than the diabetics or the old ladies with mundane urinary tract infections.

"They talk all the time about supporting you through residency, but really that's all just lip service," Josh said. "If you want to switch, go ahead. On the other hand, you might be better off finishing the year." I had heard this advice before. "Things are going to get better," he assured me. I had heard that before, too. "You have to ask yourself, Where do I want to be in ten years?" I had heard it all before; I had been working through these issues my entire professional life. After all this time, so many stops and starts, it was dispiriting that I still had no idea what I wanted, and that the insight of an older, supposedly wiser resident left me right where I'd started: knowing the pros and cons but unable to decide.

After dinner, I walked home. The night was clear, the lights bright. The cabs were weaving up the packed avenue like a game of Donkey Kong, their neon taillights randomly blinking at me like a sea of red eyes. There was a void in my life that I didn't know how to fill. My old career in physics was finished; I couldn't just pick up where I left off. My new life was all about medicine. Even if I made a big show of never talking about it, at social or family gatherings, it was there, never far from my mind, the dominant motif in my life. How could I just give it up? I had no options, no plans, just complaints.

Becoming a psychiatrist was a romantic notion, driven by a nebulous desire to find creativity within medicine, but I knew it made little sense. Not so long ago I had been experimenting on quantum dots with picosecond laser pulses. Now I wanted to become a psychoanalyst? It sounded flaky, even to me. Psychiatry was fringe, elitist, out of the mainstream—precisely what I had fled by going into medicine in the first place. Did I really want to join another profession I had little faith in? Wasn't it better to work hard and not have to apologize?

Maybe Josh was right. Internship wasn't going to last forever. It was already almost a third over. Perhaps my best option was to buckle down and focus. In photography there is a thing called a *pinhole camera*. It operates on the same principle as squinting: narrow your field of view and you are able to see more clearly. This, I decided, was what I had to do now. Instead of gazing so far into the future, perhaps I should just focus on the path directly ahead of me. Perhaps such an approach would deliver clarity.

Coming up was a rotation at Memorial, the world-famous cancer hospital allied with New York Hospital. Oncology; maybe that was my calling. Somehow I doubted it, but I told myself that I owed it to myself to give residency some more time. If things didn't improve quickly, then I would march into Dr. Wood's office and break the news. My father's injunction kept reverberating in my head: *Don't change horses in the middle of the ocean.*

cracking up

night float

Too few residents emerge from training thankful for the opportunity to practice in a fascinating and intellectually challenging field. Instead, many believe that the world owes them something for what they've been through.

—TIMOTHY MCCALL, "THE IMPACT OF LONG WORKING HOURS ON RESIDENT PHYSICIANS," *THE NEW ENGLAND JOURNAL OF MEDICINE*, 1988

At four o'clock in the afternoon, I was struggling to put on my necktie. I draped the silk band around my collar, pulling up and down to adjust the length on each side. Then I curled the wide part around the narrow, making a counterclockwise loop. I fiddled with the short end for a few seconds, trying to remember what to do next, before pulling my hands apart and starting over. On my next attempt, I experienced a faint glimmer of recall. I finally got it on the third try. Procedural memory is the last to go when you are fatigued. It means you are about to collapse. This did not bode well for my first night at Memorial. If I couldn't put on a tie, how was I going to function in the hospital?

Before heading in for my shift, I stopped by the Hi-Life to see Shannon. "What happened to you?" she said when I sat down at the bar.

I grimaced, taking off my neck brace. "Herniated disk."

Her expression softened. "How'd that happen?"

I didn't know. A few weeks earlier, a gnawing pain had developed at the base of my neck and in my right shoulder and elbow. The palm of my right hand, from the thumb to the wrist, felt numb. Josh had diagnosed me with carpal tunnel syndrome, and for a few days I had worn a wrist brace, which only seemed to aggravate the pain. It felt like a fat drill was boring into my shoulder. At first I wondered if perhaps my symptoms were psychosomatic. Interns often develop weird ailments during training, and was it just a coincidence that one of my leukemia patients had been hospitalized with similar complaints? But as the days passed, the pain steadily worsened. When it was almost unbearable, I went to Dr. Bele in the outpatient clinic. He sat me down in a chair, palmed the top of my head, and pressed downward. A hot electrical sensation traveled down my right arm, and I howled in agony. "You have a slipped disk," he pronounced. He sent me to the office of a sports medicine specialist, who told me that my right biceps reflex was almost absent, indicating significant nerve damage. She gave me a cervical collar and ordered a spine MRI, which was performed the following morning. Rajiv took a few hours off to accompany me to the test. Lying flat on the gantry, I could almost feel my eyelashes scraping against the roof of the scanner, and the loud Schumann opera being piped into the headphones did nothing to quell my anxiety. I thought of wide open spaces. I thought of romantic interludes with Sonia. I thought of the hundreds of MRI scans I had casually ordered for patients over the past few months with nary a second thought.

The MRI showed what by now everyone suspected: a severe herniation of the disk between my fifth and sixth cervical vertebrae. The gelatinous core had ruptured through the fibrous capsule, pinching a nerve root. When the radiologist showed me a sideways view of my spine, it looked like the herniated disk was partially compressing the anterior column of my spinal cord.

I went to a neurologist at my own hospital, who told me there was a slight chance the disk would heal on its own but that it was likely going to require surgery. At the very least, he advised taking a break from internship.

That afternoon on the ward, I was unable to turn my head because of my neck brace. I had to rotate my entire body to look in any particular direction or to perform physical maneuvers. My patients joked that I should see a doctor. My colleagues were mostly reserved, politely inquiring about the injury but not paying it much attention. I remembered how they'd been when a classmate claimed to have a hairline foot fracture back in August: resentful, unsympathetic, whispering that she was faking it. Of course, I was aware that one of them was going to have to cover for me if I left.

A couple of days later, I got a phone call from Dr. Wood. He had just spoken to the neurologist. "So you need some time off?" he said pleasantly.

"That's what I was told," I replied, then quickly added, "But I'm not planning on taking any."

He asked me why. I wasn't sure what to tell him. I had been contemplating quitting internship before my injury, but now the situation had become more complicated. Leaving now, I feared, would have adverse lasting consequences on my psyche. I didn't want to be forced out. I wanted to leave on my own terms.

"I'd stay home if I thought it would help," I said. "But I might need surgery no matter what."

"Take the time," Dr. Wood urged. "We all admire the way you've handled this, not drawing too much attention to yourself. No one thinks you haven't been sincere."

I didn't say anything, but his kind words lifted my spirits. Though we had little in common, I liked Dr. Wood. I admired his commitment and integrity. And I was glad that he liked something in me, too.

I told him I'd think it over. At the very least, I wanted to complete my upcoming rotation at Memorial Sloan-Kettering. The Memorial rotation was the toughest of the year, and I had been looking forward to it as one might a sickening thrill ride. Cancer was the icon of deathly disease, and as a den of illness, Memorial had a sort of mystique. The patients there were as sick as any we were going to encounter all year. If you overlooked something at Memorial—a rash, a fever—your patient could crump quickly, and no patients were more crump-prone than Memorial patients. I was hoping that taking care of such patients would deliver confidence, courage, a sense of purpose. I felt like a marathoner trying to finish a race even though his legs are collapsing.

The challenge of Memorial was multiplied by the fact that I was going to be doing "night float" there. Night float was a relatively new concept in residency training. Older physicians, like Dr. Wood, had trained under a very different system, when call was every second or third night and residents routinely stayed up for thirty-six hours at a stretch. But things started to change late one spring evening in 1984, when a young woman named Libby Zion entered the emergency room at New York Hospital. She was agitated and running a high fever. Eight hours later, she was dead.

Though the exact cause of her death remains a mystery, her case aroused intense debate over what until then had been little discussed: the way residents are trained in New York State. The residents who cared for Zion the night she died had given her a powerful narcotic, and then had been slow to respond when she developed an adverse reaction. If they had been more rested, medical educators wondered, would they have been able to save her life?

In 1987, a special commission led by Dr. Bertrand M. Bell, a professor of medicine at Albert Einstein College of Medicine in the Bronx, proposed a number of changes in residency training in New York State: closer supervision of residents in emergency rooms, more help with routine tasks like drawing blood, and strict work limits. Residents were prohibited from working more than twenty-four hours at a stretch or more than eighty hours per week. Eventually these changes spread to residency programs throughout the country. Teaching hospitals that had relied on interns and residents as medical staff were forced to grapple with the problem of cross-coverage: providing care to patients when their primary resident was not on duty. As a result, many hospitals created night floats—residents who worked the night shift for specified periods of time, usually a few weeks.

Many in the profession, including most residents, applauded the Bell regulations. Studies have shown that, under the old system, residents after a call night score lower on tests of simple reasoning, response time, concentration, and recall. Many, both inside and outside medicine, argued that residents could not provide proper care for patients if they were chronically fatigued. In an editorial in *The New England Journal of Medicine,* one educator wrote: "Few would choose to ride in a car driven by a resident coming off a 36-hour shift. It should come as no surprise that the public would question the ability of sleep-deprived residents to make life-and-death decisions."

However, some educators argued that there was no clear-cut scientific evidence showing that tired residents harm patients, either by increasing mortality rates or complications. One doctor wrote in *The New England Journal of Medicine*: "My own experience in staffing our intensive care unit both in the traditional manner and with a 'night float' suggests that errors due to faulty transfer of information are at least as frequent as those due to fatigue from being on call overnight." Educators also argued that the work limits that led to the creation of the night-float system were detrimental to a resident's training because they interrupted learning and created a kind of shift-work mentality. Of course, the shift aspect of night float was precisely the attraction for many interns. After doing night float, Vijay had told me, echoing the sentiments of many of my classmates: "I walk into the hospital empty-handed, and I leave empty-handed, and I like that."

"Are you sure you can handle it?" Shannon asked me worriedly as I drained my last sip of coffee.

"I think so," I replied.

Outside, it had started to rain, a late October drizzle that glistened on the tar-black wrought-iron railings guarding the aging brownstones in the neighborhood. Mist pecked at my skin and moistened my hair. The spray cooled my upper body, which felt hot and sweaty because of the neck brace. Under a tree, a water droplet splattered on the bridge of my nose, the intense sensation momentarily dulling the pain in my neck. The pain had been terrible all afternoon. Before leaving the apartment I had popped two pills of Lodine, a painkiller.

My shift was supposed to begin at 5:00 p.m., when residents and nurse practitioners departed for the day, and end at 7:00 a.m., when they returned. Meanwhile, I was going to be responsible for about eighty patients.

At the security desk at the front entrance of the hospital, an officer gave me a quizzical look. I rode up the escalator, passed through a waiting area where families were sprawled on green and orange couches, and turned down a corridor going to the cafeteria. Not wanting to draw attention to myself, I removed the neck brace and stuffed it into my backpack.

It was a typical hospital cafeteria, with grimy brown carpeting, potted plants, and cheap Kandinsky posters. A corkboard on the wall was plastered with announcements from various support groups, invitations to join in research studies, and urgent appeals for bone-marrow donation. Large paneled posters told the storied history of the hospital and predicted the next generation of advances from the Human Genome Project. Two New York Hospital interns were waiting for me at a table reserved for house-staff conferences. One of them, Caitlin, was a very attractive brunette from Georgia. She handed me a list of her patients with their major medical problems, allergies, and a short summary of their hospital course. "Don't worry about seeing this guy," she said, pointing to a name with a star next to it. "He's signing out against medical advice. I told him not to leave. I told him the risks, blah, blah, blah, but he wouldn't listen, so sayonara," she concluded with a flick of her hand.

"There is one patient I have to tell you about. This guy Schroeder has been hallucinating all afternoon. We don't know why; maybe he has brain mets. We gave him some vitamin H"—Haldol—"and he's quiet now, so he shouldn't give you any trouble, but if he does, just snow him with more Haldol and Ativan." I nodded intently; Caitlin had great breasts.

"I'm sorry to dump this on you," she said, gently caressing my arm.

"No problem," I replied, affecting nonchalance. "The longer you stay, the longer you stay."

Six cancer teams—Gastrointestinal (GI), Allogeneic Bone Marrow Transplant, Genitourinary, Head and Neck, Breast, and Melanoma— signed out to me. (The other night-float intern got sign-outs from Leukemia, Lymphoma, Lung, Autologous Bone Marrow Transplant, Hematology, and Multiple Myeloma.) By 6:00 p.m., everyone had left.

The first hour of night float is supposed to be relatively tranquil, the calm before the storm, but not this night. A few minutes after the last intern signed out, I got paged. *Beep . . . beep . . . beep.* "Are you covering Schroeder on GI?" a voice inquired.

"Hold on, let me check my list." I sifted through the papers as the voice kept talking. "Okay, here he is," I said. "Schroeder, patient of Dr. Raymond." Of course: he was the patient Caitlin had just signed out to me, and whom I'd so smittenly pledged to look after. "Sixty-four. Colon cancer status-post 5-FU and leucovorin. All right, go ahead."

"I just told you. He's delirious and his oxygen saturation is dropping."

There was a long pause.

"Are you coming?"

"Yes, I'll be right there," I said.

The GI ward was shaped like a racetrack, with two dimly lit corridors encircled by wooden banisters and painted a dull yellow. The nurses' station was almost deserted, save for a clerk and two nurses having coffee. In his room, Schroeder was sprawled in bed, his arms and legs tied to the rails. He apparently did not speak English—apart from obscenities—because a German translator was there, a lanky, greasy-faced fellow who was grinning nervously. "He says that things are coming down at him," the young man said, clenching his teeth to keep from laughing. "He feels that things are crawling on his skin."

When I attempted to apply my stethoscope to his chest, Schroeder lunged at me with a force that shook the entire bed. His hands turned white as the cloth cuffs cut off his circulation. "What do you want me to do?" the nurse who had paged me demanded. "I can't keep him tied up all night." *Beep . . . beep . . . beep.* I glanced at the beeper on my waist. "What's his baseline?" I asked, checking the display. About the only thing I had been signed out was that he wasn't going to give me any trouble.

"I'm just a float," the nurse replied, referring to the fact that she worked per diem shifts. "I'm meeting him for the first time, too."

At the nursing station, I answered the page. A patient's heparin drip needed to be renewed. I told the caller that I'd come by as soon as possible to write the order. Sitting down, I perused Schroeder's chart. Caitlin had written an "event note" that afternoon, but it didn't say much more than what she had already told me. When I called Schroeder's family, hoping they could clarify his baseline mental status, his daughter told me in fluent English that he had a history of alcoholism but had never behaved anything like what I was describing. "He had an MRI of his brain this afternoon," she said. Caitlin had neglected to mention that. "Can you tell me what it showed?"

Beep . . . beep . . . beep. Another page.

"I'm going to have to get back to you," I said.

"When will that be?" she demanded. *Beep . . . beep . . . beep.* Fourth page in ten minutes.

"Listen, I'm sorry but I'm covering eighty patients right now," I blurted out. "I will have to call you back."

"It's just that I live in Westchester and it takes me a half hour to—" she started saying before I hung up.

When I got off the phone, an attending physician in the nursing station took me aside. It was Jim Krank, a clinical trialist who specialized in acute leukemia and the withering stare. He was a chubby man with a brown, bushy toothbrush mustache. I had taken care of one of his patients recently, an elderly man with drug-resistant leukemia and fungal pneumonia. When the end was near, his son had tried to put restrictions on blood draws. "I know my father, and he didn't want to live this way," he had said. "The one thing he always prayed for was that he would go in his sleep." But we quickly discovered that it was almost impossible *not* to draw blood from a cancer patient. Some reason or another always came up. Eventually his family instructed us to provide "comfort care," which meant no needle sticks and a steady infusion of morphine. For a while, his condition seemed to improve, making Dr. Krank grumble thickly, "It always happens this way. Patients do better when we leave them alone." It was the most devastating critique I had heard of the profession, and though I knew it was made flippantly, it still made me think: *What is the point of all this?* All the protocols, the chemotherapy, the transplants—what was the point of it if, in the end, the sickest patients, the ones we were beholden to help, or at least not to harm, were better off without us? My first instinct when the old man started getting better was to turn off the morphine drip, but Krank dialed it up even further. I was afraid he might stop breathing, but of course that was the whole point. It was called the law of double effect. It was okay for us to hasten his death in the service of treating pain and discomfort.

"The daughter doesn't need to know how many patients you're taking care of," Krank said quietly, facing me down in the nursing station. I tried to explain but he cut me off. "The only patient she cares about is her father. So go check on that MRI."

I instructed the nurse to administer another dose of Haldol and ran downstairs to the radiology department, which was deserted at this hour. "Nice lives these radiologists lead," I thought bitterly. A resident was sitting in a darkened room in front of a workstation with a thick pile of radiographs. I asked him if he would look at Schroeder's MRI with me.

"What's the story?" he snapped, obviously annoyed by the interruption.

"Sixty-four, colon CA, delirious."

"Liver mets?"

"Not that I'm aware of."

"Any mets at all?"

"I don't know."

"Why's he in the hospital?"

"Now? I don't know."

He looked disdainfully over his shoulder. "Look, I'm just covering for the night," I protested.

"So am I," he replied coldly. Another float.

The MRI showed an abnormal marking in the right cerebellum. Could it be a metastasis? "It's nonspecific, but I guess you have to assume it is," the resident said.

"So what should I tell the family?"

"Tell them the MRI was read by a floating second-year," he replied, chuckling.

By the time I got back to the twelfth floor, Schroeder was fast asleep. "What should I do if he wakes up?" the nurse asked.

"Give him some more Haldol," I replied. I had learned my lesson last month with Mrs. MacDougal. Best to have the drugs in the body before the shit hits the fan.

I called Schroeder's daughter and told her that a preliminary reading of her father's MRI showed a vaguely abnormal speck in the brain. Bracing myself, I informed her that the scan wouldn't be officially read until tomorrow. To my utter surprise, she accepted this delay without objection.

On night float, you don't stay in one place for very long. Pretty soon my beeper was in status epilepticus. There were orders interns had forgotten to renew: IV fluids, antibiotics, nutritional supplements. Patients on blood thinners needed to have their clotting times checked. Some patients required blood tests every six hours to monitor for "tumor lysis syndrome," in which cancer cells rapidly die and flood the bloodstream with dangerous levels of potassium, phosphorus, and uric acid. At eight o'clock, I got called about fever spikes, which meant more patients to examine, chest X-rays to order, and blood and urine cultures to draw. As I pored over charts, my neck started to ache terribly, so I went to the call room and put my cervical collar back on. I furiously scribbled down tasks: type and cross-match blood, transfuse platelets, order MUGA scan, change antibiotics, replete potassium, add

Bactrim, start fluconazole. The tiny boxes were proliferating on my sheets like the pox. By the time I got around to seeing my third febrile patient, my task list had doubled, more pages were coming in, and I had given up trying to examine every single patient I was being called about.

I did manage to see a few. I went up to the bone-marrow transplant ward on the twelfth floor. The first successful bone-marrow transplant was performed in 1968 to treat aplastic anemia, a kind of leukemia. Since then, the therapy has been used to treat many cancers and immunological conditions. Success has been tempered by complications, horrific problems in their own right: graft rejection, graft-versus-host disease (where the graft rejects the host), cirrhosis, infections, death. After these transplants, patients are often at risk for life-threatening infections. Many of them are "neutropenic," with vanishing numbers of infection-fighting white blood cells, and some have "neutropenic fevers," requiring long courses of intravenous antibiotics.

Bruce Diner had recurrent pulmonary infections, bronchiolar widening, and liver failure—complications of a bone-marrow transplant. He was sitting up straight, appearing anxious and short of breath. A pressurized oxygen mask was digging into his chubby cheeks, its oppressive whooshing sound barely modulated by the loud rock music coming out of his headphones. He needed a new liver and a new pair of lungs and was waiting to hear if his name was going to be added to yet another transplant list. Lara Rand needed platelets. Red, raw skin was peeling away from her neck, a consequence of graft-versus-host disease. No one knew why her platelet count was so low, but preparations were being made to remove her spleen in case the platelets were being sequestered there. Jane Glass's skin was tightening in a scleroderma-like reaction, another consequence of graft-versus-host disease. Her face was like a mask. "I'm so confused," she sobbed when I went to see her. "Yesterday they told me I'm dying; today that I'm getting better."

Around 9:30 p.m., I went to the Department of Medicine library, where it was quiet, to answer another flurry of pages. A Mediport catheter had just blown and the nurse and the IV team had been unable to draw labs, which meant that I was going to have to do it. I was steeling myself for the patient's likely reaction to another hospital worker showing up at his bedside with a needle. "They should really teach us about this tumor-lysis stuff," I said angrily to the other night-float intern, a stocky Korean who was watching *Ally McBeal*. I couldn't believe he wasn't running around madly like me.

"It was in the packet," he said, gazing at the TV. "Yeah, it went through everything you need to know, how you're not supposed to give calcium, when to draw labs, et cetera, et cetera."

I shrugged, annoyed. "They should still teach us about it. Not everyone has time to go through the packet."

There were two kinds of interns at Memorial: those who were planning on specializing in oncology and those who couldn't tolerate the subject for even a month. My fellow night-float intern, it turned out, was in the latter camp. He was planning on specializing in infectious diseases and was eager to get back to New York Hospital.

"Everyone around here is enrolled in a research trial, but have you seen the way they get informed consent?" he said at the commercial. "The fellows are walking up to patients who are encephalopathic, and they're handing them a sheet of paper and saying, 'This is the protocol that we talked about. Now sign here.'

"They gave a Jehovah's Witness a bone-marrow transplant across the street," he went on incredulously. "She said that there were absolutely no circumstances under which she would accept blood transfusions. Now tell me, how could they in good conscience do that? She's saying, 'Under no circumstances will I accept a blood transfusion.' They should be telling her that there is a 99.9 percent chance that you will need a blood transfusion. I mean, have you ever seen a transplant patient who didn't get a blood transfusion? They're giving that 0.1 percent chance and presenting that as a reality, and what is a desperate patient supposed to say? 'Yeah, I believe in God, I'm going to be in that 0.1 percent group.' They should have told her, 'If we give you this treatment, there's a 90 percent chance that we will shorten your already short life span by three months.' "

He went on to tell me about an elderly woman with pancreatic cancer that had grown into her bile duct and metastasized through her GI tract. She had been through several rounds of chemotherapy without success and was ready to quit treatment but was afraid to tell her oncologist. "She told me, 'I don't want him to think I'm giving up.' Can you believe it? She didn't want to let him down! The last thing she needed to feel guilty about was wanting to die at home. So I told her, 'Why don't you have a talk with your oncologist?' But she couldn't do it. So when it came time for a biliary stent procedure, which everyone knew was going to be futile, I called the interventional radiologist and said, 'She has a couple of months to live. Tell you the truth, I'm not even sure of that, and she doesn't want the procedure, and neither does her daughter, but they're not able to tell their oncologist.' I presented it like, If she dies, they're going to come after you, and I got the response I wanted, which was, 'It doesn't sound like such a good idea. Sounds like the risk is too high.' If I had presented it a different way, I probably would have gotten a different response.

"So then I went to the oncologist and told him what the radiologist said and he said, 'Fine, send her to hospice.' I think he knew I was putting up roadblocks, trying to prevent him from doing what he wanted, but at least I prevented him from giving her any more chemo.

"She died two weeks later at home. One day this woman comes up to me on the ward. She had been the woman's hospice aide. She told me that the patient made her promise that the day she died, she would come find me and tell me. She said my patient wanted to thank me for encouraging her to die the way she wanted to."

A short while later I was called to the room of a middle-aged man with colon cancer who had started bleeding profusely from somewhere in his intestinal tract. His wife, grim-faced, was at his bedside. Large gobs of tarry stool were sitting in a bedpan. The muscle had eroded from his upper body, making his neck appear unusually long, like a swan's. He eyed my cervical collar with an affected curiosity. "Looks like you need a doctor," he said, forcing a smile. Cancer had cast its long shadow over everything in the room except him.

Unable to localize the site of the bleeding, doctors had been giving him radiation therapy to his entire gut. In the dim, yellow light his wife started asking me questions, but I knew so little of his complicated case that there wasn't much I could tell her. The results of a recent CT scan, the most likely sites of the bleeding, when he might go for further radiation therapy—all that information was deep in his chart, and in the mind of his sleeping resident.

Then I went to see a patient with intractable hiccups. Several months before being hospitalized, he had begun vomiting after meals. An upper endoscopy revealed esophageal cancer. Walking into his room, I felt almost relieved. After what I had been dealing with so far that night, hiccups seemed almost laughably unserious. But as with everything at Memorial, these were no ordinary hiccups. They had been going on for over twenty-four hours, leaving the patient sleepless and utterly demoralized. "These hiccups are killing me dead, night and day," he said.

I didn't know what caused hiccups, let alone how to treat them. When I asked a nurse, she mentioned that a drug called chlorpromazine was sometimes used, so I wrote an order for it. Walking through the nurses' station, I casually checked the patient's chart. There, amid his papers, was a brief note. He had once suffered a severe reaction to chlorpromazine. It wasn't documented as an allergy but was scribbled in a progress note. I immediately canceled the order, relieved that I had caught the mistake in time but alarmed at how easily it might have slipped through the system. (Later, I realized that if the hiccups would have yielded to such a simple solution, it would have been attempted already.)

That was the thing about night float. You were taking care of patients about whom you knew next to nothing. Night float was like walking along a narrow mountainous ledge. As long as you looked straight ahead, oblivious to the height, you were okay. But every now and then, you had to look down.

Patients, too, hated the night shift. They wanted answers; it didn't matter to them that you were just covering for the night. I went to see an elderly woman. "The doctor told me that I needed surgery next week," she said. (Actually, it was a bronchoscopy, where a flexible tube is inserted to inspect the trachea, but in her mind there was no distinction.) "Do you know anything about it?"

I said I didn't.

"They say they see this mass on my chest X-ray and want to evaluate it. I've had this mass for years and now they want to do surgery? Why?"

I told her I didn't know but that she could bring it up with her doctor when he returned in the morning. "I tried already, but he wouldn't say," she replied. I tried to leave but she stopped me. "See, I just want to know, why would a doctor come in and tell me what none of my doctors ever mentioned before? It doesn't make sense." I nodded. "Can you explain it?" I said I couldn't. "But why would he say it?" she persisted.

"If you don't want the surgery, you don't have to have it," I said. "Remember, it's your body."

"Yes, that's right," she said, settling back into bed. "Thank you."

I could only imagine how disruptive my ill-informed remark had been the following morning.

Later that night I was paged because a leukemia patient wanted to ask me a question. When I finally got around to seeing him, it was almost 2:00 a.m. He was an obstetrician from New Jersey who had been admitted to the hospital because of a leukemia flare, an acute "blast crisis," where the bone marrow starts to churn out leukemic cells (myeloblasts) at a prodigious rate. He had received the usual chemotherapy cocktail, until he became short of breath and doctors discovered a large collection of malignant fluid in the space around his heart. Surgeons had drained the fluid with a needle. Now he was awaiting a

CT scan to see if the pericardial membrane needed to be stripped away to prevent further fluid accumulation.

But it hadn't been signed out to me that he needed the CT scan tonight. He was sitting in a chair, wearing flannel pajamas and a gray T-shirt. His temples were wasted, imparting a forlorn look. The sign on the door read CONTACT ISOLATION. I stepped inside the room, being careful not to touch anything.

"I'm supposed to be going for a CAT scan—" he began.

"It's not going to happen tonight," I interrupted.

"Why not? Is the scanner being used?"

"No, at least . . . I don't know, but they don't do nonemergent scans in the middle of the night."

"Then why do they keep telling me I'm going for this test? They keep telling me that they need to rule out constrictive pericarditis. They're talking about pleurodesis. Doesn't that qualify as an emergency?"

"I'm not your regular doctor so I can't say," I replied lamely. "It wasn't signed out to me to have it done tonight so it's going to have to wait until the morning."

"God, I'm going to have a nervous breakdown if I don't get out of here. I've been here since July."

Beep . . . beep . . . beep. "I'm sorry, sir," I said, holding up my pager.

"It doesn't matter to them that you're a doctor. You'd think it would make a difference, being an insider, but it doesn't. You're still at their mercy."

"I'm sorry but—"

"This is a fine institution," he went on, undeterred. "I've been fortunate to be here, but there is no coordination—"

"I'm sorry, sir, but I have to go," I said, and left.

On night float, things sometimes happened in clusters. That night at Memorial was the night of the falls. First, I got called about Mr. Gurvitch, whom the nurses found kneeling on the floor next to his bed. He said that he had been walking to the bathroom when his knees buckled. "Does he need a CAT scan?" a nurse inquired. The patient insisted that his head hadn't touched the floor, so I told the nurse that a CAT scan wasn't necessary. I ordered the patient to remain in bed for the rest of the night.

A half hour later, he face-planted into the windowsill. Back in his room, I found him sitting in a chair, dabbing dark droplets of blood from his nostrils. Apparently he had again tried going to the bathroom but had again gotten dizzy. I was pretty sure his nose was broken. Now, there was no question that he needed some sort of imaging study. I phoned the radiology department. No answer. I tried again, this time letting the phone ring for several minutes. Someone finally picked up. "I need a complete facial series stat!" I cried.

"What's that?"

I hesitated. "X-rays of the face?"

In the middle of the night, hesitation to a radiology technician is a bit like blood to a shark. Suddenly I found myself on the defensive. He hurled questions at me: Why were the X-rays necessary? How were they going to change my management? How badly was he bleeding? Who was going to bring him down? Rajiv had told me that in the hospital, sometimes the best defense is a good offense. "Listen, I'm just covering for the night, but your supervisor's going to want to know why you refused to do an X-ray on a guy with cancer who just crashed into a window and has a platelet count of zero."

That did the trick. "Why didn't you tell me he had low platelets?" the tech said. "So he should have a CAT scan. Send him down; I'll do him now."

At five in the morning, I put my head down on a pillow in the call room. I popped two more Lodine pills. For the thousandth time during internship, I despaired about how rest doesn't accumulate. One terrible night and the fatigue drenches over you once again.

An hour later, as daybreak approached, I found myself in Mr. Fibak's room. A young Polish man, he too had fallen while getting out of bed. I had seen him once already that night for a fever. Inside his isolation room was a small sink, where I rinsed my hands with scalding hot water before donning gloves and a yellow gown and backing my way through a curtain.

I took a moment to look over his bedside chart. The vital signs— pulse, temperature, blood pressure, and respiratory rate—were recorded on a graph. Each number was supposed to be charted in a different color, with a different scale for each sign, but someone had recorded all of them in blue. I wasn't sure whether his pulse was 102, or his blood pressure, or if he had spiked a fever to 102.

The dawn light was seeping through the window blinds. Looking out onto First Avenue, I could see that taxicabs were moving, but most of Manhattan was still not up. The room was gray, cold, and spare, with a vaguely unwelcoming air, in keeping with the season. Under a terry cloth blanket, Fibak looked like he was sleeping. He was a thin man with sunken cheeks and short, wispy hair standing up on his scalp like young grass in a newly seeded field. Bags of multicolored liquids were hanging on a metal pole at his bedside, emptying slowly into a tightly wound cable of plastic tubes passing into a catheter in his right arm and another in his chest. His skin was pale. His body looked like it would break if I pressed on it.

I called out his name. He did not stir. Alarmed, I tugged at the blanket and he immediately sat up, appearing embarrassed for having been caught slumbering. "How are you feeling?" I asked as he shook away the sleep. "I was told you fell down."

His nose was crusted with blood and there was a small bruise on the side of his face. "You never came back to see me, Doctor!" he exclaimed.

Evidently I had promised to do so earlier that night, but I had forgotten why. "Well, I'm here now," I said, pressing gently on the bridge of his nose.

"That's because I fell. You were never going to come back to see me."

His deep-set eyes looked fearful, like those of a sick child. The inside of his eyelids had a grayish hue, a sign of profound anemia. His breath sounds were coarse, his rib cage almost unbearably bony. Shallow ulcers coated the inside of his mouth. He told me that the pain in his mouth and throat was almost intolerable. He was chronically nauseated, and he could no longer swallow. Nutritive fluids were dripping into his vein through an intravenous catheter. Unopened Tupperware containers filled with prepared foods were strewn on his bedside table. "Who brought these for you?" I asked. "My wife," he replied. "She wanted me to eat something, but I told her they have to give me morphine and Zofran first."

I told him he needed a CAT scan to rule out bleeding in his head. For a moment he was quiet. Then tears came to his eyes. "Come on," I said. "After what you've been through, this will be nothing."

"When can I leave this place, Doctor?"

"I can ask your doctors when they come back in the morning."

"I know what they are going to say. 'When your counts come up. When you stop having fevers.' I got cytomegalovirus, Doctor. I've been on these antibiotics for a month. I just want to know, am I going to leave this hospital?"

I was silent. "I will have to ask on rounds," I said.

Fibak looked away. "I know I'm never going to leave," he said, dabbing at his nose. "Just tell them to give me an answer," he said angrily. "I got a wife and kids, Doctor. It's been two months."

The teams returned to the hospital at seven o'clock. At seven-fifteen, an indignant chief resident paged me to tell me that residents were waiting for me to sign out in the library. I was in with a patient who had just gone into acute congestive heart failure. I had just administered morphine and diuretics and was pretty sure he was going to have to be intubated. Could the group come over to me? I asked. After a few minutes, interns and nurse practitioners started streaming into the room. I wasn't sure where to begin, so I took out my sign-out lists. They looked like the doodles of a bored high school student, covered with scribbles and arrows and boxes. One page was torn; another had a long streak of blood. "How was your night?" someone asked.

hole

And you may find yourself in a beautiful house, with a beautiful wife
And you may ask yourself—Well . . . How did I get here?

—TALKING HEADS, "ONCE IN A LIFETIME"

In biology, ontogeny recapitulates phylogeny. The fetal heart, through its development, reproduces the single-chambered organ of our gill-bearing ancestors. The education of a doctor similarly replays the travails of physicians of generations past. There are several reasons for this: institutional inertia; a desire for cheap labor; the punitive sensibility of senior physicians. "The brutality of the training is deliberate," a medical school professor once told me. "It forges loyalty to the profession through shared hardship." For me, it had done just the opposite. My spirit was broken after four months of toil and compromise. The pain in my neck was unrelenting; my right arm was starting to feel heavy. Midway through my week of night float at Memorial, I informed Dr. Wood that I was going to take a break from residency. I suspect he knew that more than just my neck needed to heal.

When I called Sonia in Washington to tell her, she started crying. She hadn't realized how much I had been suffering. I told her the hiatus from residency was going to be temporary, though I had no idea if that was really the case. She said she'd pray for my speedy recovery.

I was given six days off and then a reduced work schedule—call every fifth night, rather than every third or fourth, and one or two mornings off per week for physical therapy. At first I was elated. Time off! A paid vacation during internship! But my initial exhilaration was quickly replaced with a brooding melancholy when I realized that I was buried again in indecision and purposelessness. Mornings were restless. I'd wake up at dawn, unable to go back to sleep. I'd get out of bed feeling cold, listless, with a queasy, sad feeling, as though my mind had been spinning its discontents in my sleep. There was a heavy weight below my sternum—the weight of a hole—extending down to the pit of my stomach. I lay on the couch, blankly watching television, staring at the window, staring at the walls. So much effort, and now where was I—the bottom of the heap? In my journal I wrote:

Something is wrong—something. My mind is sluggish; I cannot focus. My mood is low; perhaps I am depressed; or perhaps this is just the way it is. I have felt for months that I am fighting something; I am fighting to stay up. I feel like a marble rolling around in a bowl: back and forth, back and forth, speeding up as it gets to the bottom, desperately trying to avoid what will happen if I stop. How low can I descend? There is a pit visible and perhaps I am bound to fall into it.

I had gotten so used to the daily grind, to being told what to do and where to be at every moment, that the loss of that routine was queerly unsettling. I found myself peering jealously through my living room window at my colleagues down on the street scurrying outside the hospital complex. I envied their activity, their health, their sense of purpose and continuing accomplishment. I wondered what they were thinking; did they even know that I was gone? I occupied a sort of netherworld, not sick enough to garner sympathy, but also not healthy enough to function normally.

Since I couldn't exercise, I took to walking, especially in the morning, when the fog shrouded the East River like little clouds. I could hardly believe who was out and about: high school kids in hip-hugger jeans; young professionals in James Dean leather coats; middle-aged men pushing expensive strollers with pretty blondes in fur coats and wraparound shawls carrying Louis Vuitton bags. On the promenade, I walked past bums lying on wooden benches or in sleeping bags, their faces blackened, talking to themselves with reverie. I caught their stares and walked on.

In Central Park the leaves were turning color, littering the ground in heavy, sodden piles. Birds circled slowly in the air, like vultures seeking carrion. I had always loved Berkeley in the fall: the crunchy brown leaves under your feet; the long chilly evenings walking down Telegraph Avenue, where the grimy hawkers peddled their fake llama-wool sweaters and the fat ladies sold fruit-shaped candles beside endless stalls of cheap jewelry. Walking without purpose reminded me of that time. I thought how ironic it was that I had gone into medicine to join the real world.

On my reduced work schedule, I began twice-weekly physical therapy at a nearby orthopedic hospital. Most sessions, my head was put into a traction device, which relieved the pressure from the slipped disk. Standing with my back against a spongy wall, I performed neck-strengthening exercises while young Latino therapists worked on elderly men in wheelchairs to the tunes of salsa and merengue. The goal was to help patients recover "functional status," so different sections of the treatment room replicated different environments patients might find themselves in: a "deli counter" with a cash register; a "produce department" with plastic fruit; a "dry-goods aisle" with bags of rice and beans; a "frozen-foods section" with fake cartons of ice cream. There was even a tiny space with a single bed and side table. It reminded me of the hospital call rooms I had been sleeping in.

Over the following weeks, profoundly unsure of my future, I decided to write an essay about my experience on night float. My purpose was to warn hospital administrators and future residents to the dangers of this cross-coverage system. I pitched the idea to Cornelia "Cory" Dean, the science editor of *The New York Times*, to whom I had been introduced by my journalist-doctor acquaintance Elisabeth Rosenthal. When I spoke with Cory after arriving in New York, she had encouraged me to keep a journal and write about issues related to residency. When I queried her about a piece on night float, she encouraged me to write it up.

In the essay I criticized a system that left interns in charge of a large number of very sick patients about whom they knew very little. I recounted some of my near-fatal mistakes on the night shift at Memorial, when I'd felt overwhelmed, and had been receiving inadequate supervision. In my opinion, the Bell Commission, which instituted residency work-hour limits, the impetus for the night-float system, seemed to have traded one set of problems for another. Obviously doctors could not assume round-the-clock responsibility for their patients, but having night floats seemed fraught with the kind of risks hospitals were striving to avoid: discontinuity of care, delayed tests, medication errors, or worse. Which was safer: to be cared for by a fatigued resident who knew you, or a rested resident who did not?

Cory and the *Times* accepted the essay. In fact, when she paged me to tell me, I was in a flower shop on Lexington Avenue, buying a bouquet for Sonia, who was planning on visiting me that weekend. Cory asked me where she should fax the "playback." I obviously couldn't have her fax it to the hospital, so, with the florist's permission, she faxed it right to the flower shop!

On the morning the essay was published in the Tuesday science section, I was stopped in the hospital by a medical student I didn't know, who asked me if I had written "that article" in the *Times*. I was astounded that a stranger had recognized me. During the day, I spied the newspaper in the hands of several attending physicians, wondering what they were thinking. Of course I felt proud at being published, but I was anxious nevertheless about the reaction the essay could provoke. When I ran into Dr. Carmen, he cryptically told me he had been hearing my name all over the hospital.

The essay (predictably, in retrospect) caused a firestorm. I was told it was discussed at a meeting of the medical board, which apparently thought that I may have created a liability risk for the hospital. At

Memorial, a top-level administrator reportedly instructed the chief residents to draft a press release defending the night-float system and assuring the public that patients were safe. (As far as I know, the press office never released it.) Even Dr. Bertrand Bell, who headed the original work-hours commission in the mid-1980s, sent a letter to the New York State Department of Health, a copy of which was provided to me by the *Times*:

The continued scheduling by hospitals of sleep deprivation and chronic fatigue as a feature of residency training in hospitals in New York State . . . is disturbing . . . [Dr. Jauhar's article] details the most egregious defiance of the law . . . The article is the sentinel event in demonstrating a problem hazardous to health and in need of corrective action. It is quite clear that the department must cite Dr. Jauhar's hospital for breaking the supervisory requirements of the law.

At one time I might have obsessed about the fallout, but at this point I didn't much care. Most mornings now I was waking up fantasizing an escape. That I had somehow found the energy while on leave to write the piece and get it published in the most important newspaper in the country only heightened my ambivalence about medicine: Wouldn't I be better off switching to journalism? In my diary I wrote: "I hate feeling stupid; I clam up and doubt myself. It's one thing in a field where ignorance is sanctioned, like journalism; quite another in a field where ignorance is vilified, like medicine."

I confessed these doubts to my parents when they came to visit me a few weeks later. They had come to New York for a special occasion. Sonia and I were getting "pre-engaged."

The view through my window was of a cold late-autumn day: no snow, but no movement on the streets either. My parents were sitting quietly on the couch, expressionless except for their perpetual look of worry, which faded in impact from overuse. Though impressed that I had gotten an article published in the *Times*, my father was worried about its effects on my medical career. After the battles he had waged at the university over "racialism," he had become sensitized to professional conflict and advised me to be more accommodating than he had ever been, especially with senior physicians who were going to judge me and perhaps write letters of recommendation on my behalf. "You must remember that medicine is your goal and writing your hobby," he had written in a letter. "You must never get obsessed with writing at the cost of your profession. We liked reading your article in *The New York Times*, but <u>nothing</u> will make us happier than seeing you as a great doctor alleviating human suffering."

I was sitting at the dining table, absentmindedly looking out onto the street, my head fixed stiffly in a Miami J-collar. I had just taken more Lodine and was waiting for the analgesic effect to kick in.

"If someone gets sick, I think it's a reflection on their abilities," my father declared.

"Which abilities?" I asked.

"Abilities as a doctor, as a man. I had neck problems, too. I went to all the bloody doctors. They pumped me with drugs—Celebrex, Vioxx, Fiorinal—but I stopped them all. Now I do my exercises and I feel better. It's your responsibility to keep yourself healthy. It reflects on your abilities as a doctor. At least that's my opinion."

I said nothing. There was no point arguing when my father was in one of his moods.

"So what is going on now? We are in the dark."

"With what?" I asked.

"With your career, your life!" my father cried. He leaned forward like a lawyer about to make a case he had been preparing for months. "First you wanted to do physics; you said that medicine was for mediocres. Then you wanted to do law. Law has nothing to do with physics, right?" (He did not wait for a reply.) "Then you applied to medical school. We didn't tell you to apply. I said, 'Okay, he wants to be a physicist.' But you said you wanted to do medicine. I didn't tell you to do it. But I told you, 'If you do it, you have to stick with it.' And I'll tell you, by God, you did the right thing. If you stayed in physics you would be doing post-doc after post-doc: no money, no job security, struggling at the university, like I struggled. Going to medicine was the best thing that could have happened to you. You had landed in a ditch. Now at least you have some direction."

I kept quiet. My father was nothing if not persistent. He always believed that one more warning could avert disaster, and right then I was kind of hoping it was true.

"You can fix this," my father went on. "Nothing is lost. It is not falling into water but staying there that drowns a man."

"What do you want to do?" my mother asked quietly.

"I don't know, maybe journalism."

"Journalism?" My father's face filled up with fury. He had barely tolerated this interest when it was an avocation. "What guarantee do you have that you will get a job in journalism?" he demanded. "Do you think they are going to make you an anchorman or hire you at *The New York Times*?"

"Will Sonia be happy if you become a journalist?" my mother sputtered.

"Sonia has nothing to do with it," I replied.

"She wants a doctor!"

"Leave her out of it!"

"Your mother has a point," my father intoned. "Money talks. Believe it or not, money is important."

"*Khoon sook gya hai*," my mother said, shaking her head, meaning that her blood had dried up with worry over me.

"You are always wavering, flickering, putting us through hell," my father said, obviously disgusted. "*Thanday doodh noo phook marta hai*," he muttered.

There he goes again, I thought, always telling me that I was blowing on cold milk.

"You don't know what it's like," I started.

"My dear son, did you think it would be a walk through a rose garden? They don't pay you for nothing."

"What about passion?"

"What is passion?! You can train your mind to find passion." He accused me of immaturity. I accused him of a bourgeois mentality. Back and forth it went—the recriminations, the anger. Why was I not practical? Why were they not supportive? Why, with all the promise I supposedly possessed, would I consider ruining my life by quitting medicine now?

"You have to learn to focus," my father said sadly, getting up to end the conversation. "Then and then only are you going to get somewhere. You cannot succeed by doing something halfheartedly. You cannot always do what you like, but you must like what you do."

LATER THAT WEEK—on an auspicious day, according to the gurus Sonia's parents had consulted—we drove a rental car to New Jersey for dinner and a religious ceremony with Sonia's family. The ceremony was called *roka* (meaning "to stop"), and it was supposed to signify that Sonia and I had chosen each other and were going to stop looking for other people. When I told my father about this "pre-engagement," he responded with his usual gruff practicality. "You like her, so why don't you just get married?"

Sonia's family lived in Edison, population one hundred thousand, an enclave for Indian immigrants unlike anything I had ever seen. As I drove through town, we passed Kar Parts, Patel Cash & Carry, Bombay Chaat House, and Delhi Darbar. Young women in *salwar kameez* tops and braided ponytails ambled along the road carrying groceries. Old men clad in white dhoti cloth were pumping gas. Signs on office buildings read PATEL, GUPTA, KHANNA. Sonia's parents had a busy internal medicine practice here—an empire really—with two thousand patients and three different offices. Her father had urged me to join his practice after finishing my medical training. "You must become a cardiologist," he said on more than one occasion. "Then you can take over the practice."

We took a sharp right onto a country road lined with tall oak trees. Suddenly the conventional wood-frame homes on the main road gave way to huge mansions set in landscaped plots lined with luxury cars.

We turned onto a gravel-ridden private road covered with leaves. The house was visible about a quarter mile in the distance: a rambling three-story whitewashed colonial with black shutters, long balconies, and four Mercedes-Benzes parked out front. A herd of deer looked up as we drove past. *So this*, I told myself, feeling awed, *is what a doctor's salary can buy.*

Images of our modest bungalow in Riverside, California, flashed through my mind. Our entire tract-housing block could have fit on the roadway leading up to the house. I looked at my parents' faces, wondering what they were thinking. Were they impressed? Was this the reason they wanted me to stick with medicine?

In the car, my father and I had reached an uneasy rapprochement; there was to be no more discussion of my career today. His last words on the subject were in the Lincoln Tunnel: "Your mother and I always think of you as our brilliant son—a source of light for our family. Every morning you wake up, ask yourself: What is the aim of my life? Am I heading in the right direction?"

When we arrived at the house, Sonia came out to greet us. Though I had been to the house once before for dinner, going there with my parents set the differences in our upbringings into sharp relief, and I think Sonia must have sensed my unease. A pandit was waiting for us in the ornately decorated living room. As Sonia and I sat side by side on a silk rug under a painting of Lord Vishnu, he lit a *havan*—a wisp of cotton soaked in oil—and loudly chanted Sanskrit verses. Syllables were shooting off his lips like bullets, and his brown pate glistened with the effort. Hunched over on the floor, with the pain in my neck nearly unbearable, I regretted leaving my neck brace behind in Manhattan. The pandit asked me to repeat certain phrases—"*aana maana gaana . . .*"—which I did, oblivious to their meaning. Were these another set of commitments I was destined to break? After each verse, the pandit made an offering of rice grains and flower petals to Lord Ganesh. He smeared *tikkas* of red paste and crushed seeds on our foreheads and periodically filled our outstretched palms with a *parshad* of holy water and milk. Sonia and I rubbed vertical streaks of turmeric on each other's forehead and hung flower garlands around each other's neck. When the time came, the pandit instructed me to offer a ring. I had bought it the week before at Cartier in midtown. It had three intertwining bands of yellow, white, and pink gold, signifying love, fidelity, and passion.

Afterward, maids brought out platters of chicken and lamb chops, savory *pakoras*, and curried vegetables—and bottles of Blue Label and Macallan's. I sat quietly, picking at the food on my plate. My appetite was poor; in fact, I had lost ten pounds over the past two months. The pit of my stomach burned with acidity, the first sign, I was sure, of a peptic ulcer.

Gifts were exchanged. Sonia's grandmother recounted stories from the *Ramayan*, a religious parable. The lesson seemed to be that the person who lives by his words will be rewarded; he will be king. "Never break your promises; never take the easy way out." Of course, she was talking about my relationship with her granddaughter, but I could not help but think the words equally applied to other commitments I had made.

I looked around the room. Everyone was smiling, beaming. I resented their laughter, resented my discontentment. Sonia's father drunkenly took out a microphone and started performing Bollywood karaoke. He took me aside. "Be happy," he said. "You are always so serious. When you are stuck in a mud puddle, you cannot expect it to flow like the Ganges." He offered me a set of golf clubs and told me that I would be made an honorary member of his country club. I thanked him, not having the heart to tell him that I doubted I would ever use them. I couldn't picture myself like him, a successful doctor riding down rolling fairways in a golf cart.

Under the influence of liquor and the occasion, my father looked happy, perhaps even a bit inebriated. Seeing him that way, a man who took pride in maintaining control of himself and others at all times, felt almost surreal. The smell of Old Spice on his cotton shirt transported me back to a time when I had been vulnerable to his disapproval. I remembered how he used to exhort the virtues of vitamin C. Growing up, I became obsessed with vitamin C because of my father. I gorged on fruit to prove my love for him. He sometimes reminded me of the father in Vittorio De Sica's *The Bicycle Thief*: loving, protective, but somewhat pathetic, too. Right then I felt like the boy in the film, holding his father's hand, looking at him in awe and fear while he ate a pizza to which he was not entitled.

Outside, in the backyard, a photographer set up a tripod camera and snapped pictures as Sonia, wearing a red silk *salwar kameez*, and I, wearing a charcoal gray Brooks Brothers suit, touched the bark of a holy tree. Afterward, she went inside and I sat alone on the stone steps. It was dark now, quiet, apart from a rare cricket, the nearly full moon illuminating the expansive lawn. I looked out at the parched, knolled fields singed by the cold, dotted with what looked like burial mounds, my thoughts as tangled as the skein of brown trees in the distance. *How can I quit now?* I thought. *How do I disappoint everyone, including myself? I'm not strong enough, bold enough, courageous enough, to say, Stop!*

I was flailing in a quagmire of my own making, and yet the quagmire was the only place I could imagine being. The constant cogitation was exhausting and seemingly preordained. Perhaps this was the way it had to be; perhaps the way my life had unfolded depended on who I really was, deep inside, not the part that could be changed or molded or beaten out like a pellet of ore. A lyric kept going through my head: *You may find yourself in a beautiful house, with a beautiful wife/And you may ask yourself—Well . . . How did I get here?*

In a flash, I thought of Lisa. I wondered how she was doing. At one time, I had ruminated over her illness, too. I had been racked with doubts before. I remembered discussing her with my father, crouched uncomfortably on the living room carpet, the snow packed outside, the house unbearably lonely, crying the both of us, me for my losses, he for me, and perhaps for his losses, too. But that had been a very different problem than the one I was now facing. As a good friend had once remarked, "Some problems are divine."

I felt the urge to cry, but I told myself to wait until a more appropriate time. I cleared my throat, tightened up my face, anything to keep myself from sobbing, but the tears came anyway, hot and quick, salting my face. Images were shooting in from the fringes of my memory. I had seen them before, perhaps in my childhood, perhaps in a movie. I was six years old again, running across the road into oncoming traffic, only to be whisked up into my father's arms. He was forcing me to eat an overripe banana on the way to the school bus stop, dragging me along in my starched public-school uniform. I was back in middle school, preparing to defend my title in the Math Field Day competition. After the competition, in the school parking lot near the petting farm with the one goat and a few chickens, my father took one long disappointed look at my fourth-place certificate and ordered my mother to kiss it.

I don't feel like being bold. I just want to be solemn and brooding. Being courageous takes too much effort. What's the point? When the going gets tough, the smart get out! That's what the preacher used to say on the steps of Sproul Hall. Get out, get out. I can't get out!

At one time, I had been so optimistic about my future, and so had my parents. I had invested it with so much hope, comfort, profundity—and here it was, and I had become a doctor, and it was all so muted and colorless. Everything was gray, in tone and shade. What would happen if I broke myself down again and rebuilt? I was afraid that all that would remain would be fragments of shell and dust. Everything else would evaporate.

winter blues

O Wind,

If winter comes, can Spring be far behind?

—SHELLEY, "ODE TO THE WEST WIND"

When I was a boy, I used to ponder the following question: Should a person stop doing something if there is a chance that thing could lead to disaster? For example, would I stop driving altogether if I knew that at some point in my life I was destined to crash into a brick wall? Would I consign myself to a life of immobility (especially true in Southern California) to avoid such a calamity? During the winter of my internship, I often asked myself this question in relation to medicine: Should I go on? Though I was still working in the hospital, I was just barely functioning. And I wasn't sure that disaster did not lie ahead.

In December, with the pain in my neck starting to subside, I was sent back to Memorial—to substitute for an intern who had just returned from a leave of absence for major depression. Even though she was back on the wards, the chief residents thought it best that she perform her Memorial service in the spring, so I ended up spending New Year's Eve once again on call on the leukemia ward.

That night, I saw Kayvan Patel for the last time. A middle-aged man, he had been diagnosed with acute lymphocytic leukemia two years earlier. At first his disease responded to chemotherapy and he went into remission. But the cancer returned and eventually proved resistant to all treatments. He knew he was going to die. But first, he wanted to spend a little more time with his two sons, eight and eleven, to impart lessons they could carry with them when he was gone.

He could not escape the hospital, though. The leukemia had ravaged his immune system, so every time he got a new fever—which happened every few weeks—he would be hospitalized and placed in virtual isolation. His sons were discouraged from visiting him because they were going to school and posed an infectious risk. He was given antibiotics—antibacterial, antiviral, antifungal—for weeks at a time, often becoming violently nauseated and short of breath during his daily infusions. With each passing day his frustration and sadness grew as he realized the fever was consuming the precious little time he had left.

One day, he decided he had had enough. The months of hospitalizations and the endless, mysterious fevers had taken their toll on his mind as much as his body. When he told his doctors that he wanted to go home, they discouraged him, telling him he could rapidly succumb to an infection, but he would not be dissuaded. On New Year's Eve, shortly before midnight, he called me into the small room that had become his home. Lying on sheets wet with perspiration, his face dark and flushed, he spoke to me with a resoluteness I had not seen in the three weeks I had known him. "They say I will die if I leave the hospital," he whispered. "I will take that chance because here I am already dead."

Not long ago, his words could have described my feelings, too. It had been a bleak autumn. Trying to make it through each day was like pedaling a bicycle up a steep hill, straining to keep my balance as my calves burned with heat and pain. The constant pressure to perform, to satisfy the expectations of my family, my colleagues, and myself, was too much to bear, and eventually I cracked. And once I cracked, the crisis of confidence became self-sustaining, as I began to flagellate myself over my state of mind. Why wasn't I stronger? Why couldn't I handle the stress? Why me? Why now? The lower I felt, the worse it got, as my mood seemed to feed on itself. But fortunately, even in the midst of this crisis, I knew that my dark mood was pathological. I had enough insight to know that I was clinically depressed.

Because I was miserable, I succeeded at making the people close to me miserable, too. A nugget of anger was always wedged deep in my brain, ready to explode at the slightest provocation. At times I lashed out at Sonia, dumping my frustrations on her even though we were supposed to be in the prime of our courtship, a honeymoon phase. Post-call, I'd snap if I didn't get enough sleep. One afternoon, exhausted after a difficult night on call, stress ulcers stinging the inside of my mouth, I told Sonia I wasn't going to be able to make it to a social function at her parents' house that evening.

"My parents had it a lot worse than us," she said, clearly annoyed by the change of plans. "Those were the days of the giants. My father used to be on call every night. You and I have it comparatively—"

"Stop it!" I roared, rage surging through me, momentarily clearing my mind of its cobwebs. I always hated it when Sonia compared me to her father. I was having a hard enough time in medicine without being reminded of how he had succeeded.

"Why are you yelling?" Sonia shouted.

"I don't want to hear about your father or your family! I have my own way."

Before long we were angrily circling each other in the foyer. We were in our volcanic phase, and in the volcanic phase, you didn't know where the lava would flow.

"Have you no concept of what I'm going through?" I barked.

"You act like you're the only one!" Sonia said. "I've got my own stuff to deal with."

"You don't know the pressure I'm under!"

"Don't dump it on me," Sonia retorted. "It isn't fair."

"You see how I'm working. Why don't you understand—"

"I understand, but honey, you need help. You're depressed. Remember how things were last summer—?"

"Stop it, just stop! I can't deal with this right now." And with that I stormed out of the apartment.

As was typical in those days, Sonia called me a few minutes later, and we quickly made up. That was the nature of our fights during internship: explosive eruptions rapidly followed by amends and calm. After a long nap, I apologized for my outburst, and we went to her parents'. But I still felt like a razor precariously balanced on its edge.

IN JANUARY, I rotated back to the outpatient clinic at New York Hospital. After what I had been through the past couple of months, I was glad for an easy rotation, and it was good to see some of my regular patients. Perry Richardson showed up for his normal psychotherapy session. A lumbering black man with a flirtatious manner, he had fallen on hard times after being laid off as a sales representative at a pharmaceutical company, losing his apartment and his boyfriend, even living for a while in a homeless shelter on Ninety-sixth Street. But he had started taking night classes in graphic design and was planning on starting a glossy-brochures business. Jimmie Washington came in, too, still loudly announcing in the waiting room that she was a busy obstetrician. She had a few surprises for me, like the stroke she had suffered in 1984. "Did I know about that?" I asked. "You would if you'd been listening," she admonished. "Okay, so tell me about the stroke," I said. "It was after my brain surgery," she replied. Brain surgery! I didn't know what she was talking about. It turned out that she had had a brain aneurysm resection fifteen years earlier, which I thought probably explained her eccentric personality.

That month, I made my first house call. In truth, it wasn't entirely my idea. The patient, Roberto Gonzalez, had prostate cancer that had spread to the bones. He had been coming to see me with his wife at least once a month throughout the fall and winter, but he had missed his last couple of clinic appointments. One afternoon I got a call from his visiting nurse. I had never spoken with her before. (Admittedly, I had even been a bit lax about filling out the home-care order forms that were periodically put into my mailbox.) "He's getting sicker," the nurse told me. "He would love to see you."

"How can we get him into the office?" I asked sincerely. (Did she want me to fill out another transportation form?)

"You could pay him a visit," she suggested delicately. It hadn't even occurred to me. At no time during my education had I seen or heard of a doctor making a house call.

I went to see him one evening after work. His block in Spanish Harlem had the characteristic mix of pawnshops, check-cashing stores, and dilapidated storefronts painted with colorful murals. Children were jumping rope on the sidewalk in front of the building, while old men passed the time on a nearby stoop. Standing in my white coat, I rang the door buzzer. A teenage girl popped her head out of a fourth-floor window. "Dr. Jauhar is here!" she cried.

Inside, I ascended the cracking limestone staircase. It was a steep climb; no wonder he had been unable to come see me. At the top of the stairs, I was greeted by a shawl-covered woman in her sixties. She clasped my hand. "Thank you, Doctor," she said. "Thank you for coming."

The apartment was well kept and filled with Catholic adornments and the fragrance of potpourri. I followed his wife to his room. Mr. Gonzalez was lying in bed, wearing a diaper, his crumpled body barely making an impression on the crisp sheets. His lips and eyes were coated with crust, and his face was sunken. A plate of rice and beans was sitting on the bureau, untouched. "Dr. Jauhar is here," his wife said. "He has come to see you." He extended his hand weakly, and I held it. I asked him how he was feeling. "A little better," he whispered. "But I'm sick of going in the bed. I'm sick of being a child."

Instinctively, I reached for my stethoscope, but then I realized I had left it at the clinic. In fact, I had brought nothing with me: no penlight, no blood pressure cuff, no prescription pad, nothing. I looked up at his wife's smiling face, wondering if she noticed.

Without my tools, I couldn't follow my usual procedures, so I just sat at his bedside, stroking his hand. Afterward, in the kitchen, I sat with his wife and had a cup of tea. I asked her how she was holding up. "He wants me to wait on him hand and foot," she said with a mixture of resentment and resignation.

"It takes a lot of love," I said, not knowing how to respond.

"I don't know if I love him so much anymore," she replied matter-of-factly. "Now it's more like I just take care of him."

She took a sip from her cup. "He's jealous that I'm up on my feet and he isn't," she said. "The other day I wanted to buy face cream, but I couldn't go because he wouldn't let me. When the grandkids come over, he says, 'They came to see me.' " She shrugged, like it was not in her nature to deny him such a small victory. "You know what he said to me the other day? He said, 'When I die, the spirit is going to come take you, too.' "

I nodded silently.

"That's not love," she said. "That's egoísta. You know what that means?" I could guess. "It's everything for yourself."

That night, while riding home on the bus, I felt curiously at peace. The trip uptown had filled me with a very different feeling than the ward medicine I had been practicing for months. Even though I hadn't prescribed any medicine or assisted them in any tangible way, I had learned so much about the Gonzalezes during my brief visit. House calls are a vanishing practice, but for me they were the sort of thing I had once looked forward to doing when I became a doctor.

Mr. Gonzalez died at home a couple of months later. It was two years before I made another house call. What I remember most about that first one was how impotent I felt. Outside the familiar terrain of the clinic, with no equipment or physician backup or formal training to speak of, I didn't know what to do. Later, when I mentioned the house call to a senior physician, he scolded me for having created a liability risk for the hospital by taking on this task without supervision. Overall, the experience seemed to have been a wash. So I was surprised when, two years later, I received a letter from Mrs. Gonzalez. "I just wanted to thank you again for coming to see my husband when he was ill," she wrote. "My family and I will never forget what you did." My small, reluctant act of kindness had made a lasting impression.

ONE FRIDAY AFTERNOON in the middle of January, a hospital operator paged me to tell me I had an outside call. When she put it through, I heard the uncharacteristically subdued voice of John Davidson, a close acquaintance from medical school who was now in the middle of his fourth year. He had left a couple of messages on my answering machine the night before, but I had neglected to call him back, electing to wait until the weekend, when I had more time. He asked me how I was doing. "Fine," I replied, though by now I was feeling on edge. After a long pause, he asked me to sit down. "What is it?" I demanded, irritated by the melodrama. And then, voice breaking, he delivered the bad news. Sam Stein, my best friend from medical school, had killed himself.

Feeling dizzy, I sat down. "What?"

Sam had been one of the most beloved students in our class. A Northern California native transplanted to the Midwest, he had an exuberant personality not unlike that of a Labrador retriever, always so full of energy and good cheer. We had spent a lot of time together my final year in St. Louis: marathon studying for exams, bar-hopping to meet women, cruising around town in my red Honda Civic with Radiohead blasting from the stereo. He was the one friend I had invited to my medical school graduation (since I had short-tracked, Sam was going to stay in St. Louis for another year). When I had spoken with him a few weeks earlier, there had been no indication that he was unhappy. His pediatric residency interviews were going well; he had just come back from Boston and was getting ready to fly out to Philadelphia. The residency director at St. Louis Children's Hospital had informally offered him an internship spot, which he was trying to decide whether to accept. He had so much going for him: a beautiful fiancée who was also a doctor, loving parents, a bright future. How could he have killed himself?

John told me that Sam's fiancée Heather had said that Sam had been feeling depressed for the past few weeks. For reasons that were unclear, he seemed to have lost confidence in his academic abilities, though he had always been near the top of his class. He had confessed to Heather that he didn't think he was up to handling residency. "You know Sam," John said, his voice trembling. "He always was his own worst critic."

He told me that Sam had started spending a lot of time in the library reading. A fellow classmate had seen him holed up in a cubicle one night, unusual behavior for a fourth-year medical student in the midst of interview season. Heather had made an appointment for him in the student health clinic, where a doctor had given him a prescription for an antidepressant. That was the day before he died. Sam never filled the prescription.

On the day he died, John told me, Sam had gone to the kitchen in the middle of the night. Apparently he had taken out a butcher knife, then climbed onto the counter and opened a small window over the sink. He crawled onto the ledge and jumped, still holding the knife, plunging twelve stories into a pile of garbage cans. Heather had awakened to the wail of police sirens.

My thoughts were swirling. I remembered a party Sam had had on the rooftop of his apartment building in St. Louis a few blocks from where I used to live. At the party, he had impulsively jumped over a four-foot gap onto the roof of the adjoining building, crossing over a chasm that extended down at least three hundred feet. Then, laughing, he jumped back. Livid, I had threatened to leave the party if he repeated the stunt.

"I don't understand," I finally said, my eyes filling with tears. "He was interviewing at all the best residencies."

It was an unusually warm winter day in St. Louis when I arrived for the memorial service. John picked me up at the airport, and we drove quietly to his apartment. As we were about to enter Forest Park, he pointed to the reddish brown brick building where Sam had lived. I craned to look back at it. All I could think about was the regret Sam must have felt after jumping. Twelve stories. I shuddered, imagining what my friend must have been going through.

At the service, which took place in a lecture hall on the medical school campus, friends went up to the podium to talk about Sam. Someone started off his tribute with "Dude!"—and after an uncomfortable silence explained that that was how Sam spoke. John said a few words, too, though I could not bring myself to do so. The doctor who had prescribed the antidepressant showed up. When she saw Heather, they each broke out into horrible wails.

AS WINTER WORE ON, more light streamed through the window blinds and the hospital became a generally more pleasant place to work. I rotated through various subspecialty wards: cardiology, neurology, pulmonary medicine. The patients on the neurology ward were sick—cruelly sick—and having suffered with my own neurological problem, I felt a special empathy for them. One man had Broca's aphasia. He could compose speech in his head; he just could not talk. Every time he tried to say something, he ended up quitting in tearful frustration. Another man had had a right parietal stroke, causing him to eerily neglect everything on the left side of his body, essentially immobilizing him. A woman with multiple sclerosis had such severe incontinence that she had to catheterize her own bladder to urinate. An elderly woman with Parkinson's disease smacked her lips and flicked her tongue like she was trying to dislodge a seed from between her teeth. She wanted to go home, but a psychiatrist had deemed her without capacity, and social workers had been unable to find a nursing home for her. The state was trying to get guardianship through the courts, but her lawyer was fighting it. Other patients on the ward were paralyzed from brain tumors or had Alzheimer's dementia, including one patient with a type the residents termed "delightful dementia" because it rendered her curiously passive and agreeable. The sentiments I had heard about neurologists seemed close enough to the mark. Master diagnosticians, they had depressingly little to offer their patients.

As the weeks passed and my neck healed, my gloom slowly lifted, allowing me to better judge the pluses and minuses of my situation. In the end, I'm not sure what convinced me to stick with residency, just as I'm not sure exactly what propelled me into the medical profession in the first place. It could have been inertia, my parents' wishes, pragmatism—or perhaps a combination of all three. It could have been the change of season. Fall/winter had always been the most melancholic time of the year for me. I remembered well those tortured months during my junior year in high school ruminating about whether I should believe in God. It could have been the news of Sam's death and the reminder it served that life is tenuous. It could have been the creative outlet provided by *The New York Times*, to which I had started intermittently contributing short essays. Perhaps my neck injury had something to do with it, too. For better or worse, it showed me what it was like to be a patient. Rajiv had said—and I had once believed—that doctors didn't do a whole lot for patients, but now there was refutation of that concept through my own experience. The neurologist and physical therapist provided hope and comfort to me at a vulnerable time in my life. They did for me what I could not do for myself: relieve my suffering. And once I experienced relief, I attributed to my caregivers a kind of omnipotence. It wasn't a stretch for me to realize that perhaps this was how my patients viewed me, too.

Whatever the reason, when the depression finally dissipated, it was like getting the gift of an early spring. I looked forward to going to the hospital each morning. Something was impelling me forward—a sense of discovery, perhaps, or intellectual adventure. Though medical practice might be mundane, even cookbook, I realized (realized again, really) that there were real complexities in it. There was a lot to think about—if you wanted to think. "Things are going to change," Rajiv constantly assured me when we talked about second year. "You can still become the kind of doctor you want to be." I was still curious to discover what that would be. (Ironically, my depression was probably the death knell for my interest in psychiatry. I couldn't imagine spending my days talking to people who felt like me.)

In April, Sonia and I got married in a lavish Hindu ceremony at a posh hotel in Woodbridge, New Jersey. At the end of the ceremony we took the traditional seven laps around the holy fire and recited our marriage vows. At the reception afterward, I could see the tremendous relief in her parents' and my parents' eyes. "Come on, darling," my father cooed as Sonia made her way to the head table in a red *lengha* stitched with gold thread and studded with jewels. Sonia and I made a good, culturally apposite match. It hadn't been easy being engaged during internship, but finding her had been the best thing to happen to me in an otherwise terrible year.

In June, at the end of internship, our class boarded two yellow school buses and went to Tarrytown, in the hills of Westchester County—Washington Irving country—for a daylong retreat. In a building that was a hybrid of a corporate training park and a Gothic Revival estate, we huddled in small groups to talk about the year that had been and the year coming up. We discussed the hardest rotation of internship. Someone said it was the CCU, but the general consensus was that it was night float at Memorial, because of the volume and the constant worry that patients could crump on you at any moment. In the morning, we acted out mock intern-resident encounters and watched staged videos of good and bad residents. As in typical instructional videos, the bad residents were unbelievably bad and the good residents were unbelievably virtuous. In the afternoon we attended classes on how to convey empathy, identify patients' concerns and expectations, and involve patients in shared decision-making. "The fact that we are talking about this touchy-feely stuff is a big change," Ali, a classmate, said. To me it seemed at best belated. Internship was almost over; it seemed a bit late to start talking about empathy.

At the end of the day, sitting on the grass outside, people recollected memorable moments from internship. David Jennings remembered the time he had forced a patient to go for a procedure. "He said he didn't want it," David recalled, "but I told him, 'Shut up, you need it.' I realized then that I was not his friend; I was his doctor. It was an epiphany." Cynthia, who, after much back-and-forth, had decided to stick with internal medicine, told of the time a patient had masturbated while she tried to examine him. Rachel recalled how grateful she had been when a resident put in an IV for her without being asked to. That led to a discussion about how we were going to do better by our interns next month. We were going to help out with blood draws and other scutwork; we were going to stay with them through sign-out; we were not going to dump on them the way we had been dumped on. It was a nice sentiment, but I figured that most of what we were pledging would become a distant memory come July 1. Internship had been a brutal initiation to medicine. Somehow we had gotten through it, and now those who would follow us were going to have to go through it, too. I thought about some of the residents I had worked with that year. Some, like Steve in the CCU, had been first-rate, but many others would round quickly and disappear, coming back to the wards for a quick flyby before noon conference and lunch, then off to the residents' lounge in the afternoon. I felt torn between striving to become the kind of resident I had wished for as an intern and getting by like most everyone else.

On the bus ride home, I thought once again about what I had been through over the past twelve months. Had I learned enough to move on? Dr. Wood had assured us during orientation that if we did as we were told, we'd be ready by now to supervise the next batch of interns. That time was at hand, and though I still had doubts, something told me that I was going to make a much better resident than intern. The bus entered a tunnel. I could hear the cars, the rumbling, on the roadway above us. The past twelve months, too, had been a passage through a dark tunnel. Then, suddenly, in the blackness, a shaft of light: second year.

PART III

reconciliation

difficult patients

The secret of the care of the patient is in caring for the patient.

—FRANCIS PEABODY, AMERICAN PHYSICIAN, 1927

I started the second year of residency like my first: in the outpatient clinic, not on the wards, where my classmates were already supervising new interns. Sonia was finishing up her third-year clinical clerkships at George Washington University and was planning on moving in with me next month to do her fourth-year at New York Hospital. Though I missed her, I didn't mind being apart. I felt like I needed time alone to devote myself fully to getting the hang of second year.

One evening, a young man came to see me. Because he had a walk-in appointment, I figured he had a minor problem—maybe a sore throat or a sprained ankle—that I could help him with right away. But when he sat in my examination room, his face was flushed. "I have a lump on my testicle," he announced.

Jonah was twenty-nine, handsome, with unruly brown hair, hazel eyes, and a nervous earnestness that was instantly likable. He had a kind of California surfer drawl that bespoke nonchalance, but his darting glances and stammer betrayed his anxiety. The lump was about the size of a pea, he said. It didn't hurt. He had noticed it only the night before. "I don't usually examine myself," he added sheepishly.

I was immediately concerned. A painless testicular mass, if indeed it originates from the testicle, is almost always cancer. I couldn't remember where I had learned this, but it evidently had diffused into my brain at some point during internship.

A general exam of Jonah turned up nothing out of the ordinary. His right testicle, with the lump, hung a bit lower than his left, but that was normal. He directed me to the mass. It was on the upper pole of the testicle, round, rubbery, about half an inch in diameter. It wasn't tender or mobile. It appeared to arise directly from the testis.

He asked me what I thought. I wasn't sure what to say. "I don't know," I replied after a pause. "It may be nothing. Let me consult with another doctor."

The physician supervising me that evening was a young attending who had recently completed her residency at New York Hospital. I told her that I suspected testicular cancer. Concerned, she came with me to examine Jonah. Then we went back to her office to discuss what to do. "It's probably cancer," she said, sitting down at her desk. "He needs an ultrasound to confirm it."

I nodded nervously; that was what I was going to suggest, too. "Good pickup," she said, perhaps sensing my unease. "You caught it early. He can probably be cured."

Testicular cancer is the most common solid tumor in men fifteen to thirty-four years of age. Like most malignancies, it used to be a death sentence; today, with advances in chemotherapy, it has a cure rate of over 90 percent. Even patients whose cancer has metastasized can usually be cured. Standard chemotherapy will successfully treat the vast majority of these patients. Of the remainder, approximately a quarter will be cured with second-line chemotherapy, and approximately a quarter of the remaining few will be cured with newer regimens involving high-dose chemotherapy with stem-cell transplantation.

When I got back to the exam room, Jonah was even more on edge. "What do I have?" he demanded. I decided not to burden him with unconfirmed suspicions. "I don't know," I said. "Can you come in tomorrow for an ultrasound?" A wave of alarm washed over him. "Do I have cancer?" he whispered.

I didn't want to be the one to break the bad news. "I just don't know at this point," I lied. "We need more information."

The next morning I called a urology resident and told him that Jonah needed an ultrasound. "No problem," he replied. "We'll do him this afternoon." Around five o'clock, he paged me. "It's cancer," he said. The test showed a round, well-defined mass, about five-eighths of an inch in diameter, on top of the right testicle. "Have you told him yet?" I asked. "I'm about to," he replied.

Jonah later told me how he got the news. "The resident just walked right in with his team and told me," he said, still shocked. "He was very take-charge and matter-of-fact. His attitude was, 'This is what you have, and this is what we need to do about it.' But it was sort of like— boom!—I wasn't expecting it. The scariest thing is how you can be just fine one minute, and the next have someone tell you that you have cancer and need to have your testicle removed."

I wondered whether my being more honest with him that first evening might have lessened the blow.

A short while later, a stream of residents and medical students flowed in to examine him. "I understand why they had to do it," Jonah said. "It's sort of rare, and they have to learn. But at that point I just wanted to be left alone."

Three days later, Jonah had an orchiectomy, in which the urologist removed the testicle by pushing it up through an incision on Jonah's upper groin. He was out of the hospital later the same day. After the operation, a cancer specialist told him that his kind of testicular cancer had about a 30 percent chance of recurrence and that he had two options: dissection of the lymph nodes in his groin and abdomen for evidence of residual disease, or "watchful waiting," in which he would have blood tests and X-rays every month, as well as CAT scans every three months. Jonah decided to wait.

"Sometimes, late at night, I lie awake thinking," he told me several months later. "Like, if I don't stir, it won't emerge again. Like if I move around too much, I might awaken it. Like it's this beast."

A beast, I agreed: asleep and scary, but one that can be killed.

There were days when it felt like I was grappling with my own slumbering beast. Though my overall mood was much better than it had been six months earlier in the winter, my motivation for medicine still seemed weak, ill formed, a bit suspect. At times I was feeling low again, uncertain of the path I was on. My classmates were already talking about subspecialty fellowships, moving on, getting further training. Earlier that spring, in a sort of post-depression euphoria, I had considered applying for a cardiology fellowship. I devised a reading schedule, reviewing a new topic—electrocardiograms, antiarrhythmic drugs, atrial fibrillation—nearly every day. I knew that I was going to have to perform well second year to garner strong letters of recommendation and have a chance of securing a spot the following spring. But by the start of the new academic year in July, I could no longer imagine pursuing further training. I still felt overwhelmed by the responsibilities that I already had.

ONE AFTERNOON IN EARLY JULY, I was summoned to the chief residents' office. Stuart Barton, who had been my resident on the nephrology ward, and Clarence Riley, another third-year, met me there. They were both assistant chief residents now, an honor reserved for the most brownnosing seniors. Riley, who had thin brown hair and a disproportionately wide mouth, was sitting behind a large wooden desk. I remembered him from the welcoming party at the faculty club during internship orientation. He was one of the two residents who had walked into the party in scrubs, which had seemed awfully brazen at the time, but in the intervening months I had found him to actually be quite smarmy. Barton had been a supportive junior resident, but now he was standing pompously grim-faced at Riley's side. It was sad to see how easily he had been corrupted by power.

Riley motioned for me to sit down. I didn't know what was going on, but the atmosphere in the room told me that some sort of reprimand was forthcoming. Leaning back in his chair, fingers steepled, his eyes focused on a point on the wall behind me, Riley said: "So can you tell us how you came to write the article about the ICU?"

He was referring to an essay that had just been published in the *Times*. "People were pretty upset about what you wrote," he said. "Suzanne Mendes"—one of the ICU attendings—"was especially unhappy. She came to us and complained that you shouldn't be writing this stuff in *The New York Times*." In the essay, I had discussed the case of a seventy-two-year-old woman who walked into the emergency room one day carrying a report from another hospital stating that she had fluid in the sac around her heart. While lying on a stretcher in the ER, she had briefly stopped breathing. Physicians in the ER had inserted a breathing tube in her windpipe and transferred her to the ICU. I wrote:

There things rapidly fell apart. A needle, inserted in an effort to drain the fluid around her heart and examine it for clues to her underlying disease, was inadvertently pushed too far, piercing her heart. She lost several liters of blood. Because she was a Jehovah's Witness, she refused to accept blood transfusions. Debilitated and anemic, she became dependent on her ventilator. But she found the breathing tube painful and uncomfortable, and she periodically tried to yank it out, which raised her blood pressure to dangerous levels. One morning, I walked into her room to find her unable to move the right side of her body. A CAT scan confirmed that she had suffered a large stroke.

Now she was lying in bed, heavily sedated, her wrists restrained, receiving sustenance through a tube. The attending physician looked at the woman sadly. She would have been much better off, he said, if she had never come to the ICU. "Bad things happen here. You see it all the time. It's probably a combination of patients already being sick and the terrible things we do to them."

Iatrogenic, or hospital-acquired, complications, the essay went on, had reached epidemic proportions.

ICU care, provided to the most frail and sick patients, often results in the worst iatrogenic injuries. Catheters placed in various organs and invasive procedures, like spinal and lung taps, can cause complications like bleeding and infection. Frequent blood drawing and round-the-clock monitoring often result in fatigue and depression among patients. Heavy use of medicine sometimes results in drug reactions. "Most of our patients would do better on auto pilot," a doctor completing a senior fellowship in the ICU at my hospital recently told me. "They'd be better off if we brought them in here and just left them alone."

Of course, this is an exaggeration. Many patients will do fine if they can be supported through an acute medical crisis. But even for these patients, the level of care that is safe and necessary has not been clearly defined.

In 1980, Dr. Arnold Relman, then editor of *The New England Journal of Medicine*, wrote: "The cost and psychological stress of ICU treatment would be justifiable if such units were known to reduce mortality and morbidity from levels achievable with less costly and intensive modes of hospital care. [But] there have been no prospective, randomized, controlled trials to supply such data." Almost two decades later, such studies are still lacking.

I told the story of an elderly woman in the ICU who was in a coma for a month.

She developed a blood infection, and kidney, heart and respiratory failure, but lingered for weeks with antibiotics and drugs to elevate her blood pressure. We all knew she was going to die and that our efforts were futile. Still, no one in her family was willing to give up, and so we persisted in aggressively treating her, causing her obvious pain every time we poked her with a new catheter or pushed on her belly to examine her. What finally caused her death was a catheter placed through a hole in her abdomen, which probably resulted in yet another infection. She did not live any longer because of what we had done, just ended her life more miserably.

One day, I walked into the residents' work room and saw scribbled in red ink on the eraser board: *Primum non nocere*. First do no harm.

The essay concluded:

More is not always better, especially in medicine. Less aggressive treatment may sometimes reduce the risk of injury, particularly in patients who have a good chance of getting well again. Though it runs counter to most medical training, only when doctors learn to do less, and not always more, will they stop causing inadvertent harm to patients in the ICU.

"They passed it around at morning report," Barton said gravely as Riley continued to stare at me from behind the desk. I envisioned the scene: junior and senior residents and a few medical students sitting around a long conference table with Dr. Wood and a senior physician, munching on Tal bagels, mumbling among themselves as the essay went around. "Rob Lerner"—another ICU physician—"was the attending that week," Barton added.

"What did he say?" I asked. Lerner was the head of the ventilator management team and one of the senior physicians I admired most.

"Not much," Barton replied tersely. "He sort of scanned it, but he didn't look happy. Someone asked if you were still serious about applying for a cardiology fellowship."

I shifted uncomfortably in my seat. Was I being threatened?

"Maybe you should write a letter of explanation," Barton suggested. "To Suzanne. To help her understand your point of view."

"I don't see why I need to apologize," I said defensively.

"We're not asking you to apologize," Riley said quickly. "Just explain yourself."

Since when, I wondered, did I have to answer to a junior ICU attending, let alone residents only one year ahead of me?

"The essay is pretty self-evident," I said in a measured tone. "Complications occur in the ICU. Why should it bother anyone that I pointed it out?" Of course I knew why, but I had decided to adopt a disarmingly—if disingenuously—naive approach.

"They're going to keep a close eye on you," Riley said. I wasn't sure whom he was referring to, but I assumed it was higher-ups in the Department of Medicine. For a moment I considered just writing the letter, but then I thought, *Screw it; I don't owe them anything.* In graduate school I had always been taught to think independently. Even my father had encouraged dissent, even if he hadn't always tolerated it. Giving in to their demand would make me think twice about writing more essays. My writing was too important to me to allow it to get corrupted like that.

"They're not going to give you any more slack," Riley warned. I said I'd take my chances.

When I got home, a bit shaken, I called Rajiv. Cardiology fellowships were hard to come by, and though I doubted I was going to apply for one, I wanted to keep my options open.

"Fuck 'em," Rajiv said definitively. "There are other fellowship programs in New York. Some of them might even be impressed that you wrote something for *The New York Times*.

"You know what your problem is?" he went on quickly. "And I'm shocked because it should have happened by now; you did a Ph.D. in physics for God's sake. You don't have a thick skin. You care too much about what people think. That's going to be a major problem for you, especially if you keep writing these articles."

THE MONTHLONG ROTATION in the outpatient clinic passed rather uneventfully, until one morning when a sullen young woman walked into my exam room and plopped herself into a cracking vinyl chair. "I want a referral to a chiropractor," she announced. Judging from her face, she was in no mood for small talk.

Earlier that morning, she had clashed with the doctor answering the phones at the clinic. She had requested the referral but had gotten upset when he started asking questions about her back pain. When he insisted that she come to the clinic to be examined, she told him he was wasting her time and hung up. But about an hour later, she walked into the clinic, where, after an angry exchange of words with the front desk clerk, she was quickly ushered into my room. Her regular doctor was away.

She was tall, frumpily dressed, with wavy auburn hair and narrow-set eyes. "How long have you had back pain?" I asked.

"It started this morning," she replied. "I heard a pop between my shoulders."

"Has this happened before?"

"Yes, several months ago." She had gone to a chiropractor, which helped.

"What did the chiropractor do?"

"I don't know," she replied, her voice rising. "He manipulated my spine and I felt better."

"Are you experiencing any weakness or numbness in your legs?" Nerve root compression from a slipped disk (like the one I had had in my cervical spine) was a common and potentially serious cause of back pain.

"No."

"What about shooting pains?"

"No."

"Pins-and-needles sensations?"

"No!" she shouted. "How is this important? I just want a referral."

"Okay," I replied, but first I had to examine her. I explained that if she had a pinched nerve, a chiropractor might do more harm than good. Reluctantly, she got up onto the examination table. I pressed on her back with my fingers, trying to see if I could localize any tenderness. Back pain was usually benign, but in rare cases it could be caused by an infection or tumor, and I wanted to make sure I wasn't missing anything. After finding the testicular tumor in Jonah, I had become meticulous about physical examination. I raised her straightened legs one at a time, trying to elicit pain, a telltale sign of sciatica.

"You're wasting my time!" she erupted. "Call your supervisor."

Now my supervisor that day happened to be a calm, soft-spoken doctor who had a nice way with his patients. I called him to my exam room, explained what was going on, and excused myself. In the hallway, I listened as my patient inveighed against the clinic and the doctors who had mistreated her. My preceptor's quiet manner and attention appeared to mollify her, because she allowed him to examine her. Then, calmly, they discussed her options. She was not interested in Motrin or rest as therapy. She insisted on a chiropractor.

About fifteen minutes later, he emerged from the room and asked me to please write the referral. I did, and the woman left, looking satisfied.

Afterward, in his office, he shrugged and weakly smiled. "She was a difficult patient," he said. "In such cases you listen and try to do the best you can. Sometimes patients just need to vent."

The encounter left me to wonder: Who had been more difficult, the young woman or me? After all, she was the one in pain, and I had presented an obstacle to her relief. Chiropracty was unlikely to do any harm; she told me it had already helped her. Still, for reasons I could not pinpoint, I had created hoops for her to jump through, asking irritating questions more for my own purposes than for hers. The situation demanded empathy, but instead I had been automatic, hyperrational, and detached. It certainly wasn't the way I had imagined I would be as a doctor. The right thing probably would have been to give her an unfettered referral without asking too many questions, but somehow I had not obeyed this instinct. Part of the reason was to assert my authority. Part of the reason, no doubt, was that I was wearing a white coat. It wasn't the first or last time that I felt my uniform was somehow suppressing my better instincts.

Later that month, the clinic chiefs asked me to present a case at morning report, so I decided to present the case of the young woman. Snickers could be heard in the wood-paneled conference room when I put up my title slide: *Difficult Patients*. I started off talking about a landmark 1978 article in *The New England Journal of Medicine* by Dr. James Groves, then a professor of psychiatry at Harvard Medical School, called "Taking Care of the Hateful Patient." In it, Groves described certain personality traits that kindle aversion, fear, despair, or even downright malice in doctors. He described such patients as "dependent clingers," "entitled demanders," "manipulative help-rejecters," and "self-destructive deniers." Emotional reactions to patients, he wrote, cannot simply be wished away, nor is it good medicine to pretend that they do not exist. Freud called such reactions countertransference—how doctors react to patients, not the other way around—and said these reactions could be used to explore the unconscious conflicts of doctor and patient.

Aversive reactions, I told the audience, are common in any enterprise involving intimacy: marriage, psychotherapy, the battlefield, and so it is with medicine. The difference is that doctors cannot divorce their patients, at least not easily, and for good reason. Entrusted as we are with a fiduciary duty to preserve health, we cannot dismiss patients willy-nilly. But the question demanded asking: If patients can choose their own doctors, why can't doctors choose their own patients?

There are guidelines for when a doctor can dismiss a difficult patient, and usually only the most egregious misbehavior qualifies, including threats, violence, and noncompliance. For example, courts have ruled that kidney specialists do not have to provide dialysis to violent or disruptive patients, even those who need it to remain alive. In 1987, Dr. John Bower, a kidney specialist at the University of Mississippi, was sued after dismissing from his practice a patient who regularly missed dialysis appointments, verbally abused nurses, and even threatened to kill Bower and a hospital administrator. Bower cited medical noncompliance and violent threats as grounds for terminating care. The Fifth Circuit Court of Appeals, in New Orleans, agreed with him, ruling that doctors can refuse to treat violent or intransigent patients as long as they give proper notice so that the patient can find alternative care. Forcing doctors to treat such patients, the court said, would violate the Thirteenth Amendment, which prohibits involuntary servitude.

To prepare for my talk, I had gone through the "administrative files" on ten patients who had been dismissed from the clinic over the past five years. The reasons for expulsion were noncompliance with

medical advice, threats, verbal abuse, and physical violence. One patient had punched another in the waiting room. Another patient had
forged her doctor's signature to get painkillers.

After my presentation, the fifteen or so residents and attending
physicians in the room weighed in with some of their own tales of difficult patients. A resident told of an obsessed patient who showed up
at his clinic every week and even once followed him home. An attending physician said that he had once been conned into prescribing long-
acting morphine to a patient with lower back pain. The patient claimed
to have had an extensive workup by another doctor, but when the attending checked, he discovered that the other doctor did not exist. "Always do your own workup," he warned the group. "Set strict rules,
and stick to them." Another physician said that his patients were "hy-
pomanic" and rarely on point. He didn't agree with the conventional
wisdom of letting people talk out what was on their minds. Another attending compared difficult patients to Bloomingdale's shoppers. "Give
me a thousand Kmart shoppers for every Bloomingdale's shopper," he
said to murmurs of agreement. "Kmart shoppers have their insurance,
they don't pay cash, they're not going on the Internet, they don't ask
a lot of questions, they don't have a bunch of doctor friends second-
guessing your decisions."

The atmosphere had the charge of catharsis, as one anecdote led to
another. The stories were fascinating in a baroque sort of way, and I felt
pleased that my presentation had engendered such a robust discussion. (Evidently, sometimes doctors need to vent, too.) But then a dis-
senting voice was heard. It was Sheila Jones, a young attending with a
slight frame and a wispy voice. A few months back, I had helped care
for one of her patients in the hospital, a young woman who had been
troubled for years with abdominal pain and a psychologically abusive
boyfriend. The patient had been in and out of various hospitals, under-
going X-rays, ultrasounds, CAT scans, and so forth, all of which revealed nothing.

She was angry and afraid, and frequently came to the emergency
room demanding hospitalization and painkillers. Doctors who cared

for her had grown weary of her constant complaints and started giving her morphine. Then she became addicted, and no one cared about her enough to ensure that she got the psychiatric help she sorely needed, including, in retrospect, me. It was easier to abdicate responsibility than to deal with her.

She was the quintessentially difficult patient. After a while, hers was a room we avoided. Her needs were bottomless, her pain unremitting. In the constant buzz that is ward life, time seemed better spent on other patients. Nothing seemed to be physically wrong with her, at least not anything to explain the severity of her pain. Yet she relentlessly demanded morphine. Try as best we could, it was hard setting limits. A tough approach alienated her. A conciliatory approach simply got her more drugs.

But Dr. Jones knew how to handle her. Though she had been her doctor for only a few months, she had developed an effective style with this patient. She was not afraid to be strict: if the patient yelled, sometimes she yelled back, or she was kind, as the moment required. Though somewhat unconventional, she grasped her patient's psychology like no one else, and she truly cared for her. She eventually managed to discharge her without morphine.

Jones told the now-silent group that she had several difficult patients in her practice. "Like any doctor, I do not seek them out. But they are not that hard to treat, once you figure out what is bothering them."

Patients don't always come right out and say what is wrong, she said. Sometimes they hedge or obfuscate. Often the key to treating them is to look a little deeper.

"Most doctors are reluctant to take on difficult patients," she acknowledged. When these patients are ready to leave the hospital, "business cards get tucked away and doctors duck into the shadows." Consciously or not, doctors create hoops for these patients to jump through, marginalizing them even more. "And then we say these patients were 'lost to follow-up,' " she said.

There wasn't much more discussion after Jones spoke. Soon people filed out of the room. That night, I thought about how different the real doctor-patient relationship is compared with the idealized one that had been presented in medical school. Then the emphasis had been on the heartwarming stories, the enduring intimacy. But in reality the relationship is neither simple nor neat. Every human enterprise has its share of conflict and reconciliation—and medicine is no different. I don't know what surprised me more: that there was such a divide or that it had taken me so long to see it.

Even now, years later, it remains a mystery to me exactly why one doctor can relate to a difficult patient, and another can alienate her. Another reminder, perhaps, that medicine is a field of specialties. Some doctors are better at treating certain diseases; some at treating certain patients.

CHAPTER SIXTEEN

pride and prejudice

If you are hidebound with prejudice, if your temper is sentimental, you can go through the wards of a hospital and be as ignorant of man at the end as you were at the beginning.

—W. SOMERSET MAUGHAM, *THE SUMMING UP*, 1938

If internship was about being a secretary, second year on the wards was about being a manager: ignoring the small details, seeing the forest for the trees. During internship, thoughtful reflection had been all but impossible, but being able to delegate changed all that. Now I was the one in charge of my students and interns. At one time I couldn't have fathomed delegating duties, but on the wards I discovered that I loved having interns around, and it was as easy for me to dump on them as it probably had been for my residents to dump on me. No longer was I the team's shock absorber—the one who got pimped first, blamed first, thanked last. I had always found it fundamentally unfair that the people who got interrogated on rounds were usually the least equipped to answer questions. That disparity continued, of course, but it was no longer working against me.

At the same time, individual patients started to fade from view. No longer was I the first doctor paged in a crisis. Part of me missed being more involved in the life of the ward, but I also appreciated having some distance, operating remotely from the workroom, staring at a computer screen, reading through charts one by one, scribbling a short "chart-round" note, a tiny drizzle of ink to show that I had been there. I got very efficient at finding lab results or medical records, minimizing computer time because I knew exactly where everything was. The clerks would still dress me down for hogging the charts or for getting in their way, but for the most part they were much nicer to me, and I was no longer afraid of them. At lunchtime someone would call out, "Anybody want Mexican?" and I would respond, "Count me in!" like I belonged. Fellowship descended on the ranks. As junior residents, we could afford to be congenial because we were no longer carrying the burden of the hospital on our shoulders. Even sign-out wasn't a frenzied rush to get out of the hospital. In fact, most of the time, we didn't even attend because our interns took care of it for us.

Not long ago, I had dinner with one of my classmates from residency. He was now a chief resident at a major teaching hospital in the Northeast. Over the meal, we chatted about the transition from internship to second year. "In internship, it's like, 'This doesn't make sense,'" he said. "When you think about it, as interns we were making, like, a hundred and fifty decisions a day, and as second-years we were, too, but the difference was that you knew why. As an intern, you didn't know why, which is why it was so hard. You had to collect the data, process it, massage it, fit it into an existing plan. It was psychologically exhausting.

"Another difference was that second year there was more responsibility. If they criticized you, you took it more personally. You had more invested because you had gone through internship. You were more a part of the community; you worried about what people would say. You wondered, What will happen if people discover that I'm not as smart, efficient, or competent as they think?"

I nodded. In my case, the constant comparison had been with my brother.

"One time in internship I put a central line into an old woman who was on a ventilator. She needed it for something; I forget what. She had TB or something. It was me and a second-year. We tried a subclavian approach but we couldn't get it. I tried the internal jugular ten times,

and then the resident tried, and he couldn't get it, so we just kept trying. He finally got it, and we put the line in. I don't know if at some
point he got air back in the syringe, but you can guess what happened.
We checked a chest X-ray and we had dropped her lung. It was a big
pneumothorax, so the woman ended up needing a chest tube. When
the attending came back, he was pissed. He said, 'I leave and now
look! What the fuck! She's really fucking sick now. I can't believe that
you did this. What were you thinking?' It stayed with me for a long
time—not so much what we had done, as my poor resident. As a
second-year, if I had been dressed down like that, I would have been
devastated.

"Another time, second year, I took care of this woman whose
potassium was low. We were repleting her potassium every day, several times a day even. When I left one evening, I signed out to check
her potassium level. For whatever reason—maybe I didn't impress it
hard enough, I don't know—it didn't get done, and in the middle of
the night, she had a cardiac arrest because of high potassium. Her
potassium was off the scale, and then it came to light that she had been
getting saline with eighty milliequivalents of potassium chloride at one
hundred and twenty-five cc's an hour. I didn't know it. I should have
known it, but IV fluids weren't written on the nursing medication
sheets, and I had been too lazy to check the computer. I marched
straight to Dr. Wood's office and told him what happened. I said, 'Dr.
Wood, I just killed a patient. I killed her, or at least I didn't prevent her
from being killed.' "

"How did he respond?" I asked.

"Of course, he broke it down. He told me it was because of the bad
kidney function. He said her kidneys couldn't excrete potassium properly. He said, 'If I give you potassium-enriched fluids, will your body
be able to handle it? Of course it will,' and so on and so forth. He broke
it down medically, but really what I wanted to talk about wasn't medical. I had nightmares about that death. As an intern I never felt like
that, but as a second-year, you just felt more responsibility.

"So I started this conference for residents to talk about their mistakes, away from Dr. Wood, away from the attendings. Even the chief residents weren't allowed to sit in. I wanted it to be just house-staff run. Everyone makes mistakes; even if we don't think we've made them, we've made them. People would come to the conference and talk about their mistakes in a nonconfrontational way. I saw residents cry at that conference. I talked about the lady with the low potassium. It felt good to get it off my chest. I felt like, if I don't make this public—not out in public, of course, but just to my colleagues—if I don't talk about it, then it would become one of those things that never really happened. It would cease to exist."

AFTER SPENDING JULY in the outpatient clinic, I rotated to 4-North, the cardiac telemetry ward. Ward 4-North at New York Hospital was famous for its high-volume, assembly-line medicine. Each morning, patients would be shipped off for echocardiograms, nuclear stress tests, and cardiac catheterizations by an efficient, well-trained, and highly vocal cadre of nurses whose job it was to ensure everything ran smoothly. As a house officer, if you forgot to do something—fax a requisition, for instance, or write a "nothing-by-mouth-after-midnight" order—your oversight could disrupt the whole enterprise and bring the wrath of the charge nurse down on your head.

The patients on 4-North were mostly archetypes: middle-aged businessman who developed crushing chest pain sitting at his midtown desk; elderly woman who forgot to take her medications and went into congestive heart failure; diabetic with diffuse vascular disease who needed bypass surgery. One morning, I had to present three cases of unstable angina from the night before but couldn't remember which was which. The only differences were the patients' ages and the small details, the social history, which we so often ignored. The same clinical narrative could apply just as well to my eighty-five-year-old widowed patient with Alzheimer's as to the fifty-five-year-old dentist with a family. Stuck, my mind a blank, I fumbled until Mira, the intern assigned to work with me, whispered something into my ear. "The

father of two disabled children?" I said out loud. "Oh yes, now I remember."

Mira was a fast-talking, wisecracking Jewish girl from Long Island
with a pretty freckled face who barreled through the unit as if she was
on twenty cups of coffee. She showed up at 6:00 a.m. to preround, finished her notes before I even arrived on the ward, inserted central
lines, drew blood, and generally did whatever was necessary to get the
job done. She had a wonderful mix of directness, chutzpah, and easygoing charm. With Mira around, I never worried about the "July phenomenon," where patients supposedly did worse at the beginning of
each academic year because inexperienced interns were caring for
them. She seemed to have mastered her patients much better than I
ever had.

Rounds started at eight o'clock, when we sat down with David
Klein, the attending physician, to discuss admissions from the night
before. Klein was a short, graying man with a supercilious air and a
perpetually exasperated expression that conveyed haughtiness. He
spoke with a sneer, and he seemed to relish cutting into patients and
house staff alike. One morning Mira presented a case. "The patient
came to the emergency room in the middle of the night—" she began.

Klein groaned loudly. He often said that coming to the hospital in
the middle of the night was a sign of irresponsibility.

"—after doing cocaine—" Mira continued. Klein groaned again.

"He was in his usual state of health until three a.m.—"

"Yeah, yeah, I get the point," Klein snapped. "Is he a scumbag?"

Mira stopped, looking flustered. Klein threw up his hands, as if he
had asked the most natural question in the world. "Is he a scumbag or
a solid citizen?" he demanded. Mira seemed to draw a blank. I had
never seen her hesitate before.

"I'm not sure," she finally replied.

"Well, he snorts cocaine! Where does he live?"

"Manhattan."

"Where in Manhattan?"

"I'm not sure."

"Well, you can bet he's not from the Upper East Side." Some residents laughed at this remark.

"You mean people on the Upper East Side don't use cocaine?" I interjected. I despised Dr. Klein, and he didn't like me much either. He had once warned our team to watch what they said lest I quote them in a newspaper column.

"No, not most of them," Klein replied dismissively. There was an awkward pause as he uncrossed and recrossed his legs. Then he let Mira finish.

Rounds with Klein were exercises in division—making distinctions, pointing out the differences between people, the haves and the have-nots, and in fact he was quite open about it, as if his openness somehow absolved him of his prejudices. If patients on 4-North were archetypes, then Klein, too, was an archetype: overbearing, arrogant cardiologist.

Most days on the telemetry ward, we had to obtain informed consent from patients going for cardiac procedures. We were supposed to tell them the risks and benefits and answer their questions, but the process didn't always go smoothly. Sometimes we were forced to apply "gentle coercion" for the good of the patient.

José Villegas was a middle-aged man with kidney failure who had suffered a small heart-attack. One morning, he was scheduled to go for a coronary angiogram, but apparently no one had discussed it with him. When he was told that the dye used in the angiogram could damage his already weakened kidneys, he balked. He said he didn't want the procedure; he was unwilling to accept even the slightest risk of dialysis. That much was clear, even in his broken English, but Klein and the fellow had already decided that the benefits of the procedure outweighed the risks. "You could have a severe blockage in your heart," the fellow warned.

Villegas said he would take his chances.

"You could have another heart attack," the fellow intoned gravely. Villegas's resolve appeared to crack. "You could drop dead!" Klein shouted. Few patients can resist that kind of pressure, and Villegas wasn't one of them. "I guess I have no choice," he said resignedly, signing the consent form. We filed out of the room. In the hallway, barely out of earshot, Klein chuckled. "We can make them do whatever we want," he said. "As long as they agree with us, they're not crazy."

Though I detested such strong-arm tactics, I was aware that my own conduct as a physician was hardly blameless. I thought back to Jonah and his testicular mass. When he had asked me if it was cancer, I had lied and said that I did not know. I too was learning that deliberate half-truths are a part of the doctor's armamentarium.

Chest pain was the most common reason for admission to 4-North. Some of it was benign, like the hysterical Mexican women who screamed *"Ay, ay, ay."* (Residents termed this "status hispanicus.") But most of it was serious, and sometimes quite mysterious, too. One night I admitted a burly Russian man with a thick accent who was lying in bed, clutching his chest, looking very uncomfortable. He told me he had been experiencing chest pain at home that frequently got worse when he exerted himself and sometimes was relieved by nitroglycerin tablets under the tongue. Although his EKG and blood tests were normal, with no signs of heart damage, his story was too good, too characteristic of angina, to dismiss. I told him he was going to need a coronary angiogram. "Have you had one before?" I asked.

Yes, he replied. In California, Nevada, Arizona, Kansas, even New York. Every one was normal. My puzzlement must have been obvious. So was his annoyance. "They tell me it is Syndrome X," he growled.

The next day, I obtained a tape of one of his angiograms from a nearby hospital. It confirmed what my patient told me. His coronary arteries were pristine, not a trace of obstruction anywhere. So what was wrong with him?

Most people with angina have atherosclerotic plaque in the large coronary arteries that supply blood to the heart. But up to 20 percent of angina sufferers have normal coronary angiograms, a condition cardiologists have dubbed *Syndrome X.* These patients often have chest pain that mimics coronary angina and even abnormal stress tests. There appears to be a problem with their hearts, but no one knows exactly what it is.

One theory is that Syndrome X is a disease of coronary arteries too small to be seen by angiography. In one study, researchers using magnetic resonance imaging found that adenosine, a drug that dilates coronary arteries, does not increase blood flow to the inside surface of Syndrome X hearts, an area mostly fed by small arteries. They concluded that these arteries did not dilate appropriately and that the angina in Syndrome X was therefore from inadequate blood flow, not in the major branches of the coronary tree but in the twigs.

This theory appears to unify the mechanism of Syndrome X with obstructive coronary artery disease, the leading killer in the Western world, but there are holes. For example, if the chest pain in Syndrome X is due to diminished blood flow, then ultrasound studies of the heart during painful episodes should show some abnormalities, which they do not. EKG studies should reflect this inadequate blood flow electrically, but they do not. Another theory is that Syndrome X is a result of abnormal pain sensitivity, the so-called *sensitive-heart syndrome*. The chest pain in some patients can be evoked by electrical stimulation of the lower right heart chamber, which should have little effect on blood flow.

So which theory is correct? Maybe both. Syndrome X is probably not a single disorder but a constellation of disorders with many different causes. There is even evidence that psychological factors come into play. It is well known that patients with atypical chest pain often have an abnormal preoccupation with their health and anxiety or depression. One study found that two-thirds of patients with chest pain and normal coronary angiograms also have psychiatric problems.

It would not be the first time that a common cardiac symptom was thought to be predominantly psychological. In the 1990s, Dr. Arthur Barsky at Harvard Medical School studied patients with frequent palpitations. In one study he hooked up 145 patients to a continuous, twenty-four-hour EKG monitor and instructed them to record the exact time of their palpitations in a diary. He found that only 39 percent of their palpitations were accompanied by an objective arrhythmia. The patients whose symptoms had the weakest correlation to EKG abnormalities also had the most hypochondria and other psychiatric problems.

Although Syndrome X can be debilitating—not to mention a drain on hospital resources—patients who have it tend to experience normal life spans. I tried to tell my Russian patient that despite his symptoms, he did not have a life-threatening disease, but this did not mollify him. Like the difficult patient in the clinic the previous month, he accused me and other doctors of insensitivity. He demanded another angiogram to make sure his disease had not progressed. After several days of intensive but ineffective medical therapy, the team finally acquiesced. He was taken to the cardiac catheterization lab once again, where more pictures were taken of his coronary arteries. Shortly after the procedure, he went home. He was still feeling chest pain but had a clean bill of health, a reminder that even in a field as highly developed as cardiology, some symptoms retain their essential mystery.

WHEN I WAS ON CALL on 4-North, Sonia, who had recently moved in with me, often came to the hospital to bring me dinner. I'd meet her downstairs, in front of the library, where she'd hand off the curried chicken or lamb kebabs, or sometimes daikon paranthas with spicy cauliflower, courtesy of her mother. Occasionally she'd bring a plate for Mira, too, and sometimes even for the medical students on my team, and then we'd all sit in the conference room and scarf it down. She was now on a fourth-year GI elective, and it was good to see her in the hospital during the day. I always waited for her page; it was the one number I always called back immediately, no matter what I was doing. We sometimes discussed her difficult cases, and my advice was usually accompanied by a few words on appropriate etiquette for a fourth-year medical student. Afterward, I'd bask in the same sort of glow I'm sure Rajiv enjoyed when he advised me.

One night when I was on call, I was paged to the ER for a chest-pain consultation. I hated going down to the ER because the staff was so surly, so hardened by the constant swirl of illness drifting through the sliding doors. I walked past the resuscitation rooms. Stretchers bearing patients were already lined up in the hallway, even though it was only nine o'clock. An elderly woman was bellowing, "Help me, help me," over and over, but people were ignoring her. ("Who's screaming? Is that a cat?" someone joked.) I scanned the admit board next to the nursing station: sprained ankle, pancreatitis, vaginal odor for one week, depression, alcohol withdrawal, swollen eyelid, motor vehicle accident, flank pain, shortness of breath, hematuria, earache, fever, palpitations, allergic reaction to drug, stroke, vaginal bleeding, foot ulcer, syncope, lung cancer/failure to thrive, asthma, bloody stools, nausea/vomiting/diarrhea, and ascites. No chest pain. I walked over to the other side of the ER, where a nurse pointed me in the direction of a small, curtained space. I jerked open the drape. A middle-aged man, round as a beach ball, was sitting at the edge of a stretcher, panting. He looked up when I entered. It was Ira Schneider, a man I had taken care of a few months back after his heart attack.

"Well, hello," I said, closing the curtain behind me.

He took off his oxygen mask. "Hi, Doc," he said, his face brightening. He must have weighed at least four hundred pounds. Thick, fleshy folds encircled his belly, falling out of a hospital gown, which functioned more like a bib. Numerous streaks zigzagged across his abdomen and back like thick wrinkled worms. His legs resembled small tree trunks with hyperpigmented patches of skin, like tiny whorls in bark, probably a consequence of chronic edema. Large gaps interrupted his teeth. Even his mouth seemed to be too big for him.

I asked him how he was doing. "Not well," he replied, shimmying his body on the stretcher to face me. Since I had last seen him, his angina had been getting more frequent and more severe, and it was now often accompanied by an oppressive sensation of breathlessness. He had been popping nitroglycerin pills like Tic Tacs. I remembered that six months ago, in February, when he was hospitalized, he had undergone a coronary angiogram, but the pictures came out fuzzy because of the fat around his chest. Still, there appeared to be severe limitations in blood flow to several parts of his heart. His coronary arteries looked like sausage links, sectioned off by numerous tight blockages. Cardiologists had tried opening one of the blockages with a balloon catheter, but the procedure failed because of the poor view. So Schneider had been transferred to the wards for medical management, which meant drugs but no further invasive procedures.

But what he really needed was bypass surgery. A surgeon, a short, stocky man who in manner and deportment resembled a bulldog, was consulted, but he said that heart surgery would be too risky. Since Schneider was already almost totally immobilized by his weight, wound healing and physical rehabilitation would be prohibitively slow. To compound the problem, Schneider had severe atherosclerosis in the arteries in his legs, which further inhibited his mobility. "This guy isn't even a candidate for a haircut, let alone bypass," the surgeon had said. When someone argued that Schneider would die without surgery, the surgeon answered: "He's going to die anyway, but I don't have to wear the black hood. This isn't a Chinese restaurant; we don't take orders. We're doctors. We have to do what is right."

So surgery was shelved, Schneider's drug regimen was tuned up, and he was sent home.

Earlier that evening, Schneider now told me, he had experienced a protracted bout of chest pain while watching television. The pain started out as "ten out of ten" and was accompanied by a drenching sweat. Two hours later, he vomited four times and then took a sublingual nitroglycerin tablet, which brought the pain down to a seven or eight out of ten. He took two more nitroglycerin pills and two aspirin, with no further relief, so he called 911. The paramedics gave him supplemental oxygen, which helped a bit, but when he arrived in the ER, his pain was still present: four out of ten. He took one more sublingual nitroglycerin in the triage bay and only then, a few minutes later, did his pain finally go away.

I turned a green knob controlling the flow of oxygen to his mask. A tiny ball bearing shot up in a plastic meter, suspended by the increased flow of air. I asked Schneider if he had seen any doctors since being discharged from the hospital.

"Just my cardiologist," he replied. And what had the cardiologist told him? "He said I had to learn to live with the pain."

"Have you consulted with another surgeon?" I asked.

He shook his head, puzzled. "Was I supposed to?"

"No . . ." I hesitated for a moment. "I mean, you could have, but . . . well . . . let's just talk about it when you get upstairs." Frankly, at this point I didn't think getting a second surgical opinion would be a bad idea. Surely something, I thought, even risky surgery, would be better than waiting for the time bomb in his chest to go off.

Schneider was transferred to 4-North, where Mira and I wrote his orders. We started him on a blood thinner and intravenous nitro-glycerin, and continued the rest of his medication regimen. But even though he was pain-free now, I was pessimistic that drugs alone could manage his disease.

The next day, I spoke with Dr. Carmen, the CCU attending, Schnei-der's cardiologist. Conceding that medical management had failed, he said he was going to consult the surgical team again; perhaps now, with Schneider's condition worsening, they would see things differ-ently. I was skeptical. The surgeons had been firm and persuasive in their arguments, and I didn't expect them to change their minds.

"Still, I wonder if the surgical option was dismissed too quickly," Carmen said. "Sometimes we look at a patient like this and make a judgment that isn't always fair or rational or even medical." He left, but his comment stayed with me. Had we discriminated against Mr. Schneider because of his weight?

It didn't appear that our prejudice, if it existed—I wasn't sure—had been conscious. Granted, his obesity had been on our minds in de-ciding on his treatment. It would have been impossible, not to mention bad medicine, for it not to have been. But had we been hyperconscious of his obesity, to his detriment? Had we made a value judgment that, because of his weight, surgery would be wasted? Or worse, that he was somehow less deserving of surgery because he was unable or un-willing to control his weight?

Doctors can be a judgmental sort, a point that had been driven home to me by the discussion on difficult patients the previous month. Of course, it can be argued that making judgments is the essence of what doctors do. That elderly man in the intensive care unit: Should we treat the patient aggressively or pull back? Should that alcoholic with liver failure get a transplant? These are medical judgments but moral ones, too.

Judgments about personality, character, and worthiness are re-flected in all aspects of the doctor-patient relationship, from the lan-guage doctors use to describe patients (hysterical, difficult, solid, scumbag), to the attitude they take into the examination room. Every day, in clinics and emergency rooms, doctors encounter drug addicts with endocarditis, smokers with lung cancer, and others seemingly bent on self-destruction. To treat them with perfect equanimity, with-out any trace of moral or value judgment, would be impossibly Zen. But to act upon these judgments, to allow them to alter treatment, would be to violate fiduciary responsibility.

Personal judgments, however, can lead to prejudgments and preju-dice. Not long before I admitted Schneider to the hospital, Sheila Jones, the clinic attending, had given a lecture on disparities in health care. She presented several studies on health outcomes in various patient populations that suggested that subtle prejudice might be widespread in medicine. For example, a study showed that blacks not only waited longer than whites for kidney transplants, they waited longer to get on a kidney transplant waiting list, even though they suffered dispropor-tionately from kidney failure. Why do doctors delay? There was more: compared with whites, black women were twice as likely to receive in-appropriate treatment for ovarian cancer, and they had a worse prog-nosis; blacks with lung cancer were less likely to receive possibly curative surgery; and blacks with heart disease got fewer cardiac an-giograms and bypass operations, had worse outcomes after a heart at-tack, and were less likely to receive standard drugs like aspirin and beta-blockers. The difference in angiogram rates was independent of the doctor's race, and it persisted even after correcting for disease severity, insurance status, geography, and income.

The disparities were not limited to race. Women with heart disease got fewer cardiac angiograms and catheter procedures than men, and they were more likely to die from heart attacks and unstable angina. A recent study had shown that women with chest pain waited longer than men did for emergency room examinations. Perhaps, influenced by behavior stereotypes, doctors were more likely to minimize symptoms in women and attribute them to emotions.

The list went on, encompassing gays, the elderly, and other groups. These and other studies suggested systemic discrimination in medicine, though it was hard to draw any firm conclusions from them. Why did it take longer for doctors to put black patients on the kidney transplant list? Was it racism, or was it because blacks have a higher rate of transplant rejection? Why were doctors more likely to withhold artificial ventilation, dialysis, and surgery from seriously ill elderly patients than from their younger, equally ill counterparts, even after preferences regarding aggressive treatment were accounted for? Was it ageism, or rational, merciful medicine? Bias, unconscious or not, might account for these disparities, but it was camouflaged, which was perhaps why it was so hard to root out.

I couldn't help but wonder: Had our own bias toward Ira Schneider been camouflaged, too?

In the hospital, Schneider continued to have severe chest pains—small heart attacks, really—that were inadequately relieved by medications. One morning, he nearly doubled over while washing up. The surgeons, reconsulted, turned him down again. Rajiv told me it was because agencies monitoring surgical outcomes were putting tremendous pressure on cardiac surgeons to produce good results. Over the past decade, while surgeons with higher-than-expected mortality statistics had lost operating privileges, others with lower-than-predicted rates had taken to advertising on the radio. Because surgeons who had been aggressive about treating very sick patients like Schneider had incurred higher mortality rates, they had been penalized. Apparently this was an insult many surgeons could no longer countenance.

I didn't know what to do, but I knew I had to do something. I thought of Dean Dowton in St. Louis and his commencement address. "Believe in something," I remembered him saying. "What are you willing to compromise? Where are you going to take a stand?" If there was one ethic I was sworn to uphold, it was to do whatever I could to prolong life.

I knew I couldn't go talk to the surgeons—they would have no patience with my second-guessing—so I decided to talk to Schneider himself, in the hope that I could spur him into getting a second opinion. In Dr. Klein's world, there were private patients and service patients. Fortunately for Schneider, he was a private patient with good insurance. He would have no problem finding another doctor.

I went to his room one afternoon. When he saw me, he tried sitting up, transferring his weight this way and that, as if trying to fall upward. With a heave that almost pulled me off my feet, I helped him up.

"I wanted to talk to you about something," I said. He leaned forward on the bedside table, pushing his lunch tray aside. I hesitated. "I should have talked to you about this before, but—" I stopped.

"What is it, Doc?" he said, sounding worried.

"It's nothing, really. It's just, I wanted to make sure—do you know that you can go somewhere else for a second opinion?" He stared at me with the same puzzled look he had had when I tried to bring up the subject on the night he was admitted.

"You can go somewhere else to have surgery," I went on in a hushed, conspiratorial tone. "You can see another doctor. You're the one in charge. You can do what you have to do to protect yourself."

He continued to stare at me silently.

"It's just one surgeon's opinion, see," I said, feeling treacherous. "You can go to another hospital. For another opinion." I wasn't sure he was getting it. "Maybe another doctor will agree to operate. Do you understand what I'm saying?"

"Yes, I understand," Schneider replied testily. "You're telling me that I can go to a surgeon who is willing to operate on me." He paused. "Listen, I'm just grateful to God for being alive. Look at me! I would never survive an operation!"

TODAY, AFTER MORE THAN TEN YEARS in medicine, I am no longer surprised by the small injustices I see in the hospital. Ours is a multi-tiered system, and the tiers can be defined any which way. I once cared for an Indian man with metastatic colon cancer who was in his early thirties, had been born in New Delhi, had gone to Berkeley as an un-dergraduate, where he studied physics, and later moved to New York for a job. For all the obvious reasons, I saw myself in him. Whenever I had a spare moment, I would steal away to his room, where we remi-nisced about college or about life in New York. I looked through his medical record with a keener eye than I did for my other patients. For him, I was willing to read up on experimental chemotherapy protocols or make an extra phone call to ensure that his tests were not delayed. Did it make a difference? Probably not—at least not in any tangible way—but the extra attention gave him solace, even if it didn't change the outcome of his disease. If doctors discriminate against patients, then it follows that sometimes they have favorites, too.

Frankly, what surprises me now are the rare doctors who treat the drug-abusing homeless person with the same care as the Madison Av-enue socialite. They are the kind of doctors who seem untouched by bias, or at least recognize their biases and fight to disentangle them from medical decisions. Like their colleagues, they appear unaware of their behavior and how much it matters.

informed consent

Down, down, down into the darkness of the grave
Gently they go . . .

—EDNA ST. VINCENT MILLAY,
"DIRGE WITHOUT MUSIC," 1928

In September, I returned to night float, this time as a second-year.
At 9:00 p.m. each night, I'd wander over to the emergency
room, where Dr. Chou or one of the other ER attendings would
give me a thumbnail summary of a patient I was supposed to admit.
The ER workups were typically quick and dirty. Blood tests were usually missing; X-rays or electrocardiograms had often not been done.
One time, I watched a third-year resident argue bitterly with Dr. Seymour, the tall, overbearing night physician, because Seymour wanted
to admit an anemic patient for gastrointestinal bleeding without even
checking the stool for blood.

In addition to admitting patients, I was also responsible for helping interns overnight. The first time I got called for backup was by an
intern in his third month who needed help interpreting a tricky EKG. I
liked reading EKGs. Unlike most problems in medicine, you could apply strict logic and reasoning to them. On the ward, with the intern
raptly looking on, I took out my metal calipers and placed the sharp
tips on two P waves. Then I advanced the calipers across the page, one
arm over the other, showing how the tips landed squarely, sequentially,

inevitably, on the downstream squiggles. It was a thing of beauty, really, and then I launched into an explanation of what it all meant. To the intern, the tiny markings had meant nothing, but now, thanks to my simple demonstration, they meant everything. If only the rest of medicine could be so straightforward.

One night, around 10:00 p.m., I was called to the Memorial ER, across the street from New York Hospital, to admit Armen Izanian, a man in his late thirties with salivary gland cancer that had spread to his lungs and bones. As I looked over his chest X-ray, which showed "cannonball" lesions throughout the lung fields, the ER attending said: "Sad case. Young couple, no kids. All they have in the world is each other."

Izanian's wife, Anna, was sitting with him. A small chocolate cake with caramel spears sat on a small table by his bed. It was his birthday.

He was of Middle Eastern descent, bald and gaunt, with a slightly pitted face but otherwise handsome features. A long scar coursed down the side of his face, where, I assumed, he had had surgery. The bones in his face were unusually prominent because of his wasted musculature. His eyes were dark brown and large, conferring on him a look of amazement. An oxygen mask was strapped to his mouth. The flow through it produced a steady hum, like a leak from a tire.

He answered my questions politely. He said he had been having fevers for the past couple of days. In the ER, he had been given intravenous diuretics and a medicated mist to open up his airways, and though he was feeling better, he still was unable to speak in full sentences without stopping for breath. In fact, he was taking in about thirty breaths a minute, even though the oxygen in his mask was nearly at maximum concentration. Given his debility, I wondered how much longer he was going to be able to continue at this rate. If he tired, the next step would be intubation: insertion of a breathing tube into his trachea for artificial ventilation. But a respirator wasn't going to help a man with disseminated lung cancer, at least not for long. I decided to broach the subject of DNR (Do Not Resuscitate): whether to try to revive him if his heart stopped beating or if he stopped breathing.

"If . . ." I hesitated, though I knew exactly what I wanted to say. ". . . in the event that you could not breathe on your own . . ." I paused again. ". . . would you want us to insert a breathing tube and put you on a respirator?"

Izanian stared through me. For the past few minutes he had been friendly, even good-humored, but now he appeared annoyed. "You're saying I'm in trouble?" he growled.

"I'm not saying anything is going to happen imminently," I said, quickly backtracking. "I just wanted to ask the question so that we do everything in accordance with your wishes."

"No one talked to us about it before," his wife interjected. She was stylishly dressed, with short brown hair, thick-rimmed designer glasses, and a pious reserve I found appealing. In different circumstances, I might have described her as sensual. "But we want to try everything," she said, looking at her husband. "Right, Armen? We don't have a choice in the matter."

The choice, of course, was to limit aggressive measures if the end was near. I thought of what Dr. Omar Morales, the young Puerto Rican attending with pockmarked skin and a gangster's demeanor, had once said to the wife of a cancer patient being admitted to the ICU. Initially she, too, had wanted everything done. "He will get intubated," Dr. Morales told her with glum conviction. "Then we will not know his volume status, so we will have to insert a catheter into his lungs. He will get an infection. We will give him antibiotics. His blood pressure will drop. We will give him intravenous pressors. His kidneys will fail. He will need dialysis. And, despite everything we do, his cancer will not go away. Eventually you will make him DNR, but by then he will have suffered for no good purpose."

He spoke like a clairvoyant looking into a crystal ball. The course was tragically stereotyped; there were no surprises, no miracles; he had seen it over and over again. The wife agreed to DNR that day, and the patient died a few days later. But even though Izanian was in similar straits, I knew that I had neither the experience nor the fortitude to hold such a discussion.

"Do you need an answer tonight?" he demanded.

"No," I replied, though in fact I probably did. "Why don't you think it over and discuss it with your doctor?"

Anna followed me to the workstation. "We are scared," she said apologetically. "We know he is dying, but we want to hold on for as long as we can."

I told her that DNR did not mean we would stop treating her husband. It only meant we would limit life-prolonging interventions in case of a cardiopulmonary arrest. (Even though this was technically true, I wasn't sure how well it was implemented in practice. Too often I had seen nurses and doctors use DNR as an excuse for laxity.)

"He is all I have," Anna said, her eyes moist but steadfast. "I want everything done to keep him alive."

The encounter reminded me of a patient I had seen at New York Hospital a couple of weeks prior. One morning, around 2:00 a.m., I was hanging around the ER when paramedics wheeled in a ninety-year-old woman named June Steinway on a stretcher. She was having severe chest pain, which an EKG immediately confirmed was a massive heart attack.

The ER staff sprang into action. Doctors whisked her into a treatment room, placed a monitor on her, slapped an oxygen mask over her face, and began an IV drip of nitroglycerin. Though in pain, she was alert, clearheaded, and quiet. The only indication of an emergency was in the buzz of the many doctors and nurses around her.

Doctors began preparing her for cardiac catheterization. The chest pain had started only three hours ago, so there was still time to open the blocked artery that was cutting off blood flow to her heart. The cardiology fellow, an earnest man, stepped outside the room to talk with the woman's middle-aged daughters.

"Your mother is in critical condition," he told them. "If nothing is done, she could die." Angioplasty probably offered her the best shot of surviving this crisis, but it was risky, particularly in an emergency. Their mother could die on the table or suffer brain damage or end up on a ventilator. No one could predict with any certainty what would happen.

"She can also be treated with a thrombolytic drug to dissolve blood clots," the fellow said. It was administered through a simple injection and required no invasive procedures. But it was not as effective as angioplasty in this situation, and it carried a risk of causing bleeding, especially at her age, into her head.

So what did they want to do?

The daughters asked for a couple of minutes to talk it over. When the fellow came back, the elder one faced him squarely. "We can't bear to watch our mother go through any invasive procedures," she said. "She is ninety years old. If she was sixty, it would be a different story."

The fellow nodded. "So you want us to give her the thrombolytic then," he said.

"But you said there was a risk of stroke with the drug," the elder daughter said.

"Of course there are risks," the fellow replied impatiently. "But you have to weigh the benefits. She could recover from this and go on to live a few more years."

"We want her to live as long as possible, but with quality," the younger daughter said tearfully. "We don't want to see her on a ventilator."

"I can't offer any guarantees," the fellow said. "My job is to tell you the options. The final decision is up to you."

The daughters looked perplexed. "We can't make this decision," the elder daughter said. "Perhaps you should ask our mother."

Now ordinarily, in an emergency, doctors are not supposed to waste precious time discussing risks and benefits. They—we—are taught to treat first and ask questions later, on the assumption that rational people would prefer treatment to prolong their lives. But this emergency was different. The patient was awake and seemingly competent. The fellow could decide how best to treat her heart attack, but only she could decide whether the effort would be worth it.

In the treatment room, Steinway's blood pressure had stabilized and she was a bit more comfortable after receiving a shot of morphine. She was an obese woman with thinning, salon-done brown hair, lying on a narrow gurney dressed in a faded teal hospital gown. A tangle of EKG wires snaked across her chest, terminating on green electrodes pasted to her hefty, exposed breasts. A nurse was struggling to place an oxygen tank under the stretcher in preparation for transport to the catheterization lab. The hubbub in the room had given way to a sort of heaviness as everyone waited for a directive to proceed or not. If the decision was for angioplasty, an attending cardiologist and the catheterization staff on call were going to have to be summoned. Everything was on hold until a decision was made.

Steinway smiled as her daughters approached. They hugged and kissed her and stroked her hair. She clutched their hands and beamed at them. The fellow took his position at the foot of the stretcher. "You are having a heart attack," he announced, bringing a hush to the room. "There are some things we can do to treat you but we need your consent."

He quickly went through the treatment options and risks. Cardiac catheterization, thrombolysis, groin puncture, local anesthesia, simple injection, contrast dye, blood thinning, vascular complications, allergic reactions, bleeding, infection, stroke, renal failure, heart attack, death. Steinway listened but did not say anything. He repeated the options. She nodded. So what did she want to do? She shook her head. "What is best?" she asked.

The fellow's speech picked up nervously. "It's difficult to say what is best in this particular situation," he said. "Studies comparing angioplasty and thrombolytics have shown advantage for angioplasty if it is performed by an experienced cardiologist within three hours of the onset of symptoms. Death rates are lower, and angioplasty results in an open coronary artery much more often than thrombolytics. And angioplasty also reduces bleeding complications, especially in the brain."

He paused for a second, waiting for her to process what he had just said. "But," he went on quickly, "your blood pressure is low, which makes angioplasty riskier. And people in your age group might not get the same benefit, though we don't know this for sure."

Steinway turned her attention back to her daughters. The younger one asked for a blanket for her mother, but the nurse replied that she wanted to keep Steinway's chest exposed.

"I know I'm presenting a lot of information," the fellow said evenly. "But we have to proceed quickly if you're going to get any benefit. The longer we wait, the more your heart is jeopardized."

Steinway stared at him blankly, as if expecting him to say something else. When he didn't, she turned away again.

The fellow moved in closer. A sense of urgency crept into his voice. "Is there any other family you want me to talk to?"

"We are her only family," the elder daughter replied.

"Then tell me what you want to do," he said sharply. The attending physician was surely going to chew him out for taking so long to obtain consent. "If she were my mother," he added almost parenthetically, "I would tell her to have the angioplasty."

"But you said there is a risk of kidney failure," the younger daughter said. "You said she could end up on dialysis."

"Of course there are risks!" the fellow cried. "There are risks with everything we do. But there is a risk of doing nothing, too."

The elder daughter cleared a strand of hair from her mother's perspiring forehead. "What do you want, Momma? Do you want the surgery?"

Though it wasn't clear how much of the complicated situation Steinway understood, it was pretty clear that she didn't like any of her options. She wanted assurances the fellow could not give. And he wanted a decision she could not make. Finally, she looked out at the room of white coats, slowly shook her head, and said she didn't know. She was taken to the cardiac care unit for observation.

To me, this outcome was hardly a surprise. Hospitalized patients have a hard time weighing their options under the best of circumstances. In an emergency like this one, where the stakes were high and the time frame to make a decision so compressed, how could we expect a ninety-year-old or her suffering daughters to make the proper choice, any more than I could have expected Armen Izanian and his wife to decide on the spot whether to authorize a DNR order?

I remembered how the cardiology fellow used to obtain "informed consent" for procedures on 4-North. He told the patients the risks and benefits, but rarely did this prompt any sort of meaningful discussion. Patients invariably told him, "You're the doctor. I'll do whatever you say." Most of them seemed to think informed consent was a sham, demanding they either ratify decisions that had already been made or make decisions they were not equipped to make. Even when patients were not agreeable, they could easily be persuaded to change their minds, like the Mexican man who was bullied into having a catheterization against his better judgment. The words Dr. Klein, the attending physician, had used after wresting consent from him were emblazoned in my memory. He said we could get whatever we wanted from patients. "As long as they agree with us, they're not crazy."

The next night, around 3:00 a.m., I stopped by Armen Izanian's room to see how he was doing. I expected to find him asleep, but when I peeked in, he was sitting bolt upright in bed, eyes closed, hands folded, in an almost meditative pose. A pressurized mask was strapped tightly to his face, its plastic straps digging deeply into his neck. A machine whooshed like a steam engine with each breath. His wife, Anna, was standing at his bedside, stroking his perspiring forehead. Feldman, an intern, was also in the room. He was a young punk with pointy eyebrows who talked so fast he stammered. He had a reputation for being a cowboy, confident and cocksure.

"Who called you?" he demanded when he saw me in the doorway.

I told him I had admitted Izanian the previous night and wanted to see how he was doing.

"Well, look at him!" Feldman exclaimed, walking out into the hallway. Izanian was breathing over forty times a minute. Though he was receiving pure oxygen, his pulse oximeter was reading only 90 percent, critically low.

"He probably has pneumonia," Feldman said. "The chest X-ray

shows a new infiltrate." This did not surprise me. Lung tumors can obstruct the breathing passages, causing fluid and secretions to build up, a disorder called postobstructive pneumonia.

Wondering why he hadn't called me for backup, I asked Feldman which treatments he had given Mr. Izanian so far.

"Lasix, Solumedrol, Atrovent, albuterol," Feldman replied rapid-fire, counting out the interventions on his skinny fingers. "But he's getting tired. I think he's going to crap out pretty soon."

"Have you called the ICU?"

"He's DNR!" Feldman cried indignantly. "Right now, I just want to keep him comfortable."

I assumed the DNR order had been issued earlier in the day. "Did you start antibiotics?"

Feldman shook his head, as if the thought had occurred to him but he had decided it wasn't worth it.

"DNR doesn't mean we're not going to treat him," I snapped. "Start him on broad-spectrum antibiotics. Let's see if we can get him through this."

As Feldman headed over to the nursing station, I heard his beeper go off. *Beep . . . beep . . . beep.* The sound transported me back to a year ago, when I had been the night float at Memorial. For a moment I felt a pang of sympathy for him. Night float during internship had almost broken me; I was thankful those days had long passed. But from what I could remember of it, I was certain that the last thing Feldman wanted to do that night was spend precious time on a patient who was DNR.

Back in the room, Anna was waiting expectantly for me, her face pale and drawn. I told her we were going to order some medicine to help her husband's breathing. "I understand you discussed intubation with your doctor," I said.

"Yes, this morning," she replied.

"And you decided to make him DNR."

After a pause, she said, "What does that mean?"

An eerie sense of calm enveloped me, like the sensation one often has before a shock. "That if he stops breathing, there will be no attempt at resuscitation," I replied carefully.

This time the pause lasted several seconds. "No, we never agreed to that," she said firmly. "We want full resuscitation."

My breathing quickened and my heart started to pound like a drum. I asked her what they had discussed with their doctor. I didn't know if she had misinterpreted the conversation or if she was now changing her mind.

"We talked about what to do if he becomes a vegetable. But we want to do everything possible right now. Right, Armen?" It was not so much a question as a tragic, plaintive demand.

Izanian's face had turned a sort of reddish blue, the color of a hematoma, a sign of profound hypoxia. "We had—" he said, pausing for breath, "a discussion—we agreed—to—DNR—but then—we changed—our mind."

I sprinted to the nursing station, where Feldman was leafing through the chart of a different patient. He told me he had written the order for the antibiotic.

"I'm calling the ICU," I said, grabbing a phone.

"Why?" Feldman cried. "I told you, he's DNR!"

"No he's not!" I shouted. "His wife said they want a full code." A couple of nurses looked up from their late night snacks.

For the first time that night, Feldman appeared fazed. "They—they can't do that," he stammered.

"They just did," I snapped. I swiped Izanian's chart off the rack. In the front was a DNR form. Scribbled on it was an attending physician's signature but not Izanian's or his wife's. "Look," I hollered, rapping my knuckles on the sheet. "They didn't even sign the form. They agreed to something, but it wasn't DNR."

Feldman dropped what he was doing and ran to get an arterial blood gas (ABG) kit. Maricel Gomez, the critical care fellow, was surely going to require an ABG before accepting Izanian to the ICU. I called her in the unit and quickly summarized the case. I told her about the metastatic cancer and the fevers that had brought him to the hospital. "Something obviously got mixed up with the DNR," I said breathlessly. "I guess the family didn't realize what they were agreeing to. Right now he is tachypneic, breathing thirty-five times a minute on positive-pressure ventilation. His oxygen saturation is about ninety percent. We're drawing a blood gas, but I think he's getting tired, and I wanted to let you know sooner rather than—"

Gomez cut me off before I could finish. "I can tell you that he is not a candidate for the ICU," she declared in a thick Filipino accent.

I started to speak but froze in mid-sentence. Had she not heard me? "He is not DNR," I repeated.

"It does not matter," she replied calmly. "In a cancer hospital, everyone could end up in the ICU. But we have to make choices."

I had never heard of a patient being rejected by the ICU because he was too sick. "So what do you want me to do?" I stammered. "The family wants everything done."

"You should try to make him DNR."

"They don't want it!"

"Then you can intubate him on the floor. But there are no ICU beds for this patient. He will not benefit from ICU care."

I couldn't believe how cavalierly she was dismissing him. "Are you going to write this in the chart?" I demanded. The medico-legal threat worked sometimes, but not this time. "Of course," she replied.

"Can you at least come see him?" I pleaded. I had never intubated anyone on my own.

"I'll come by and take a look," she said. "But it will not change my decision."

She soon appeared at the nursing station, a stocky Filipino woman carrying an array of beepers on the waistband of her tight gray scrubs. Without acknowledging me, she sat down with Izanian's chart. After a couple of minutes, she told me to take her to him.

In the room, she bore down on Izanian, who was now gasping for breath. She started off by reviewing his medical history as Feldman and I stood stiffly behind her. Though her tone was icy and monotone, I was impressed by how quickly and accurately she had digested the complicated chart.

"If we put in a breathing tube, there are two courses," she explained to Anna. "If it is the cancer that is making him like this, he will not get better. The breathing tube will not make the cancer go away, of course. If it is pneumonia, then the tube may help—but when we take it out, he still has cancer." She made the last comment with a rhetorical flourish, like a debater who has just made a clever point. Izanian and his wife stared at her, saying nothing. Feldman looked away, appearing bored.

Gomez repeated the options, describing a decision tree where all paths lead to the same outcome. "We can intubate him if you wish," she said to Anna. "But he will have to stay on the floor. There are no ICU beds available."

Like June Steinway's daughters, Anna seemed paralyzed by the choice before her. "What do you recommend?" she asked softly.

"I cannot tell you what to do," Gomez replied sharply. "But I can tell you that not everyone gets a breathing tube. When my father died, he did not have intubation."

"How long would the tube have to stay in?" Anna asked.

"I cannot say," Gomez replied impatiently. "It all depends on what is making him like this. If it is pneumonia, maybe a few days. If it is cancer . . ." Her voice trailed off.

Anna patted her husband's cheek. He opened his eyes. "What should we do, Armen? Should we try the breathing tube?" Behind the mask he scowled, appearing lethargic and confused, probably due to a lack of oxygen. Anna turned back to the fellow. "We want to do everything possible—"

"Then we have to intubate him now," Gomez interrupted.

"But could we wait a little longer to see if he gets better on his own?"

"No!" Gomez barked. "Now is the emergency, now is the time. We do not want to intubate him in the middle of a respiratory collapse."

Anna looked at me helplessly. My vision momentarily clouded as tears filled my eyes. The death of a spouse is hard enough to accept without having to sanction it in the middle of the night. I thought once again of Lisa. What if we had gotten married? What if I were the one standing in Anna's shoes right now? Medicine, I was beginning to learn, is about life. In the struggles of your patients, you can find yourself.

"You can sign the DNR form now," I whispered, trying to break the impasse. "We can intubate him later if you change your mind."

Gomez spun around and glared at me, as if I had committed the worst mistake. Then she turned back to Anna. "Once you sign the form, we will not intubate him," she said.

"And we cannot decide for intubation later?" Anna asked.

"No," Gomez replied firmly. "If we are going to intubate, we must do it now. So what do you want to do?"

Anna did not say anything.

"Are you prepared to sign the DNR?"

Anna nodded, blinking away tears.

"We can try calling the attending," I offered, receiving another icy look.

"Yes, okay," Anna said, appearing relieved. "I would like to speak with him."

"So do I understand you correctly?" Gomez said threateningly. "You do not want us to intubate him at this moment? You want to wait to speak to the attending?"

Anna nodded, trembling.

"And what about CPR? What if he has a cardiopulmonary arrest before we can reach the attending?"

"CPR is okay," Anna said. "Just no intubation right now."

"You can't say yes to CPR and no to intubation," Feldman blurted out. "That makes no sense."

Gomez ordered us to step outside.

"Basically they want us to intubate him when he codes," Feldman said mockingly in the hallway.

"That's their right," I said quietly.

"But they have incomplete information!" Feldman cried. "They don't know what it means to say no to intubation and yes to CPR. The first thing we're going to have to do in a code is secure his airway. A, B, C," he said, condescendingly raising three fingers. "Airway, Breathing, Circulation."

"It's still her decision," I said, hating the ill-mannered punk. "Whether it is right or wrong."

Gomez put up her hand, signaling an end to the discussion. Her expression toward me had turned from contempt to pity, as though she thought me pathetically naive. "I'm going to call the attending," she announced quietly.

The attending physician on call that night had never met Izanian or his wife. Back in the room, we struggled to put the phone to Izanian's ear, but the oxygen mask kept getting in the way, and the noise from it made it impossible for Izanian to hear or be heard. When the mask was removed, his blood oxygen saturation started to plummet. After multiple attempts, Gomez finally passed the phone to Anna. She listened for a few seconds. "Yes," Anna finally said into the receiver. "We want to fight. We have no choice but to fight."

Gomez bolted out of the room to get an intubation tray. Feldman went to answer a page. Finally we were alone.

Medicine is a stochastic science—no doctor can predict the future—but in this case the outcome was never in doubt. Advanced cancer patients who end up on ventilators die during their hospitalizations. Life support was futile, and the idea of inserting catheters and tubes into this man seemed inhumane. Even though I despised Gomez's approach, I knew she was right. DNR was the only acceptable choice in this case. A breathing tube was going to mean a lot of suffering without any realistic possibility of gain.

Fatigue was setting in. In the dim dawn light, Anna asked me what to do, and I told her.

The next morning, I stopped by the room. The priest had left; Izanian's body had been moved to the morgue. Anna was still sitting at the bedside. Her hair was mussed, her jewelry askew. She had on the same outfit as when I had met her two days ago. I sat down and told her that I was sorry.

"He was supposed to be my friend for life," she said softly. "I wish I could have done something for him."

"You did a lot," I said.

"But did I do the right thing?"

I had asked myself that same question. "Putting him on a ventilator would have prolonged his suffering," I said.

She nodded, blinking away tears. She noticed my wedding ring. "You are married?" she asked.

I nodded.

"Live each moment like it is your first," she said. "Sometimes it is hard, but you have to try."

OVER THE YEARS, I have come to appreciate how problematic informed consent can be, and not just in emergencies. When I started residency, I viewed patient autonomy as an absolute good, an ethical imperative that trumped all others. In medical school I had learned about some of the infamous breaches of autonomy in the history of medicine: the Tuskegee study in the 1940s in which black men with syphilis were intentionally left untreated, despite the availability of penicillin, in order to study that disease's complications; or the Willowbrook study where developmentally disabled patients were intentionally infected with hepatitis. Even today, patients continue to be enrolled in experimental drug studies without proper consent, or under tacit intimidation.

Informed consent was supposed to guard against such abuses. But informed consent is practiced very differently from the way ethicists envisioned it. It was supposed to protect patients from doctors. Instead it is used to protect doctors from patients or, rather, from the hard decisions that patient care demands. Doctors nowadays sometimes use informed consent as a crutch to abdicate responsibility.

A few years later, when I was a cardiology fellow, a patient of mine had an angiogram. He was still lying on the operating table, catheters in his groin. A cardiologist called me over to review the film.

When I got to the cardiac catheterization lab, two attending physicians and a senior fellow were studying the angiogram on a computer monitor. The coronary arteries were sectioned off by five narrow blockages.

What to do? The senior physician favored angioplasty. Two blockages could be opened today, he said, and three at a later date. The others thought bypass surgery was the better option. Someone asked my opinion.

I thought about it for a few minutes. Surgery was probably the more durable solution. Bypass grafts could last a decade or more, longer than most stents. Plus, surgery for my patient meant one procedure, not two.

Still, there were risks. Because of his advanced disease, my patient probably had about a 10 percent chance of dying in surgery. If he survived, he could be left with memory deficits or chronic chest-wall pain. Plus, it would take longer for him to recover from surgery.

Since we couldn't reach a consensus and it wasn't an emergency, the senior attending physician made what seemed like a reasonable proposition: give the patient the options and let him decide. After all, he was the one who was going to have to live with the consequences.

He was lying on a long, narrow table, a middle-aged man covered from neck to toe by a sterile drape. His face had a strangely disconnected look, which I attributed to anxiety and sedation. He smiled as I approached. "The angiogram is done," I started off saying.

I told him he had five blockages in three arteries and two options. Angioplasty could open the arteries without surgery, but he would need two procedures, one of which could be started right away. Open-heart surgery, on the other hand, probably offered him the best chance of not having to undergo another procedure in the future. "But it's a big surgery," I added.

I didn't want to bias him one way or the other. A few months before, I had convinced a patient to have heart-valve replacement surgery, which had resulted in serious complications. I didn't want another bad outcome on my conscience.

He listened intently but did not say much. I repeated his options. He nodded. So what did he want to do? He looked puzzled. "What is best?" he replied.

That I was having this conversation at all is testament to how much medicine has changed in the last two or three decades. In hospitals today, "patient autonomy" is the ruling ethical mantra, even superseding beneficence. But it can be a problem.

For one thing, patient autonomy often seems to be more important to doctors than patients. Sometimes patients want to hear their options and make their own decisions, but just as often, in my experience, they want doctors to guide them through the tough decisions and, yes, sometimes, tell them what to do. The father of a friend of mine died a few years ago from lung cancer. My friend told me that when he asked the doctors about chemotherapy, they gave him numbers and statistics but assiduously avoided giving advice, which was what he really needed.

"What is best?" my patient asked me again. "I can't tell you what to do," I repeated. He stared blankly at me. I shifted my weight, feeling frustrated. Then I decided to start acting like a doctor.

"What are you afraid of?" I asked. It turns out his uncle had had open-heart surgery a few years back. Judging by his tone, he wanted no part of it. "It sounds like you're scared of surgery," I said. He nodded. "So we should do the other thing," I said. The patient agreed, so we did an angioplasty. It went well.

Another issue I continue to struggle with today is how to balance patient autonomy with the physician's obligation to do the best for his patient. As a doctor, when do you let your patient make a bad decision? When, if ever, do you draw the line? What if a decision could cost your patient's life? How hard do you push him to change his mind? At the same time, it is his life. Who are you to tell him how to live it?

In my second year of residency, I took care of a gay man who had a CT scan of his head because of weakness in his legs and difficulty concentrating. It showed signs of a brain infection often associated with AIDS. I advised the man to have an HIV test. "If you are infected," I told him, "it is better to know early." But my patient refused. He said he didn't believe that HIV caused AIDS. When I pressed him, he emphatically stated he didn't want to discuss the matter any further.

My patient was neither psychotic nor delusional. For the most part, he spoke calmly and rationally. I didn't want to force him to take a test he didn't want, yet I didn't want his disease to progress to the point that it would be untreatable. I wasn't sure what to do, so I did what most doctors do in these situations: I called a psychiatrist.

The consulting psychiatrist that morning was a tall man with a serious, deliberative style befitting his line of work. I spoke with him in the hallway after he evaluated my patient. "Clearly he's making a bad decision," the psychiatrist said. "But that isn't enough to deem him incompetent." My patient's thoughts were not grossly disorganized, and he wasn't obviously depressed or psychotic. "He is showing impaired judgment," the psychiatrist went on. "But we all have impaired judgment from time to time." In other words, my patient could make a bad decision if he wanted to.

I felt torn. How far should a doctor go to make a patient do the right thing? When do the demands of beneficence outweigh those of patient autonomy? First, do no harm, I had been taught, but what about the harm a patient can inflict on himself?

Medical decisions necessarily involve value judgments, and who better to make those judgments than the patients involved? If a fashion model doesn't want surgery because it will leave a scar on her face, it may make sense in the context of her value system. Even though I may not agree with her, I can understand her reasoning and abide by her decision.

The problem with my gay patient was that I couldn't understand his reasoning. It seemed arbitrary to me, borne out of flawed reasoning and misinformation, not careful logic. It was the wrong decision for the wrong reasons, but by the ethics prevailing in medicine, I couldn't force him to make a better one. Even so, hardly a week goes by that I do not wonder if I should have tried harder to persuade him to have the test.

Over time, my views on informed consent have evolved. I no longer view paternalism as suspiciously as I once did. I now believe that it can be a core component of good medical care.

Not long ago, as an attending physician in the CCU at the hospital where I now work on Long Island, I got an early morning call from a cardiology fellow. Mr. Smith could not breathe. Bright red blood, filling up the air spaces in his lungs, was spewing from his mouth whenever he coughed.

"So what are you waiting for?" I asked the cardiology fellow on the phone, trying to rub the sleep out of my eyes. "Intubate him."

"He says he doesn't want a breathing tube," the fellow replied.

"He's going to die without it," I hollered.

"I know," the fellow said matter-of-factly. "And I think he knows, too. But he still doesn't want it."

I sank onto my living room sofa. What to do? Mr. Smith had come so far since his heart attack. Cardiac catheterization. A drug-coated stent to open up a blocked coronary artery. Intravenous blood thinners to keep the stent from clotting. Was it going to end like this?

"This is a reversible complication," I told the fellow. I had seen such bleeding before with aggressive blood thinning. With a few days of ventilatory support, the bleeding should stop, we would be able to pull out the tube, and he would walk out of the hospital.

"What do you want me to do?" the fellow replied. "He's refusing." He said that he had already tried the usual measures short of intubation: supplemental oxygen, diuretics, a pressurized face mask.

"Do you think he has decision-making capacity?" I asked. If not, we could make the decision for him.

"I think so," the fellow replied, his voice thick from lack of sleep. "He apparently told the residents several days ago that he never wanted to be intubated."

"He can't do this to himself," I said. "Try to talk to him again. I'm coming in."

Outside, the sun was rising. Speeding to the hospital on a lonely stretch of highway, I mulled over the options. As far as I could tell, there were only two: we could continue the current treatments and watch him die; or we could intubate him against his wishes.

From my car I called my brother, who had performed the catheterization. "Intubate him," Rajiv said immediately. I explained that Mr. Smith did not want a breathing tube. "Who cares?" he cried. "He's going to die! He's not thinking straight."

Perhaps Rajiv is right, I thought. After all, who in his right mind wants to die? Were we not asking too much of Mr. Smith? In an emergency like this, how could we expect him to make the right choice, any more than the cardiology fellow could have expected June Steinway or I could have expected Anna Izanian to do so years ago? As an experienced cardiologist, wasn't I in a better position to make Mr. Smith's decision than Mr. Smith?

When I got to the cardiac care unit, a crowd of doctors and nurses was at the patient's bedside and an anesthesiologist was preparing to insert a breathing tube. My brother took me aside. "He was breathing at forty times a minute and his oxygen saturation was dropping, so I made the decision to intubate him."

I nodded quietly. I had made the same decision in the car.

Once the breathing tube was in, blood started rising in it like a red column. Nurses had to scramble for face shields and yellow gowns to protect themselves from the red spray. Pretty soon someone was pouring brown antiseptic soap onto Mr. Smith's groin in preparation for a central intravenous line. As needles started piercing his skin, Mr. Smith started swinging wildly. In intensive care units, the steamroller of technology starts moving quickly, flattening all ambivalence.

Eventually, with sedation, Mr. Smith settled down, and the critical care unit staff settled in for a long period of observation. If we had gambled right, he would recover within a few days. "If you get through this," I whispered to Mr. Smith, "I hope you can forgive me."

Mr. Smith had a rocky hospital course. The bleeding in his lungs continued for several days, requiring large blood transfusions, but it eventually stopped. His blood pressure was too low, then too high. He had protracted, unexplained fevers.

After a few days, I rotated off service as the attending physician in the CCU. Over the following week, Mr. Smith remained intubated. A week later, I heard that his condition had improved. A week after that, a fellow stopped me in the hall to tell me that the breathing tube was out.

When I went to see him, I realized that I had never really looked at him as a person. He was a tall, muscular man in late middle age, with a broad forehead, a flat nose, and high, handsome cheekbones. I went to his bedside and introduced myself. He didn't recognize me.

"When you were really sick, I was one of the doctors who made the decision to put in the breathing tube," I said. He nodded, eyeing me curiously. "I know you didn't want the tube," I went on, "but if we didn't put it in, you would have died."

He nodded again. "I've been through a lot," he finally said, his voice still hoarse from two weeks of intubation.

"I know," I replied.

"But thank you," he said.

Some months later, I was asked to attend a meeting of the ethics committee at my hospital, of which I am a member, to discuss my actions. On the committee were nurses, social workers, physicians, and a rabbi wearing a yarmulke who often quoted the Talmud. My hands were clammy as I walked into the room that morning, mulling over how I was going to respond to their questions. When my case came up, I told the group I had decided to intubate Mr. Smith because I was not convinced that the CCU house staff had had the proper discussion with him before making him DNR. Not having had the conversation myself, not knowing whether he had been properly informed of his choices or truly informed when he made his decision, I decided to err on the side of preserving his life. "I feel at peace with myself," I said. "I feel justified that I made the right decision."

A discussion ensued about the nature of paternalism. The head of the committee, a graying, grandfatherly man, explained that paternalism derives from the image of the paternal figure, the father, in a family. The father is motivated by an interest in his children's welfare. He acts on their behalf, but not at their behest. The beneficiaries—his children—may even repudiate the actions taken on their behalf. "Are we saying that as doctors we can reject patients' preferences by saying that their directives do not apply to their current circumstances or by saying they lack capacity because it is an emergent situation?" he asked. "Are we saying that as doctors we are all-knowing and that we have the last word?"

He wrote "patient > doctor" on a large sheet of paper. Autonomy trumps everything, he said, if the patient has capacity, but who decides? "The doctor, of course," he answered, "so ultimately the patient can decide only if the doctor says so." In the end, he said, the power structure in medicine is such that only doctors can decide whether patients have the right to exert their autonomy. And how do doctors decide? "Well," he said, "it's based on their experience, their prejudgment, their prejudice; and some doctors have the prejudice that patients cannot make medical decisions for themselves. So in these cases, paternalism rules, and it's a slippery slope toward a situation where autonomy is always undermined."

"All too often," he added, "when we judge that what the patient wants is reasonable, we decide the patient has capacity. That means we ultimately decide that they should be respected only when we agree with them." The words of Dr. Klein rang through my mind: "We can get them to do whatever we want. As long as they agree with us, they're not crazy."

A doctor with spiky gray hair said he agreed with me about intubating Mr. Smith. "I respect my patients, their choices, what they tell me," he said. "But it can't be black or white. I would have done the exact same thing as you did. It's about informed consent. If you are not comfortable it was done properly, I too would have erred on the side of intubation."

A social worker said: "My mother had been on a ventilator. The resident came by to talk to her, asking if she ever wanted to be on a ventilator again. It was like he was trying to finish another task, like he was checking off a box. There was no substantive discussion. I applaud you for doing the right thing. I think your behavior was perfectly ethical."

An ER physician said that patients were often brought in with life-threatening conditions. "One young woman said she didn't want to be intubated. I intubated her anyway. When her family came in, we talked about it, and they were thankful. And when she woke up, she was obviously happy that she didn't die."

In response, the head of the committee said it was important to distinguish hard from soft paternalism. Hard paternalism, he explained, was when physicians did not believe that patients have the capacity to understand the decisions before them. "You think, 'They will better understand when they think like me.' Like with children when you say to them, 'Why do you have to do this? Because I say so.' As a parent, you are duty-bound to prevent your kids from making bad decisions or doing harm to their bodies. Soft paternalism is different. Here you aren't sure if the patient understands. In soft paternalism, you have negotiations. You try to persuade the patient to see things from your viewpoint.

"For Mr. Smith, I might even advocate a position of hard paternalism. The standard for decisional capacity goes up the more severe the consequences of the decision. For the trivial decisions, we don't demand such a high standard. 'Oh, the patient refuses an IV? Okay, fine.' But here the consequences were catastrophic, and fortunately there was a good outcome."

He shuffled his papers together. "I feel compelled to have the last word. We want to be careful about saying patients can never make the right decisions or cannot give informed consent because their past directive is no longer applicable. We run the risk of saying, 'Patients have to listen to us. We are the first and last authority.' There is always a danger that doctors decide that they know better.

"But in this case, I think Dr. Jauhar passed the test. Final question for the committee: Should we allow Dr. Jauhar to remain a member? All in favor raise your hands." Most hands went up, I'm happy to say.

bloody penguins

Don't just do something. Stand there!

—ICU MAXIM

After almost four months as a second-year, I was beginning to get comfortable with the job. But I did not want to go back to the intensive care unit, which I had last rotated through almost one year earlier. "Maybe it'll be different this year," Sonia said, flipping through a magazine as we watched HBO one Sunday night. After all, I was no longer an intern. "Maybe," I replied skeptically.

My father-in-law called to buck up my spirits. "Critical care is simple," he said with characteristic nonchalance. "There are only a few things to keep track of: blood pressure, oxygenation, fluid status." In his world, patients were defined by their physiologies, a concept that did not comfort me.

The main reason for my reluctance, though I didn't want to admit this to anyone—least of all Sonia's father—was that I did not want to carry the code beeper. All through residency I had dreaded the day I would have to be a code leader—the one who resuscitates patients, the fearless leader barking orders, making snap judgments, saving lives. Somehow it seemed beyond my capabilities.

I phoned Rajiv for some words of encouragement. "Just be sure you're not the first one to get to a code," he said, chuckling. That was the extent of his advice.

That night in bed, my mind drifted back to medical school and my first code, on my first clerkship in internal medicine at the St. Louis VA Medical Center. Early one morning, I was dozing in the call room when a high-pitched chirp awakened me. I reached in the dark for my beeper, randomly pushing buttons until a number appeared on the display. When I punched the number in and was connected, a nurse informed me that a code was going on in the surgical intensive care unit. She had tried paging me several times, as I had requested before going to bed, but apparently I had slept through her calls, as well as an announcement on the hospital intercom. *Shit*, I thought, jumping out of bed. *How is this going to look for my grade!* Throwing on my white coat, I raced downstairs. I passed through a set of double doors and sprinted down a long hallway, spilling paraphernalia from my pockets along the way, before arriving in the ICU. It was a brand-new ward, brightly lit, a modern affair. Under an intense ceiling lamp, a rather long man was being resuscitated by a group of doctors and nurses. His skin was dry, scaly, dirty-looking. He must have had cirrhosis because his belly was horribly distended; even his belly button protruded outward. Black fecal matter was smeared on the mattress. I stood off at a distance, my eyes watering from the stench, hoping no one would call on me. A senior resident was running the code. "Okay, hold compressions," he said casually, almost like a photographer giving instructions at a group portrait. He stared at the monitor. "All right, he's still fibrillating. Push another round of epinephrine and charge up the paddles."

"Oh, let him die already!" a nurse cried out. She was riding the dying man's chest, thumping up and down on his sternum with her short arms. The code leader just chuckled and continued to give orders. There was no fear or urgency in his voice. He might as well have been directing an exercise on a mannequin.

After a few minutes, resuscitation efforts ceased and the patient was pronounced dead. I went back to my call room, but for the remainder of the night I couldn't sleep. I kept thinking about the code, not so much about the dead patient as about the code leader. He had been so calm, so cool, so composed under pressure. How was I ever going to be like that?

Besides codes, there were other reasons I didn't want to work in the ICU. Though I was almost halfway through residency, I still wasn't sure whether I even *believed* in intensive care. So much of what doctors did in the ICU seemed to be of marginal benefit, action for no good, clear, definable purpose. In the ICU, doctors were prone to an irrational compulsion to do something—anything—no matter how futile or inane. It was a reflexive impulse, like taking a step backward if someone yells out "X-ray!"—regardless of where you are standing. It didn't seem to matter that clinical data was often incomplete or difficult to interpret. The stakes were high, the patients were sick, and you were supposed to act with conviction, even if there was no basis for it. And the therapies employed were hardly benign. Ventilators caused pneumonia, intravenous pressors caused arrhythmias, central lines caused infections and collapsed lungs, bed confinement caused blood clots and deconditioning. And what to say of the noise, the stress, the sleep deprivation? *Primum non nocere.* It was a fundamental dictum, a boundary never to be crossed, but in the ICU sometimes it was impossible to do no harm.

One thing I had learned the last time I had been in the ICU was that it wasn't just doctors who hurt patients. More often than not, it was their families. I thought of Rose Reynolds, a nonagenarian who had been admitted to the pulmonary ward in the winter with a bad case of pneumonia. On her first night in the hospital, I asked her family if they wanted to make her DNR. Frankly, I wasn't sure she'd even survive the night. "No," her son, a lawyer, replied. "We want heroic measures to keep her alive."

Just before her ninety-second birthday, she was transferred to the ICU. When I saw her next, almost two months later, she was still there. She had suffered numerous complications during her prolonged stay, including respiratory failure, congestive heart failure, and a severe abdominal infection, but she was still alive, though it was hard to tell where her body ended and the tubes began.

"We want her kept alive indefinitely," her son, speaking for his three siblings, said on more than one occasion. One afternoon, my classmate Cynthia stormed into the conference room in tears. She had just performed the weekly ritual of replacing Reynolds's intravenous catheters with fresh, sterile ones. "What are they thinking?" she cried, frustrated that Reynolds's family had once again refused to discuss DNR. "They must really hate their mother!"

In the ICU, one gets accustomed to families that push, that focus on the tiny upticks in a patient's condition, even in the face of inexorable decline, but Reynolds's family stood out in their zealotry. Her condition never fluctuated; there were no peaks or plateaus to justify hope. "Let her die," I yearned to tell them. "What you are doing is much worse than death." Behind their backs, the nurses whispered that they were probably compensating now for care they had not provided earlier.

When her heart finally stopped one Sunday evening, my senior resident Reva ran the code. "Should we start chest compressions?" I said breathlessly when I entered the room. "In a minute," Reva replied. Her tone told me everything I needed to know. This was going to be a "slow code." A nurse filled a syringe with epinephrine, meticulously flicking the plastic barrel with her forefinger to get rid of the bubbles. Then she turned to Reva and signaled that the drug was ready, should we decide to use it. Reva gazed at the monitor. The squiggles of ventricular fibrillation had dampened to an almost flat line before we started CPR. With the slightest bit of pressure, I heard a sickening crunch, as Reynolds's calcified ribs cracked like eggshells under the weight of my arms. "Not so hard," Reva scolded me. "We don't want to hurt her."

We went through the motions of a code, performing shallow chest compressions. After about ten minutes, Reva said, "Let's call it. Are we all agreed?" and the nurse and I nodded. We went out to the waiting room to talk to the family. "I'm sorry, but she didn't make it," Reva told them matter-of-factly. "We tried but we could not resuscitate her." The children stared at us blankly. The son who had insisted on heroic measures walked out, taking out a cell phone.

A few minutes later, he stopped me near the conference room. "What happened in there?" he asked pointedly.

My face flushed. "What do you mean?"

"I mean, was there a chance?"

"No," I replied. "There was no chance." Of that much I was certain.

He looked perplexed. "But I thought resuscitation meant that you could keep her alive indefinitely. Couldn't you have put her on a heart-lung machine?"

WHEN I ARRIVED in the ICU Monday morning to start the monthlong rotation, the team had already assembled in the conference room. There were two third-year residents, two second-years (including me), four interns, and a medical student. I had worked with some of them before, and despite my polemic against ICU medicine in the *Times* a few months back, they greeted me with friendly nods. I smiled nervously, aware that we were about to embark on an intimate adventure together. Sonia later told me that when she worked in the ICU, the women on her team developed such intense camaraderie that their menstrual periods got synchronized—in less than a month.

The attending physician was Omar Morales, the pockmarked Puerto Rican who was adored by the house staff for his teaching and for his blunt, if impolitic, opinions. If patients grimaced, he would tell them to smile. If they groaned, he would turn exasperatedly to the house staff and say, "Why is he doing that?" Once, when a patient with blood clots in her lungs didn't want her oxygen turned off, claiming to still be short of breath, Morales ordered us to turn it off anyway, saying she was just "addicted to the noise." Another time, I was told he referred to a patient as a cockroach because she had managed to survive yet another cardiac arrest.

When Morales arrived at eight o'clock that morning, we started our rounds. There was a patient with AIDS who had respiratory, kidney, and heart failure, and was also deaf, blind, and comatose. His brother, residents whispered, was keeping him alive to collect his Social Security checks. There was an unconscious woman with terminal leukemia whose family wanted to withdraw care, but her estranged husband, who reportedly had beaten her, wouldn't permit it. Another man had fallen off a bicycle and gone to an emergency room, where a doctor sent him home without checking for a vertebral fracture. Now he lay awake, paralyzed from the neck down, staring up at the ceiling.

The ICU, more than any other place in the hospital, was where sickness and tragedy converged. Of course, lives were saved, but most days it was suffused with death, family politics, and pain. In Robert Zussman's 1992 book *Intensive Care: Medical Care and the Medical Profession*, an ICU intern reported a dream. In it, he finds penguins in a basement. The birds need to be in a cold environment or they will die, so to save one, he takes it, puts it into a blender with some ice and turns the blender on. The penguin is suddenly floating in a slushy pool of blood. The intern wakes up. The dream's interpretation is clear enough: in the ICU, sometimes the cure is worse than the disease.

After rounds, we went back to the conference room to finalize patient assignments and delegate tasks. By the luck of the draw, I was assigned to be on call the first night.

IN THE EARLY AFTERNOON, I was paged. A man with HIV was in the ER after vomiting blood. I went down to see him. He was middle-aged, of slight build, with wide-set eyes and blotchy, old-man skin. His family was sitting with him. About three days earlier, they told me, he had developed a "sticking sensation" in his throat while eating solid foods. For the past two days, he had been retching frequently, vomiting about a cupful of blood at a time. Over the past twenty-four hours, despite several transfusions, his blood counts had continued to drop, raising concern that he was still bleeding internally. I pulled down one of his eyelids; the inside was almost gray, reflecting severe anemia.

The management of acute gastrointestinal bleeding is straightforward: two IVs, in case blood has to be transfused rapidly; a blood count every few hours; drugs to quench stomach acidity; and watchful waiting. Earlier in the day, an upper endoscopy, in which a flexible camera-fitted tube is passed through the mouth and into the stomach, had revealed several shallow gastric ulcers. One was "necrotic and friable," according to the report, and even though it was no longer bleeding, it had been cauterized for good measure. "If his condition remains stable," I told his family, "he can probably go home tomorrow." I told them to go have lunch while I arranged for a bed in the ICU.

Sitting down at the doctors' station, I stared at the code beeper on my waist. I knew it could go off at any moment. I averted my gaze, worrying that it might start ringing just by my looking at it. I glimpsed my reflection in a sliding glass door. Painted on my face was a sort of anxious half smile. Feathery black curls winged upward over my ears. (I needed a haircut.) Cold droplets periodically splattered against the side of my rib cage. A sensation of heightened alertness and unease coursed through me. I did not want to carry this responsibility.

I was still writing up my admission note when I heard the shouts. I saw residents running; then I heard more shouts. I stopped at the doorway of my patient's room as if I had hit a brick wall. My patient was bleeding, like a coffee-colored fountain, out of his nose and mouth. He was unconscious. A nurse was trying to sit him up to keep the fluid out of his lungs, but his head kept flopping backward. Blood dripped onto the floor. "Call a code," someone shouted.

People rushed in past me. His heart was beating, but he had no pulse. Someone started chest compressions. A nurse put an oxygen mask on him but it wouldn't seal properly, and every time she squeezed the bag to which it was attached, it made an ineffective grunt. "Who's running the code here?" someone asked.

"I am," I replied softly.

Someone asked me for my stethoscope. I stared at him blankly; his gloved hand swiped it off my neck, smearing blood on my green scrubs. Someone started putting in a central intravenous line without my instructions to do so. "He's HIV!" a nurse shouted, dispensing gloves and masks. An intubation tray appeared, and then someone was prying open my patient's mouth with a metal laryngoscope, trying to visualize the vocal cords while a nurse assisted him by suctioning blood clots to clear the field. Periodically their heads would lurch backward, like a boxer ducking a jab, as chocolate-colored mist splattered their face shields.

People were holding bags of saline over their heads and squeezing them into his veins. Nurses were getting orders to give drugs—epinephrine, atropine, sodium bicarbonate—but not from me. My code was running like clockwork. Without me. I felt like the host of a dinner party with nothing to say.

I tried to push myself, bark orders, do something—but the tip of my tongue quivered uselessly. A breeze was blowing through my mind, which had been expunged of all thought except for the belief that everyone was watching me, cataloging my every deficiency. As the code wore on, my disconnection from it became more complete, as I was forced, with the rest of the onlookers, to the periphery of the room. People in front of me were yelling out, "How much epi has he gotten?" "Which atropine is this?" "Did he get the bicarb push?" A nurse threw up her hands. "Who's running this code?" she cried. I remained silent.

Bags of blood arrived, and doctors in the pit discussed whether it would transfuse quicker through an IV or a central line. I didn't know the answer, but I found myself thinking about the conductance of fluid-filled tubes. My patient's nostrils were trickling like a faucet, leaking blood much faster than it could possibly go in. His heartbeat was slowing down: seventy . . . sixty . . . fifty . . . Blood was everywhere—on stethoscopes, socks, scrubs. I worried that someone would slip on the floor.

After thirty minutes, his heart stopped beating entirely. A surgeon proposed cutting open his chest and performing direct cardiac massage. No one said anything except for a surgical intern, who clapped his hands with glee.

Then, suddenly, I found my voice. "It's time to call it," I murmured.

"What was that?" the surgeon demanded, turning around.

I was surprised anyone had heard me. "I said it's time to call it," I repeated, forcing the words out a little louder.

"Let's just do it for the practice!" the surgical intern cried, his eyes darting back and forth between the surgeon and me.

Emboldened by the attention, I shook my head and said, "It's too much of an exposure risk." There were murmurs of agreement.

"You're the code leader," the surgeon said, stripping off his gloves, and just like that, people stopped what they were doing and started filing from the room.

The first and only decision I made in my first code was to stop it.

Afterward, I surveyed the damage: bloody gowns, test tubes, syringes, blood-soaked gauze, central-line kits and procedure trays torn open and discarded, towels, masks, gloves, needles, my stethoscope coated with blood—and a dead body. The blood on the floor had clotted. Custodians arrived to clean up before the family returned. I went to the bathroom to wash up, not sure what was making me feel worse: that the patient had died or that I had looked like such an incompetent in front of my colleagues.

When the family showed up about a half hour later, a social worker intercepted them at the double doors and led them to a private room. "Why? What's happening? What happened?" Since I had been the code leader, it was my responsibility to break the bad news. "He started bleeding after you left," I told his wife, who was perched nervously at the edge of a cracking-vinyl couch. "We did everything we could but we could not save him." I had been steeling myself for her response, but it was nothing like what I expected. Her wails reverberated through my mind for days.

code leader

The important thing is to make the lesson of each case tell on your
education. —SIR WILLIAM OSLER

S elf-destructiveness is a staple among patients in the ICU. Over
the course of my month there, we saw many patients—
alcoholics, anorexics, drug abusers—who had treated themselves with such disregard that their bodies were literally falling apart.
None more so than the old woman from Ecuador. She answered my
questions with a shrug of resignation, as if we were talking about the
price of beef or the inevitable loss of youth, not her breast cancer. Her
words and body language conveyed a clear message: it was no big
deal.

The tumors had sprouted on her left breast like mushrooms in a
dank forest: different shapes, sizes, colors. A couple of them were
nodular, like little thumbs pushing up against intact skin. One had
cracked open, like an overripe plum. Two were covered with pink
granulation tissue, a sign of wound repair. The oldest one glistened,
reflecting the jaundiced hospital light off its smooth surface. The sight
of them eating away at her breast was as ghastly a thing as I had ever
seen.

But the old woman didn't seem to mind. As they were mostly on
the underside of her breast, she claimed not to notice them, even
though they stained her clothes and the crucifix hanging from a chain

around her neck with bloody discharge. She had obviously grown used to their rancid odor.

She would turn over every morning to let me examine them. *What was it she saw when she looked at them?* I wondered. What inside her— fear, ignorance, madness—had allowed this to happen? I thought of the words of the doctor in Aleksandr Solzhenitsyn's *Cancer Ward*: "Why didn't you come earlier? Why come here when you were practically a corpse?"

In the annals of denial, the old woman's history was not so unusual. When she, a former registered nurse, first felt a lump several years earlier, cancer apparently didn't occur to her. The lump grew to the size of a Ping-Pong ball before she showed it to a doctor—and then only because she was already at a clinic accompanying a sick friend. At the time, it was painless and surrounded by healthy tissue. If it had been removed then, in an early stage, and she had received radiation and hormonal treatment, she probably would have had a 50 percent chance of cure. But a biopsy proved inconclusive, she said, and she was all too ready to forget about the problem. She left America soon afterward for her native Ecuador, where her terminally ill husband had wanted to go to die. While there, she claimed, the tumor shrank and disappeared.

When she returned to America two years later, fronds of tumor were beginning to sprout from her breast. Soon they began to ulcerate and give off a foul smell. She went to an herbalist, who prescribed an assortment of creams. For a while the tumors seemed to regress with the application of the ointments, but then they grew quickly, breaking through her skin. Friends and family insisted that she see a doctor, but she ignored them. The tumors discolored her blouses, but she ignored that, too. Several months later she developed severe pain where the cancer had metastasized to her hip. She took ibuprofen for months without relief, still refusing to see a doctor until the pain became unbearable. Then, when she heard the diagnosis of breast cancer, she said she was surprised.

Now the tumors had invaded through blood vessels. Sometimes

when the bandages were removed, arterial blood spurt forth. An oncologist—short, squat, imperious—took one look at the tumors and told the ICU team that there was nothing she could offer besides palliative chemotherapy. The cancer had spread to the bones and lungs; the old woman's breathing was becoming more labored; the end was surely near. "It's very bizarre," the oncologist told me later. "These women look at their breasts and it's like a shadow comes over their eyes. They don't see what we see."

All diseases provoke denial, but something about breast cancer drives some women to such extreme denial that when they first see a doctor, tumors are literally growing out of their breasts. The literature on the subject is vast and has been accruing for at least thirty years.

Exactly what provokes this response isn't clear, but studies have shown that fears of disfigurement, dependency, and death play big roles. A study of Nigerian breast cancer patients showed that fear of mastectomy was the most common reason for delays. Studies of American women have shown that a third or more who feel a breast lump do not seek help for at least three months. A family history of breast cancer has been linked to delay in seeking help.

In small doses, denial can have its advantages, mitigating severe anxiety and depression. (I had experienced this myself in the early days of internship, when I had denied my own misgivings about being a doctor until my crisis forced me to confront my true feelings.) But when denial extends more than a few months, it rapidly becomes harmful as tumors grow and spread.

I didn't want to be on call when the old woman finally had a respiratory arrest. How would we perform CPR? Where would we even put our hands? I told her about the option of palliative chemotherapy. It wouldn't be curative, but it might shrink the tumors, help her breathing, ease her pain. But she said she wasn't interested. "I'm not the type to worry because it's all up to God," she said, fingering her crucifix. "It always was and always will be. So why should I worry?"

But unfortunately for the old woman, there were no miracles in the ICU that month. After a couple of days, the oxygen tension in her blood dropped and she was put on a pressurized ventilation mask. It dug deeply into her face, making her appear even more uncomfortable. One afternoon, I visited her in her room. She was in severe distress. The base of her neck had become a scalloped-out triangle as she hungrily sucked air into her lungs. A miniature Bible with an orange cover was resting on the pillow beside her. She tried to talk but the words were muffled. I handed her a pen and clipboard, and she scrawled on it with her left hand. (Her right, dominant, hand was incapacitated because of a blood clot.)

"How long?" she scribbled. I said that I didn't know.

She signaled for me to remove the mask. I undid the straps around the back of her head, and the sound of leaking oxygen filled the room. "What am I—?" She stopped, unable to continue. I pressed the mask back on her face. She took a few breaths and directed me to take it off again.

"What am I—going—?" The mask went back on. Tears were streaming down her cheeks.

We tried again. "What am I going—to do—?" she pleaded.

"We can give you chemotherapy," I said, my heart heavy. "It will shrink the tumors so you will be able to breathe a little—"

She raised her hand, signaling for me to take the mask off again.

"—today!?"

"What are you going to do today?" I said. She nodded, sobbing. My own breath quickened. How could she not have known that it would end this way? "You are going to lie here. You are going to let us give you medicine. The cancer in your lungs is making it hard to breathe, so—"

She shook her head, her face contorted by grief. The mountain of denial was collapsing in a landslide. "What am I going to do—today?" she pleaded again.

I had nothing left to say. I sat with her awhile but soon I had to go.

She signed a DNR form later that afternoon. A couple of days later, she had a respiratory arrest. No code was called.

"DO YOU WANT TO KEEP EATING, even if it means dying of pneumonia?" That was the question I posed to Mr. Caner as he consumed the rest of his lunch. "Yes," he replied without hesitation.

A wizened seventy-seven-year-old with fiery eyes, he had been admitted to the hospital short of breath. Initially it wasn't clear why. Except for a stable manic-depressive condition for which he was being treated, he seemed healthy. He did not smoke and had no cough. Though his breath sounds were coarse, there was nothing suggesting asthma, pneumonia, congestive heart failure, or other common causes of breathlessness.

His chest X-ray gave it away. Littering both lung bases were opaque speckles that looked like shards of glass. It turned out to be barium, a metal used to expose internal organs on X-rays.

But why was it in his lungs? He said he had undergone a barium-swallowing test a few months earlier when doctors suspected he was aspirating food into his lungs. To rule out esophageal narrowing, a common cause of swallowing difficulties, he ingested barium and had X-rays. Some of it accidentally went down his lungs, and stayed there.

His breathing trouble, I suspected, was caused by intermittent aspiration of barium, food, or whatever else. I told him he should strictly regulate his diet, avoiding thin liquids that are easily aspirated. He would have to eat sitting up, and in small bites. But he said he had already found such a diet too burdensome.

When a person swallows, both voluntary and involuntary mechanisms ensure the food ends up in the stomach and not the lungs. First, the tongue pushes the chewed-up food to the back of the throat, where sensory receptors cause muscles in the pharynx to contract. As the muscles tighten, the epiglottis, a flap of cartilage, flexes protectively into place over the larynx, preventing food from entering the windpipe. The food is propelled into the esophagus, where contractions usher it down to the lower esophageal sphincter, which allows entry into the stomach.

Several things can disrupt this reflex. Cancer or blockages can narrow the opening so that food does not pass easily to the stomach but backs up in the pharynx, where it can be aspirated into the lungs. Muscular dystrophy and other muscle disorders can paralyze the pharyngeal muscles. Neurological dysfunction, too, from nerve diseases like polio and Lou Gehrig's disease, or brain disorders like Alzheimer's dementia or strokes, can disrupt the complex signaling.

The reason for Mr. Caner's swallowing trouble wasn't obvious. A brain scan revealed no strokes. There was no esophageal constriction. Nerve studies were normal. In the end, we were faced with a condition we could neither explain nor treat very effectively. The safest treatment was to stop him from eating and insert a feeding tube. It seemed the only surefire way to prevent him from aspirating and getting repeated pneumonia and developing respiratory failure. But he so loved to eat— it was one of the few remaining pleasures in his life. He even raved about the hospital food. I presented the option of a feeding tube to him. He said he wasn't interested. It was too high a price to pay, even for a longer life.

One night a nurse called to tell me that Mr. Caner had choked on his dinner. When I saw him, his breathing was labored and he looked miserable. A chest X-ray showed a new "infiltrate" in the right lung, where the pea soup, sliding down his windpipe, had finally come to rest. I ordered IV antibiotics, supplemental oxygen, and a dose of steroids, and in a few hours his breathing and blood gas concentrations had improved. But I knew that it was only a matter of time before he aspirated again.

After discussing it on rounds the next morning, the team decided to make him NPO—"nil per os," or nothing by mouth—and schedule the insertion of a feeding tube. I felt conflicted about this. It was our duty to protect him—perhaps even from himself—but there seemed something barbaric about not allowing him to eat. He had no family, few friends, and no hobbies. Some mornings his only complaint was not being able to eat fast enough. In medicine, I had learned, there is often a fine line between the barbaric and the compassionate.

The following night, a nurse paged me to tell me that Mr. Caner had aspirated again. Somehow, even though his diet orders had been rescinded, he had obtained a dinner tray, and while gulping whipped potatoes, he had become acutely short of breath. When I saw him he was wheezing again and his blood oxygen tension was dangerously low. His chest X-ray showed yet another infiltrate—it even looked like a smear of mashed potatoes—at the base of the right lung.

Security was tightened. Signs were posted reminding the staff of his NPO status. Food delivery people were given strict instructions not to enter the room. At first Mr. Caner appeared to take the restrictions in stride, but after a few days of emulsified feeds through a nasogastric tube, he became mute and distant. "Why are you here?" he'd say when we made rounds, curling up in a fetal posture, pulling the blanket up to his chin.

On the morning the feeding tube was supposed to be inserted, I snuck into his room. I brought a couple of small juice cups with me. "Drink this," I urged, handing him a six-ounce carton. Without a word, he took a sip. "Try again," I said, ready to slap the cup out of his hand if he started choking. This time he drained the carton. Giddy, I handed him a piece of bread. He chewed it to extinction without coughing. Elated, I offered him other foods, all swallowed successfully. His swallowing trouble had somehow abated! Perhaps he had willed himself to get better, and just in time, too; transporters were on the way to take him to the operating room. That morning I wrote in the chart that Mr. Caner had passed a swallowing evaluation. It was supposed to have been conducted by a trained occupational therapist, but I had just done it myself. I had risked his getting aspiration pneumonia—risked his life, really—out of pity, sentiment, but the outcome seemed to have been worth it. I wrote an order to start an aspiration-type diet. I called the gastroenterology team and canceled the feeding tube. No one objected. By then I think everyone realized that a feeding tube was going to kill him a lot faster than aspiration ever would.

THE DAYS IN THE ICU ROLLED ON. "We changed the artificial tears from twice a day to three times a day," an intern quipped on rounds one morning, describing the treatment plan for a comatose patient. I perfected my technique for inserting central lines, even supervising the interns on a few. One afternoon I performed a lung tap with the ICU fellow. The patient was a frail elderly man with bad, cyst-ridden lungs. I knew what had happened as soon as I pulled back on the syringe and got nothing but air: a partial collapse of the lung. The patient had to have a tube inserted through his ribs to evacuate the air. I felt bad; I probably shouldn't have done the tap. There was no reason for me to do it; the fellow could have done it much better than me. But I had to learn.

Most of the patients we had started the month with were gone. The paralyzed Russian man with the raccoon eyes was transferred to a rehabilitation facility. A young woman with severe brain damage developed sepsis and died. The plastic surgery fellow had tended to her bedsore, slicing away dead tissue like a butcher, deeper and deeper, until white bone was visible, but eventually it got infected, leaking bacteria into her bloodstream and causing her demise. Even the woman with terminal leukemia finally had her ventilator turned off. For weeks her family had maintained steady pressure on her estranged husband. "I respectfully request you to stop life support," her father wrote in an appeal placed in the chart. "My daughter trusts her family to act in her behalf to do what she would want. She would not want her body maintained with life support. I am asking that she be allowed to go in peace."

Her brother added: "We had an uncle that died in the hospital when we were young children. We talked about how he looked on that machine, and we said that we would never want to look like that. I've known my sister for many, many years. She did not like having to ask for assistance but was always there to assist. If she knew she was being supported this way, she would be extremely unhappy."

In the end, her husband relented. "I now doubt that my wife will be able to sustain the meaningful life which she always lived," he wrote in a note that was cosigned by a notary public. One afternoon, she was put on a morphine drip and her breathing tube was removed. At first her breaths were rapid and shallow, but they quickly turned deep and sonorous, a sign of imminent death. About fifteen minutes later, they stopped altogether.

But one patient lingered on. Curtis Williams had as torturous a medical history as any patient I had ever encountered: AIDS, syphilis, hepatitis C, pneumonia, infective endocarditis, kidney failure, and cirrhosis. He was also blind, deaf, and brain-damaged from a bout of meningitis. He had been hospitalized with a blood infection, likely from an infected dialysis catheter, and despite intravenous antibiotics, his condition had deteriorated. He eventually developed respiratory failure requiring the insertion of a tracheotomy tube in his throat. On rounds, when nurses changed his bedsheets, the ravages of his many life-threatening diseases appeared in excruciating view. Mouth wide open in an impossibly wasted face, he looked like he was emitting one long, continuous wail.

He had a cardiac arrest on the one call day I happened to be fifteen minutes late to work. "Cardiac team, 5-South . . . Cardiac team, 5-South . . ." the intercom blared. *Goddammit!* I shouted in my head. What were the chances of a code occurring between seven and seven-fifteen? I raced down the corridor, spilling my coffee into a brown paper bag, which got warmer and wetter with every stride.

It was the moment I had been waiting for since the debacle of my first code in the ER that first day on call. I had practiced for it, committing the resuscitation protocol to memory. At night in bed I had envisioned various code situations: ventricular fibrillation, bradyasystolic arrest, pulseless electrical activity. I had mastered everything else as an ICU resident. I had gotten the hang of inserting Swan-Ganz catheters and interpreting hemodynamic data. I felt comfortable managing a ventilator. I could even intubate on occasion. I was doing a competent job supervising interns and medical students. But running a code was a skill that eluded me. It was a rite of passage, seemingly the last major hurdle in my education. I had to prove to myself that I could master it before moving on.

When I arrived in the room, the code team was in its usual positions. An intern was squeezing oxygen from a balloon into the tracheotomy tube, while another was performing chest compressions. "He needs a central line," Paulie, a third-year resident, called out, and almost immediately a resident pulled open a triple-lumen catheter kit and started pouring brown antiseptic soap onto the groin. "Glad you could make it," Paulie said when he saw me. He was a wise guy from the Bronx with an affected macho bravura. People called him a code monkey because he liked coming to codes, even when he wasn't on the code team, which he wasn't that morning.

I stared at the monitor. Tiny squiggles were meandering across the screen. Ventricular fibrillation. "How many shocks has he gotten?" I asked. "Just one," someone said. Defibrillator pads were affixed to his chest, charged up and ready to go. "All clear," an intern announced. Everyone took a step backward, she pressed a red button and Williams's whole body hiccupped. I looked at the monitor. Still fibrillation. "Push a round of epi and lidocaine," I said to no one in particular.

"God, are we really going to do this?" a nurse said, shaking her head in disgust. I did not respond. This was my code, and I had something to prove.

The rhythm briefly normalized, but after a minute it degenerated once again into ventricular fibrillation. "All right," I called out. "Epi, lido, amiodarone. Epi first."

"I think I blew the line," someone said, holding a giant syringe of sodium bicarbonate.

"So put in another one," I commanded, surprised at how easy it was to issue the order.

Then Paulie spoke up. "You, Manetta"—she was still doing chest compressions—"tell us when you need a break, and you"—he pointed to an intern who was standing and watching—"take over. You"—he pointed to another intern—"continue bagging. You finish getting that line in. What's taking so long? You over there, help him. I want every-one who doesn't need to be here to leave," he announced like a drill sergeant. "And keep it down. I can't hear myself think." His tone was crisp and forceful. The coup was smooth and bloodless. I did not resist it.

Paulie ordered injections of calcium gluconate, sodium bicar-bonate, and epinephrine. The EKG continued to show disorganized electrical activity. "He's still fibbing," Paulie bellowed. "Charge the machine." Williams's whole body jumped as electrical current dis-charged into his chest.

Someone said he thought he felt a pulse but he couldn't be sure. "Check the blood pressure," Paulie shouted. An intern wrapped a cuff around the arm and placed the bell of a stethoscope at the crook of the arm. "I'm not getting it," he said nervously.

"Get me a Doppler probe," Paulie cried. "We need a blood pres-sure." He waited for about three seconds. "Hello! I need a Doppler probe in here!"

"We need to run and get it," a nurse said, looking annoyed. Paulie made a face. "Is the bicarb in? Hello! Is it in?"

The person who was pushing medications into the central line said, "I just pushed it. We need a flush."

"You heard the man, get him a flush!" Paulie shouted. "Watch the needles, guys. There are too many hands in the field." He grabbed an errant needle and plunged it into the mattress. It was the sort of im-petuous, decisive behavior I seemed incapable of. A thought passed through my mind like an evanescent gust: *Will this mattress be reused?*

More drugs went in as I silently looked on. I resented Paulie for usurping my authority, but at the same time I felt relieved. At one point Williams regained a weak pulse, but it quickly disappeared. "Want another round of epinephrine and atropine?" I asked softly. Paulie looked at me askance. He didn't want suggestions; he wanted people to do as they were told. With fluid running into several IVs, he ordered escalating doses of epinephrine. Soon people started murmur-ing, "How long has it been? When did we start?"

"Hold compressions," I finally said, staring at the monitor. Wide electrical complexes raced across the screen. "Ventricular tachycardia," I said. "Get the paddles ready."

"That's not ventricular tachycardia," Paulie cried, squinting at the screen. "That's electromechanical dissociation!"

The squiggles looked like a sine wave with plenty of noise. "It's VT," I murmured.

"No it's not," Paulie shouted. "It's EMD. That is not a shockable rhythm!"

An intern was standing tiptoe on a step stool, waiting for the order to shock or not. Doubt started creeping into my mind. What was EMD? How were you supposed to distinguish it from slow VT? How was it treated? Atropine? Epinephrine? The confidence was draining out of me quickly. I found myself wondering what people in the room were thinking. What kind of impression was I making in my second attempt as code leader?

Then I turned to Paulie. "Who's running this code?" I snapped. I turned back to the intern. "Give him the shock." She hesitated. "Give the shock," I insisted. An alarm sounded, and Williams's body jumped up and down as the defibrillator discharged into his chest. On the monitor, the blips narrowed. Sinus tachycardia. A picket fence. A normal rhythm.

A resident had his hand wedged into the groin. "Pulse . . . pulse . . . pulse," he yelled out. A trembling relief washed over me. This time, the pulse did not go away.

Before the code team dispersed, Paulie went on a rant. "This was the worst code I've ever seen," he bellowed. "You guys are shocking EMD! You're not doing proper chest compressions." He put one hand over the other and pumped up and down to demonstrate how it should be done. "This poor guy will be lucky if he doesn't lose the two neurons he has left." I glared at him but did not say anything. Williams was alive, after all. I had made the right call, and I had done my job.

After ordering an intern to ventilate Williams with an oxygen bag,

I went out to the nurses' station to call Williams's brother. I had never met him. In fact, I had never even spoken with him.

When he answered the phone, I told him that his brother had had another cardiac arrest. I explained that the high potassium level in his blood, a consequence of kidney failure, had probably been the cause. "We revived him but he is obviously in critical condition," I said. "Will you be coming to the hospital to see him?"

"I can't come today," he replied.

"Well, when you do come in, would you please ask a nurse to page me? I'd like to talk with you about your brother's long-term plan."

"What plan?" he asked suspiciously.

"I'd like to talk face-to-face, if possible."

"Let's talk now."

"All right, if you prefer—" I hesitated. "I just wanted to know . . . Has anyone talked to you about DNR?" I knew the subject had been brought up, but I couldn't think of a better way to get the conversation started.

"We're not talking about that again!" he said fiercely.

"I'm sorry, sir, but we need to talk about it because your brother just had a cardiac arrest."

"I told the doctors before; I want everything done to keep him alive."

"That's fine; we can do that, but—" I decided to try a line I had heard Dr. Morales himself once use. "Some people think that when the heart stops beating, it's like the person is already dead. I'm not saying we won't treat him. I'm just talking about not trying to revive him again if his heart were to stop or if—"

"Who do you think you're talking to?" he interrupted angrily. "You're trying to bullshit a bullshitter."

"I'm not trying to bullshit you," I replied. "Your brother is terminally ill. Continuing to resuscitate him won't prevent his death. It's just torturing him for no good purpose."

"You guys have been trying to make me kill my brother for years.

Curtis wanted to live for as long as possible. 'Don't let me die,' he told me. Now how am I supposed to go against his wishes?"

"Do you think he'd still feel that way if he could express himself now?"

"It doesn't matter," he snapped. "It's what he told me. Look how many times you guys thought he was gone and then he turned the corner. He'll surprise you. I'll count him out when they pull the sheet over his head."

"Sir—"

"Put him on a heart-lung machine if you have to. I don't want his blood on my hands." Then he hung up.

That afternoon, I found Dr. Morales at the nurses' station writing notes. I told him about my conversation with Williams's brother. I asked him if we were going to have to resuscitate Williams again in the event of another cardiac arrest. I did not want to be involved in another code on him.

"He's Dr. Batton's patient," Morales said defensively. "She should have made him DNR years ago. Now we're at the mercy of that nut brother."

"Can't we still make him DNR?" I asked. I had read somewhere that two physicians could issue a DNR order against a family's wishes if they thought further resuscitation attempts were going to be futile.

"It isn't easy," Morales said gravely. "There are very strict criteria."

"What about taking him to court?"

Morales replied that the courts, with their adversarial approach, were not the right place to resolve these kinds of disputes. "Call Dr. Batton and see what she has to say," he suggested.

Some primary care doctors regularly came to the ICU to see their patients, but Dr. Batton wasn't one of them. When I called her, she said she had tried talking with Williams's brother on many occasions, but he had been equally intransigent with her. When I asked her about issuing a DNR order over the brother's objections, she suggested I speak with the hospital's legal department.

When I called that department, a staff member told me that two physicians could issue a DNR on the basis of futility, but that the definition of futility was very narrow. Two physicians had to agree that even if the patient were resuscitated, he would still die imminently. "In our experience, it's hard to get two physicians to agree to that," she said.

She added that the only way to withdraw medical care from a patient without decision-making capacity was at the behest of the patient's health care proxy—and then only if there were clear evidence of the patient's prior wishes. There was no way to withdraw care on "moral grounds"—for example, on the argument that a patient has no quality of life. "The department is very concerned about imposing medical judgments against a family's wishes," she said.

Over the next couple of days, Williams made no spontaneous movements. He remained unresponsive to painful stimuli. He made no spontaneous respiratory efforts. He had no gag or corneal reflex. His deep tendon reflexes were completely absent. A couple of nights later, he had another cardiac arrest when I wasn't in the hospital. This time, an intern nearly got stuck with a needle during the resuscitation. The next day, I heard Morales talking on the phone with the legal department. "This patient is a high exposure risk," he said, seething with frustration. "We can't keep resuscitating him. Someone is going to get stuck with HIV."

Because Williams was still in a coma, Morales decided to perform an apnea test. In this test, the ventilator would be disconnected to see if Williams made any effort to breathe on his own. If not, he could be declared brain-dead and be removed from life support. When Morales placed a call to Williams's brother to explain the purpose of the test, the brother hung up.

The following afternoon, Williams was hyperventilated for ten minutes and the ventilator was disconnected. After a few minutes, a blood gas measurement showed a precipitous rise in the carbon dioxide level, signifying severe acid buildup. Despite this powerful respiratory stimulant, Williams did not take any spontaneous breaths. After

several minutes, the ventilator was reconnected and the test was repeated, with the same result. Morales tried calling the brother to in-
form him of the results, but the line was busy. When he asked an
operator to intervene, he was told that the phone was off the hook. An
emergency telegram was sent.

Now we could act, but Morales wanted to move cautiously. He
asked for a note from Patient Services ratifying the decision to withdraw life support. A representative from that department came by and
wrote that it was "clinically inappropriate and disrespectful" to continue to resuscitate Williams. Morales himself wrote that Williams's
condition was "hopeless" and that further cardiopulmonary resuscitation would be "futile." Morales even called a neurologist to perform a
confirmatory apnea test. Nigel Caldwell had a crisp British accent and
a sharp, decisive manner. In the ICU, he was known as the executioner.
After evaluating Williams, he wrote: "The patient has failed the apnea
test. He has had three cardiac arrests. It is inappropriate to resuscitate a
patient who has failed test #1→ it goes against the natural course of illness."

He performed another test anyway. This time, Williams's carbon
dioxide level rose to ninety, more than twice normal. After ten minutes,
he had still made no attempt to breathe. The doctors watched for an
awakening, but there was none. At seven-fifteen in the evening, he was
finally declared dead. His brother declined an opportunity to view the
body.

ON MY LAST WEEKEND in the ICU, I rounded with Isaac Sweeney. Dr.
Sweeney was a portly, avuncular attending physician with a mischievous grin. Despite the miseries of the ICU, he always maintained a relentlessly upbeat manner.

It was a brilliantly sunny day, perfect weather for sailing. Midway
through long, protracted rounds, Sweeney called us over to a window.
He pointed down at a sailboat on the river. A man was standing on
the deck, looking up at the hospital. He looked like he was about

Sweeney's age, though fit and tan. He was holding a drink, and a party was going on onboard. "See that guy?" Sweeney said. "Do you know what he's thinking?"

No one ventured a guess.

"He's thinking, 'I should have been a doctor.' "

Before I left, I surveyed the unit one last time. I had seen so much over the past month; things I had never seen before, that I had never expected to see. I had changed. And yet I was leaving the place essentially as I had found it.

gentle surprises

The most essential part of a student's instruction is obtained, as I believe, not in the lecture room, but at the bedside.

—OLIVER WENDELL HOLMES

The monthlong rotation in the ICU was a turning point. Like a
phase transition, the transformation was almost impercepti-
ble, yet the results were striking. When I got back to the wards
I discovered a level of comfort I could never have imagined as an intern, or even early on in my second year. I was actually looking forward to going to the hospital each morning—devising a plan for my
patients, conferring with attending physicians, "running the list" with
my interns, holding teaching rounds with medical students ("That's
your differential? Major depression? What about autoimmune disease,
vasculitis, tuberculosis, lymphoma . . . ?"). New admissions no longer
generated armpit-drenching anxiety. Palpitations and dizziness? No
problem. Altered mental status in the setting of prostate cancer? I could
handle it. Of course, I was following established protocols, but it was
becoming clear to me that clinical medicine wasn't just cookbook algo-
rithms, as I had once imagined. There was a discretionary element to it
that could not be captured in a flow chart or a decision tree. It was a bit
like chess: the openings had long been worked out, but you could still
improvise. As a doctor, how you talked to your patients, guided them,

advocated for them, was up to you. That was how your personality could be expressed.

Ward rounds in the morning were a mad dash with my interns and students in tow. With usually twenty or more patients to see, the visits were mostly flybys during which I would interrogate patients about their symptoms and overnight course while my interns scribbled down tasks for the day: "consult Psychiatry," "curbside Renal," "check sodium at 4:00 p.m.," "inject urokinase into loculated pleural effusion." We got adept at getting in and out of patients' rooms quickly, efficiently, not making them feel like we were dismissing their complaints but really saying and doing very little at the same time. Each case had a teaching point, so most mornings I had my medical students prepare a topic to discuss on rounds: lupus pneumonitis, lithium toxicity, cortisol stimulation testing, respiratory stuff. After almost a year and a half of residency, I no longer felt insecure about the gaps that remained in my knowledge base. The set of unknowns was shrinking, and the fact that there was still so much to learn actually energized me. Ignorance was no longer the bugaboo it had once been. It now served the opposite function: it gave me hope.

There was that time in the early evening when patients were settling into bed, watching television, when I felt the most comfortable; that was when I felt the hospital was a village, and I most enjoyed making my rounds. The lights were on; patients were fed, getting ready to turn in for the night. It was the best time to visit, the time in the day when you were least likely to encounter rancor or resistance. Patients had accepted their stay in the hospital—and so had I.

At the same time, I felt more relaxed with my resident colleagues, chatting with them in the corridors or commiserating with them over bagels and coffee at morning report. "Six-hitter last night," someone might say, and I would grin and empathize, proud to be a member of a clique that knew exactly what those words meant. (Admitting six patients in one night was quite a feat.) The struggles of ward life forged bonds—not friendships always, but a kind of intimacy that was accelerated by the daily grind. Finally, after so many years, I was beginning to feel connected—to the same people from whom I had previously felt so estranged.

I was also beginning to participate more in the social life of the hospital. Something as simple as running to the coffee stand with my interns after rounds became an activity I looked forward to intensely. One morning, Lane, a stocky Australian intern with long sideburns and a Captain America haircut, said to me: "This is the first time I've worked with people that I like. You're the first person above me that I haven't feared." Some nights I'd lay awake, smiling at a joke someone had made on rounds or recounting to Sonia the antics of a member of my team, like the medical student who did a great impersonation of a fat man with abdominal pain. At first I disapproved, but he was hilarious, and in the end I succumbed to the humor like everyone else. Doctors make fun of patients for many reasons. Sometimes as a defense mechanism, and sometimes just because they can. Though I was lapsing into some of the same behaviors I had once found objectionable, I rationalized it by telling myself that the job would suck if you didn't have fun with the people you work with.

One week, I was assigned to work the night shift in an emergency room in the South Bronx. The hospital, affiliated with New York Hospital, was in a neighborhood not far from where Son of Sam, the serial killer, started his murderous spree in 1976. Some nights when I was sipping coffee in the ambulance bay during my break, I could hear the rat-a-tat-tat of gunshots. In the emergency room, it was not uncommon to encounter drunks swinging at nurses, drug addicts shouting, and handcuffed prisoners under armed escort.

It was my job to try to drain excess fluid from the belly of a young woman with alcoholic cirrhosis. I hadn't done an abdominal paracentesis in over a year; the last time was on 10-North, when the catheter had fallen out of the patient with AIDS and I had almost stuck myself. This time, I set up my instruments carefully: catheter-tipped needle, rubber tubing, plastic buckets. When I was ready, I cleaned the woman's belly with iodine soap. She shivered; it was cold. Then I pierced her abdominal wall with the catheter and started filling the buckets. Midway through the third bucket, I got paged. "Whatever you do, don't move," I said to my patient, whose breath still smelled of alcohol. "I'll be right back." If the catheter comes out, I told her, I wasn't going to put it back in. She nodded. I left the room and stopped by the nursing station. "Just keep an eye on her while I'm gone," I told a nurse.

I was away for only a couple of minutes. When I returned, the buckets were upturned and puddles of liquid were all over the floor. The catheter was out, and the drain tube was coiled uselessly on the tiles. "I told you not to move," I said angrily, tiptoeing across the mess.

"I didn't," my patient replied unconvincingly. "A man came in here and had a seizure on the buckets."

Exasperated, I stalked out to the nursing station. "I thought I asked you to keep an eye on her," I said to the nurse.

"I did," she replied, "but then a man wandered into the room and had a grand mal seizure on the buckets."

Another night I was assigned to the midnight–4:00 a.m. shift in the "salon de asthma," a treatment room in the back of the ER. The hospital opened it in response to the mysterious rise in asthma in the Bronx, where the prevalence once was eight times as high as the national average. (Today it has declined, probably because of more vigilant monitoring and treatment.) Patients could walk in right off the street and get treated without unnecessary delay. The largest influx occurred at dusk when teenagers started filing out of neighborhood playgrounds and basketball courts and sought help for asthma attacks brought on by exercise.

In the large room, patients were sitting on purple chairs of cracking vinyl, inhaling a mist of albuterol, a drug to open airways, from plastic pipes connected to oxygen outlets in the wall. A nurse was there, administering medications and checking vital signs. "In the asthma room, the patients don't fight," she told me during a lull in the activity. "The tough guys are outside, the drunks. They always want to bite us, to cut us. Here it's different. Here everybody gets along."

The atmosphere actually was more like a party. At 3:00 a.m., two middle-aged men—one having his first asthma attack in twelve years, the other a "frequent flyer"—were in rapt conversation. A young woman—not wheezing, just "a little tight"—was walking in and out of the room, talking on her cell phone. Near the entrance, one of the patients, a fifty-two-year-old man, started doing a stand-up routine.

Dressed in jeans, a plaid shirt, and white sneakers, he delivered his lines in Spanish with Seinfeldian exasperation. His audience wheezed its approval. Between laughs, the patients translated for me. He was telling them about the time he was riding on the train, chewing gum. When he tried to spit the gum out the window, out flew his false teeth.

A sixty-four-year-old homemaker from the Bronx, a regular visitor to the asthma room, gasped for breath. "I can't believe it, he makes me laugh," she said, pausing to inhale after every few syllables. She tried to explain the story to me but the laughter overcame her. "I'm not used to it," she said, before putting the pipe back in her mouth. "I'm a serious person. I never joke."

Two seats away, a sixty-year-old man from Venezuela leaned forward in his chair and wiped away a tear. "When he got home, he covered his mouth," he translated. "When his wife finally noticed, she asked him, 'What happened to your teeth?' " Then the whole group laughed and coughed in unison.

I watched in quiet amazement. The ways people cope with illness always produce gentle surprises.

IN THE FALL I rotated through the geriatrics ward. One of the attending physicians was an irritating woman whose idea of the Socratic method was pimping you with really vague questions, then acting like she had already thought of whatever answers you gave and that you were only telling her what she already knew. The other attending was a throwback to "the days of the giants," when pneumococcal pneumonia was diagnosed by injecting sputum into mice and antibiotics for urinary tract infections were tested on agar plates. One morning, one of my interns presented a case to him of an elderly man who had been hospitalized with fever and a cough producing green sputum. "He has pneumonia," she proclaimed confidently. "Take a look at this chest X-ray." She pulled up a digital image on a computer screen showing a distinct pneumonic streak. The senior physician waved it off. "First tell me about your lung exam," he said.

It was a common scenario on the wards: young doctor ignoring physical examination to the chagrin of an older and wiser counterpart. At one time, keen observation and the judicious laying on of hands were virtually the only diagnostic tools available to a doctor. Now, on the wards, they seemed almost obsolete. Technology—ultrafast CAT scans, nuclear imaging studies, and the like—ruled the day, permitting diagnosis at a distance. Some doctors didn't even carry a stethoscope.

There was a growing disconnect between the older and younger generations of physicians on this issue. While residents were apt to regard physical examination as an arcane curiosity, like an old aunt you've been told to respect, a few physicians proselytized on its behalf, claiming for it a power it probably no longer has. These anachronisms wanted to hear about whispered pectoriloquy or some such esoteric finding of the lung exam before letting you describe the results of a chest X-ray. Our apathy seemed to fuel their fervor, increasing their fear that exam skills would atrophy and die.

"Medical students don't know how to listen for breath sounds," our attending complained. "It's not that they're bad students; it's just that no one is teaching them. When I was a resident, you had to know physical diagnosis because we didn't have any other tools. CAT scans were just coming out. You had to cut someone open to figure out what was wrong with them."

One morning I shared one of my favorite medical stories with my team. We had just finished examining an elderly woman with a cardiac rhythm disturbance when I mentioned that Karel Wenckebach, a Dutch physician at the turn of the twentieth century, discovered the arrhythmia later named after him by timing a patient's arterial and venous pulsations. Wenckebach's discovery preceded the advent of the EKG and still stands as one of the most astute clinical observations in the history of medicine. Isn't it amazing, I asked my team, what doctors were once able to do?

"Today we'd get an EKG," an intern shrugged. "It's more accurate anyway."

"Who has the time to stare at a patient's neck?" another said. "They'd think you were crazy!"

It is true that teaching hospitals are busier than ever, and residents probably have less time to spend examining patients. And it is true that physical examination is often inaccurate. But these facts only partly explain its apparent demise.

The major reason for it, I have come to believe, is that doctors today are uncomfortable with uncertainty. If a physical exam can diagnose a slipped spinal disk with only 90 percent probability, then there is an almost irresistible urge to get a thousand-dollar MRI to close the gap. Fear of lawsuits is partly to blame, but the major culprit, I think, is fear of subjective observation. Doctors today shy away from making educated guesses on the basis of what they see and hear. So much more is known and knowable than ever before that doctors and patients alike seem to view medicine as an absolute science, final and comprehensible. If postmodernism teaches that there are many truths, or perhaps no truths at all, postmodern medicine teaches quite the opposite: that there is an objective truth that will explain a patient's symptoms, discoverable provided we look for it with the right tools.

Of course, technology itself can be inaccurate, its results irreproducible. In the ICU, our catheters could often produce spurious data because of poor positioning. It wasn't uncommon for us to discard the information, pull out our stethoscopes, and make a clinical decision based upon what we saw and heard, not the numbers on the screen. Moreover, the readings always had to filter through our eyes and minds, where, inevitably, they were contaminated by the very subjectivity from which we were trying to escape.

Perhaps, then, this is the new role of the physical exam: helping doctors decide when to go beyond it.

IN DECEMBER, Dr. Wood invited me to his office for my semiannual evaluation. Sitting behind a large wooden desk, he handed me a manila folder. As residents, we were judged in seven categories: clinical judgment, medical knowledge, clinical skills, humanistic qualities, professional attitudes and behavior, medical care, and overall clinical competence. The ratings were on a scale from one to nine, with written descriptions for each scale, like "indecisive in difficult management situations" or "reasons well in ambiguous situations," "pedestrian diagnostic ability" or "establishes sensible differential diagnoses."

My evaluations were excellent, mostly sevens, eights, and nines across the board. I was credited with being a good manager and getting along well with my colleagues. One attending commended me for "not giving in to the urge to put down [my] patients." It was faint praise, and not entirely accurate, but from what I had seen over the past year and a half, I took it as a compliment.

Dr. Wood asked me about my plans after residency. Some of my classmates were already filling out applications for subspecialty fellowships. I told him I had been thinking about applying for a fellowship in cardiology, but that I hadn't yet made up my mind. "Why cardiology?" he asked, surprised. Judging from his tone, he didn't think it was a good fit. I muttered something about how cardiology had powerful therapies, a solid evidence base, a good mix of inpatient and outpatient work, etc., etc., but Wood appeared unconvinced. Those were personal-statement reasons, he said, reasons to give in a fellowship interview.

The real reasons were a bit more complicated. Part of it was family pressure. I had married into a family of doctors where one's standing was measured in part by one's degree of specialization, and cardiology was at the top of the list because of its prestige and high earning potential. In my own family, my mother wanted me to become a cardiologist so that I could work with my brother. She wanted us to be equal, to have the same capacity to enjoy things, which in her view meant having comparable salaries. Unwittingly, she had encouraged us to think about cardiology since we were boys. My brother and I had grown up with her dire warnings that my father would develop "heart failure" if we were too rowdy or didn't do our chores. We grew up with a fear of the heart as the executioner of men in the prime of their lives.

But a bigger reason for my interest in cardiology, which I didn't want to admit to Dr. Wood, a general internist, was that I had become disillusioned with primary care. In the outpatient clinic I was arranging colonoscopies, checking prostate-specific antigen levels, giving pneumonia vaccinations, and counseling smoking cessation—all important activities, to be sure, but not how I wanted to spend my professional life. There was so much to do in the clinic: disability forms, insurance letters, home-care orders, depression screens, cholesterol testing, mammograms, Pap smears. The physicians there seemed harried, overworked, and ours was an academic clinic with interns and residents, social workers and nurse practitioners, good clerical staff, and computerized medical charts. What to say of the real world, where ten- or fifteen-minute office visits were the norm? With decreasing reimbursement and increasing medical liability costs, the thought among my classmates, which I shared, was: Who needs the hassle?

General internists, my classmates whispered disparagingly, were jacks-of-all-trades, masters of none. There was an appeal to being able to focus on one area of medicine and do it well. I often thought of an experience I had had on the cancer ward. One morning, a nurse paged me during rounds. A patient with leukemia that had transformed into what was called *blast crisis* was in her room screaming. She had been on a morphine drip to control the severe pain in her bones, but her IV had fallen out. Could I come quickly and put in another one?

Her room was on a dingy ward in an old part of the hospital. When I got there, she was writhing, oblivious to my presence. A bag of morphine liquid hung uselessly from a metal pole near her bed. She said her legs felt as if they were going to explode. As a resident, I had been taught the importance of treating cancer pain aggressively, but until then it had just been a concept.

I told the nurse to give her an intramuscular morphine injection, but she said she already had, twice, with no effect. I grabbed an IV and jabbed it into the woman's arm, but because it was so swollen from cancer and chemotherapy, I couldn't find a vein. I tried repeatedly, in her arms and feet, deep and shallow, this way and that, desperately trying to draw back a red blush, but with no luck. Her shrieks were becoming more piercing as the morphine was running out in her body.

"Call the pain team!" I shouted.

When they arrived, they immediately gave my patient a shot of a very potent narcotic, which calmed her down. Then they put in an IV and started a morphine drip she could adjust for her own comfort. They also started her on a long-acting narcotic that was particularly effective for cancer pain. When I visited my patient a few hours later, she was sitting in a chair, watching television.

The situation was emblematic of ward medicine. So often the key was simply to know whom to call for help. If you couldn't interpret an EKG, you called the cardiology fellow. If he couldn't help you, you called the cardiac electrophysiology fellow. If you didn't know how to administer a cortisol stimulation test, you called the endocrinology fellow. Even for something as commonly encountered as pain, there were specialists who knew what to do. There was always someone, somewhere, who knew more about your problem than you did.

Subspecialty medicine had a kind of glory which I desired for myself, and I wasn't alone. Residents across the country were increasingly forgoing primary care for subspecialty practice, especially lucrative procedure-based ones like cardiology and gastroenterology. In fact, roughly a third of my class was applying for a cardiology fellowship.

"Be sure about what you want," Dr. Wood said gravely. He didn't seem to think that I was cut out to do a subspecialty. To him, I think, my interest in writing was evidence of my generalist tendencies. I appreciated his frank, forthright manner. He was all too aware of the many detours I had taken so far in my professional life. A cardiology fellowship was a bit like doing residency all over again. Was this really what I wanted?

I made the decision a few weeks later, when Sonia and I took a vacation to the seaside town of Mystic, Connecticut. I picked the spot randomly out of a *Weekend Getaways* book Sonia had given me after our honeymoon. Mystic is an old whaling and shipbuilding town surrounded by an almost incandescent beauty. That weekend, we went hiking through hills shimmering with the most brilliant colors: oranges and yellows and rust browns and maroon reds. We visited the seaport, where we toured the old sailing boats, tall-masted schooners and sharp-bowed clippers, which were preserved in a sort of museum on the docks. On a wooden deck, an old shipyard hand demonstrated to us the fine art of tying and untying knots.

It was a sorely needed break—our first vacation since our honeymoon, in fact. Internship had been tough on our relationship. During my depression, I had grown impatient, critical of the slightest delay. For a while Sonia and I had stopped talking, except when we were fighting, and even then we weren't talking as much as shouting and maintaining silence. On more than one occasion, I came home to find wet tissues wadded up in a big ball on the coffee table, along with a few half-smoked cigarettes. Sonia had gone to bed, angry and dissatisfied with my apologies.

But, fortunately, we had survived my internship. We were spending more time together, going out to concerts and dinners, talking more. The morning after we arrived, we took a long hike, climbing to the top of a vast clearing where we happened upon a meadow, brilliant with color. We sat down on a large rock, looking out over a valley.

"You're relaxed for the first time in a long time," Sonia said as we shared a bottle of water. "You're finally smiling."

I took in a deep breath of cold mountain air. I felt buzzed. Freedom, escape—I had almost forgotten how it felt.

As we sat up on the hill, I told Sonia I had decided to apply for a cardiology fellowship. For the first time in my professional life, I was happy. For as long as I could remember, I had carried a sense of dislo-

cation—in graduate school, in medical school, in internship. Now, finally, I felt like I was finding my place. Finally, I was using tools that
were mine, not borrowed. I had been longing for this moment for four
long years. It felt like a release, a rebirth after a long period of intern-
ment. The static in my brain was finally clearing. And when Sonia
leaned over and said, "You've come a long way. I'm very proud of
you," it felt all the more sweet.

CHAPTER TWENTY-ONE

fellowship

April is the cruellest month, breeding
Lilacs out of the dead land, mixing
Memory and desire, stirring
Dull roots with spring rain.

—T. S. ELIOT, *THE WASTE LAND* (1922)

By the time I got to Bellevue Hospital, it was early evening. On the main road, city buses and yellow taxicabs whizzed by as I climbed out of the subway. Tires crackled on the wet street, throwing up a dirty spray. Rainwater splashed out of potholes. I passed by a homeless shelter where, through a grimy window, I spied a line of disheveled men in a dimly lit room being watched over by security guards. The garden in front was overrun with weeds; the only movement was a couple of enormous rats scurrying ravenously through the garbage. This definitely was not the Upper East Side. No manicured lawns here.

The medical center was a vast complex of old brick buildings spanning several city blocks on First Avenue. The hospital itself was a twenty-five-story behemoth garnished with whorls of ivy. I marched down a concrete footpath, past a stone sculpture filled with brackish water, and entered a high-ceilinged atrium. Painted on the tan limestone walls were colorful murals of farmers picking tomatoes, holding rabbits, herding cattle—the agrarian life. The images seemed strangely out of place in such a hissing urban setting. At the security desk, an officer asked to see my ID. As I fumbled through my cotton scrubs for it, nervously trying to explain why I had come, he good-naturedly waved me in.

I marched down a long tiled hallway stained with footprints from the recent spring rains and got into an elevator going to the CCU. I had been here once before, last month, on a tour of the hospital on my fellowship interview day. That day, a dapper cardiologist with English-butler features had asked me if I was still interested in doing basic research. Since I had been told that Bellevue was looking for research-oriented fellows, I said yes. I said I was fascinated by the electrical properties of cellular ion channels, and I drew similarities between these structures and the quantum dots I had studied in graduate school. Of course, it was a ploy—I had no inclination to return to the research bench—but it was a competitive year, too. My Ph.D. had always been my trump card, and so I decided to play it again for all it was worth.

The cardiology "match list" was due in a week, and I still hadn't decided how I was going to rank the hospitals I had applied to, which is why I had come to Bellevue that evening to take a second look. In the match, applicants and fellowship programs submitted a rank-ordered list of names to the National Residency Matching Program (NRMP) in Washington, D.C., which paired them up by computer. The process was the same for residency, but now the stakes seemed higher because of the increased competition. For weeks my classmates had been discussing the optimal strategy for constructing a match list. Should you take into consideration where programs were going to rank you? Where should you put your "safety hospitals"? The official instruction from the NRMP was to rank programs based on personal preference alone, but lack of a clear understanding of the match process generated considerable anxiety and the sort of paranoia one might expect when neurotic, high achievers compete for a limited number of jobs. My classmates had been having hushed conversations in the corridors about where people were interviewing, who had received an unofficial offer, who was likely going to match at New York Hospital, and so on. I tried my best to avoid the gossip, but as the deadline for the match drew near, I was starting to get nervous, too.

My family had mostly rallied behind my decision to apply for a fellowship. In fact, Sonia had pushed me whenever my confidence wavered. Now that we were married, she wanted to know that I was on the right track. The ambivalence that had once seemed charming to her was now worrisome. On the phone, whenever I had second thoughts, my mother would say: "Nothing is too difficult for you. Are you saying that everyone can do this, and my son cannot?" My father, though proud, had warned me about the tremendous effort a fellowship was going to require. "I hardly need to repeat that there is no substitute for hard work," he intoned. "It is work that sustains us." Rajiv, on the other hand, had seemed underwhelmed, even a bit apprehensive. "You've got to get your act together if you want to do cardiology," he had lectured. "It's time to stop being immature and focus. You can't live with your head in the clouds your whole life."

In early March I had received a letter from the chairman of the Department of Medicine at Bellevue. He said that his department was looking to expand its research efforts in cardiology and that he was looking forward to meeting me if I joined the program at his hospital. "He's offering you a spot," Rajiv declared knowingly when I showed him the letter, but I responded with my usual uncertainty. Though I wanted to stay in Manhattan for further training, I wasn't sure if I was ready to leave New York Hospital.

At the twelfth floor in Bellevue, the elevator doors opened and a teenage girl got on. Tall and pretty, she was whimpering softly, her long, dark eyelashes fluttering over impossibly large, bloodshot eyes and tearstained cheeks. When I asked her what was wrong, she broke down sobbing. *"Mi madre está muerta!"* she cried, as though I (in my green scrubs) were somehow responsible. I remained quiet, unsure how to respond. By the time the doors opened on the sixteenth floor, she was wailing. She got out of the elevator, turned left, then spun around to stare at me helplessly. Not knowing what to do, I reluctantly stuck out my hand as the doors were closing and stepped out.

The sixteenth floor was quiet, seemingly deserted, except for an elderly man with an IV pole talking on a pay phone. He eyed us suspiciously. The corridor smelled of cigarette smoke and antiseptic. I asked the girl where she was trying to go. "ICU!" she bawled. Apparently she had just learned that her mother had died. I put my hand on her shoulder and told her I would take her there. As we were leaving the elevator bank, a middle-aged man walked up. The girl broke free and ran to him, burying her head in his arms. Another man, about my age, also arrived. His arms were folded across his chest and his face was drawn; he regarded me skeptically. I shifted my weight uncomfortably as they embraced, trying to think of something to say. Nothing came to mind, and by now I had become inured to scenes of grief in the hospital. When the elevator doors opened again, I whispered, "I'm sorry," and jumped in. The older man raised his hand in gratitude. The family was still weeping in the hallway when the doors clanged shut. ICUs, it seemed, were the same everywhere.

In the elevator, I thought of what an intern had told me about Bellevue. The culture, the patient population, everything was very different than at New York Hospital. "The patients are indigent," she had said. "Residents perform most of the procedures. You know how it is: high autonomy, low liability."

The CCU fellow, an Indian woman with a toothy smile, was still writing her daily progress notes at 7:00 p.m. when I arrived—not a propitious sign for a prospective fellow. She flashed a quizzical look when I told her why I had come, but gave me permission to walk around. It was a twelve-bed unit with small sinks and a faintly third-world feel. Office chairs and old respiratory equipment were stacked untidily in a corner. The patients, mostly brown-skinned, were lying in sectioned-off spaces along a main wall. A fair number were intubated, and I was greeted with the familiar ringing of ventilator alarms. The view through the window was of a vast housing project and the slums of Alphabet City. The flowing waters of the East River had always provided succor on call nights at New York Hospital, and I felt vaguely sad that the view would not be transported with me if I came here.

From the CCU I started wandering around the hospital. I went up two flights to the prison ward. A guard was seated in front of an iron gate under a dingy sign that read PRISON HEALTH SERVICES, MEDICAL/SURGICAL UNIT. A group of cops was coming off patrol, stashing their revolvers in a padlocked metal box. Here, several years later, I was going to meet Robert Castillo, a small-time drug dealer, HIV-positive, hospitalized with another bout of endocarditis. The first, from shooting heroin, had destroyed one of his heart valves, requiring open-heart surgery to replace it with a pig valve. Now this pig valve was itself infected.

He was lying in the corner of a four-bedded room, not far from the toilet. The window was slightly open, though it was freezing outside; dried blood and grime stained the sill. The room, as usual, smelled like a pile of dirty socks. Castillo had been living with relatives in Staten Island before his intravenous drug habit landed him in jail. He was a frail man in his fifties with white hair and piercing narrow-set eyes, one of which had stopped moving normally. Doctors thought he had had a stroke but they didn't know why. An echocardiogram, an ultra-sound of the heart, provided the answer. Sitting on top of one of his heart valves was an infected mass of tissue—a *vegetation*—that was flapping around wildly, like a flag in the breeze. A portion of it had probably broken off and gone to his brain.

The echocardiogram also revealed an abscess, a collection of pus, around the valve. Few conditions in medicine absolutely require sur-gery, but this is one of them. Antibiotics cannot penetrate into an ab-scess because there are no blood vessels to deliver the drugs. Left untreated, it is bound to grow, eating away at surrounding tissue. In fact, the abscess had so weakened a portion of Castillo's heart that that part of his heart had turned into a thin-walled aneurysm, bulging out with every heartbeat. If the aneurysm ruptured, he would almost cer-tainly go into congestive heart failure and die.

Surgeons who had been consulted said that Castillo was too sick for surgery. It was going to be a complex operation, involving excision of the infected valve and a portion of the aorta, the major blood vessel emanating from the heart, and replacement with tissue grafts. Besides being a diabetic and a "re-op," Castillo had had a stroke and a recent bout of congestive heart failure. All that added up to a surgical mortality risk of about 50 percent. "I don't know whether it's ethical or unethical," the senior surgeon had said in turning down the case, "but in this day and age we are not rewarded for taking care of sick patients."

At the bedside, I asked Castillo how he was feeling. "I'm breaking up," he said softly. I took out my stethoscope. "Let's not do this here," he said. He led me down the hall, past a security guard, to the treatment room. He sat down on the exam table and took off his light blue pajama top. "Angela," the name of his mother, was tattooed above his left pectoral muscle.

His lungs sounded clear. His heartbeat was fast, but otherwise okay. "What's happening with the surgery?" he asked as I put away my stethoscope. I told him that the surgeons had decided not to operate. "Didn't they tell you?"

"Yes," he replied, "but it went in one ear and out the other." I looked away, frustrated.

"Listen, I'm sorry," he said. "I've had a problem with drugs all my life. It's hard for me to stop."

I asked him if there was anything he wanted me to do. "Yes, please find out when my mother is coming," he said. I told him I would ask his nurse to call. But back at the nursing station, the nurse said, "Give me a break. He can walk. He knows how to use the pay phone."

I sat down to write my progress note. Nearby, a surgical fellow and a second-year resident were having a heated discussion. The fellow was saying he knew Castillo had little chance of surviving without surgery, but that he didn't think an operation was going to change his long-term outcome. The resident replied that he was uncomfortable with doctors playing God.

"Look, we're not doing him again!" the fellow shouted. "He has an incurable disease. He is always going to shoot up. We don't operate on these people because they reinfect. You're going to expose the staff and the surgeons to this guy's blood, to HIV, for what? To treat an incurable disease?"

"What about people who really do want to stop doing drugs?" the resident countered. "Are you saying you're going to condemn someone to die?"

"This guy had a chance but he failed," the fellow said angrily. "Why should I take the risk to my family, to my child, because of him?"

"It depends on whether you view drug abuse as a personal failing or a real disease," the resident said.

"Whatever!" the fellow erupted. "He has himself to blame. I didn't put the needle in his hand."

The vague outlines of a memory started to form in my mind.

"He says he wants to stop doing drugs," the resident insisted. "He says he'll enroll in rehab."

"Look, we've worked with shooters," the fellow said, obviously frustrated by the resident's stubbornness. "They say whatever they're supposed to when they're in trouble. You can't trust them. Besides, you told me he wanted to go back to that hospital in Staten Island."

"I spoke to the Staten Island surgeon. His secretary left a message that he would not operate."

"See!" the fellow cried, throwing up his hands. "You can call anyone you want, but I can tell you right now that no one is going to do this surgery. A valve isn't like popping in a piece of bubble gum. You don't give a new liver to an alcoholic."

"Valves are not in limited supply. You could say livers are."

"Yes, but someone who's a recidivist!" the fellow shouted. "It's unfortunate but you reach a point where you have to develop some kind of policy."

And so it went, back and forth, for several more minutes. The memory I had was of Ira Schneider, the morbidly obese man I had taken care of on Ward 4-North when I was a second-year resident. So much had changed since I had advocated for Mr. Schneider to receive a bypass operation over the objections of his surgeons. At one time, I too had felt passion like this resident. I too had felt deeply disturbed by a surgeon's refusal to operate. Now, listening to this discussion, I wondered if the resident wasn't just a bit naive. It was a transformation that troubled me.

In some ways, I probably ended up becoming the kind of doctor I never thought I'd be: impatient with alternative hypotheses, strongly wedded to the evidence-based paradigm, sometimes indifferent (hard-edged, emotionless), occasionally paternalistic. Kind of like my brother. Early on in my training, I had unrealistic expectations of other doctors—and also of myself. I thought I was going to make big changes, more of an impact, reform the profession somehow, but in the end I adapted to the culture around me. I came to accept the workings of the hospital and of my colleagues. I became less judgmental—of doctors, not patients (there was a time when it had been the other way around)—and more forgiving of, more faithful to, my guild. Medicine, I learned, is a good profession, not a perfect one—and there are many ways it could change for the better—but most of its practitioners, like my brother, my wife, my classmates, were fundamentally good people trying to do good every day. Sure, there were doctors who were only interested in making a buck, who didn't approach each case thoughtfully, but thankfully they were in the minority. Most doctors really did want to care for their patients in the right way.

I have often thought of the conversation Rajiv and I had when I toured the ICU in San Diego just before I decided to apply to medical school. I had accused him of insensitivity after a remark he made about a dying patient. "So you'll be a different kind of doctor," he shrugged. "Once you get out of the ivory tower."

In the end, I probably fell short. Once I embraced my profession, my behavior naturally grew more aligned with that of my colleagues. I wasn't strong enough to change the culture, or even to resist its embrace. For most of internship, I had been tormented by an ideal, which

I had to get rid of in order to survive. All my life, if things weren't perfect, I was apt to dissect, try to find larger meaning; if I wasn't perfect
every moment of my life, then I was nothing. I had to let go of that
to be free, let go of the past, the missteps, and the false starts. In my
weaker moments, I often told Sonia with regret that I had become a
different doctor than the one I originally wanted to be. "You're nice,
you're caring," she'd reply sympathetically. "Your patients love you."
Her words, automatic, provided some solace, but I still often wished
that I had held on to my earlier ideals.

From the prison ward I walked through the cardiac catheterization
suites, where I would spend a lot of time over the next few years, and
then I went downstairs and exited the building. It was getting to be
dusk. The sidewalk outside Bellevue was like an enormous Jackson
Pollock painting, splattered with the most mysterious splotches. The
faint light streaming through the cloud formations was an allegory of
what my life had been as a resident: bleak, but always with a glimmer
of hope to remind me of why I was here.

Near the ER I ran into the CCU fellow, who was waiting for a
friend. "How was your tour?" she asked pleasantly. "Good," I replied.
Bellevue was very different from New York Hospital, but I was beginning to wonder if I wouldn't benefit from a change. The fellow invited
me out to talk some more about the program, but I politely declined.
The evening was temperate, and I wanted to walk home alone.

My shadow stretched long across the concrete squares. The landscape appeared surreal, almost two-dimensional, like it had been
painted onto a canvas. I ambled past delicatessens and parking structures, past the UN Building, whose green-tinted face rose to the sky
like a giant domino about to topple over, and through midtown, where
the office buildings shimmered like black jewels. Each block was like a
tableau on a filmstrip, with some unseen force turning the reel. I marveled at the swirl of humanity on the streets: teenagers riding skate-
boards, young urban professionals carrying briefcases, pretty blondes
in wraparound shawls, their designer glasses pushed off their faces

and wedged into their straightened hair. A couple was having dinner at the counter of a gourmet food shop. I stopped to watch them. Did they know how lucky they were for this moment?

Near Fiftieth Street, the neighborhood changed, becoming more residential. Classic walk-ups with rusty fire escapes sat perched atop storefronts with multicolored awnings. Each shop was like an old acquaintance, one that I hadn't seen in a long time and for which I had been longing. I walked under an overpass where homeless men were camped out in sleeping bags. Thoughts flitted through my mind like gnats after the recent rains. What was it, I wondered, that had kept me on this road, through the dark days of an internship winter, through my neck injury and subsequent depression, through the ICU and the CCU and night float? A desire for experience? A sense of service? Pragmatic considerations? Obligation to my parents? The absence of a viable alternative? Or perhaps just the promise that I would make it to this point, when I would finally feel content with the choices I had made. Internship had been a difficult time, but a hopeful one, too—new career, new city, new marriage—and, in the end, it was that hope that had gotten me through it.

What a strange experiment I had conducted! Bailing out of a promising physics career in my mid-twenties to go to medical school. And then a clinical residency in internal medicine when I wasn't even sure I wanted to be a doctor. It had been a foolhardy mission, and yet it occurred to me that I would do it all over again. Becoming a doctor had strengthened me in all the ways I had hoped for. I discovered a physical hardiness I didn't know I possessed. I learned how to cope with—and inflict—pain. (Residency had toughened me, but it had coarsened me, too.) I learned how to withstand pressures—mental, physical, and moral. I learned to become passably competent with my hands. I learned how to think in schemata and to simplify—perhaps oversimplify. And finally I learned how to make big decisions—and not always after ponderous reflection. At one time I had worried that my ruminative nature would impair me as a physician, and no doubt it hurt me

when I was an intern. But in the end, my unwillingness to act reflexively probably made me a better doctor. The very characteristic that
had been least adaptive when I was an intern probably helped me the
most afterward.

There had been other benefits, too, of a more personal nature. I'd
met and married a doctor, and though our mutual interests extended
well beyond medicine, our common profession served as a comforting
backdrop to our relationship. Rajiv and I had gotten closer, too. Being
in the same profession as him had helped me become more accepting
of his brash behavior. (For better or worse, I had become more like him
than I ever expected.) Finally, it was good to see Mom and Dad so
proud. I was "on the right track." I had climbed "out of the ditch." I
had fulfilled their dream for me, and though they could never know
what I had been through, I embraced their pride. Though I still thought
they were hopelessly naive about medicine, I also believed that they
probably had been right all along in encouraging me to become a
doctor.

I had seen so much in the past year and a half. I had learned so
much about a profession that had once been inscrutable and intimidat-
ing to me. I learned that patients will almost always tell you what is
wrong with them, if you're willing to listen. I learned that the most important thing in clinical practice is common sense. And I discovered to
my surprise that the practice of medicine is its own ivory tower. Whenever you delve into something deeply, it achieves its own fortified, rarefied status. And as in academia, the ivory tower of medicine is loaded
with mystery. Most things we don't understand; much of our knowledge is incomplete. I often thought of what an attending physician
once said to me on the geriatrics ward. I had been caring for an elderly
woman who had fallen at home and could not get up, so, as part of
the workup, I ordered telemetry monitoring, an EKG, and a head CT
scan, all of which were unrevealing. I told the physician I was planning
on getting an echocardiogram and maybe a tilt-table test. Far from
being impressed with my thoroughness, he shrugged. "Sometimes

elderly people just fall," he said. But what was the reason, I asked: an arrhythmia, a transient ischemic attack? Was it a shutdown of signaling from the brain to the limbs? He shrugged again. "Sometimes they just fall."

I had learned so many lessons these past twenty months, and perhaps the biggest one of all was that medicine was a lot more complex than I had ever imagined. It was a glorious, quirky, inescapably human enterprise, with contentious debates, successes and failures, villains and heroes, oddities, mysteries, absurdities, and profundities. It was a testament to the power of my profession that now I could not imagine a life without it.

Was the pain, the ordeal, of residency worth it? When I was buried in internship, depressed and hopeless, I didn't think so. But once I got through the first year of residency, I came to realize that there probably isn't a better way to learn medicine. Internship is a classic apprenticeship of immersion. Some of the suffering may be gratuitous—thirty-six-hour shifts and hundred-hour weeks endanger patients and doctors alike—but there is only so much you can ease away and still preserve the core of the experience. In learning to become a doctor you have to work hard and stay late and devote yourself to medicine to the near exclusion of everything else in your life. You have to see a patient's illness through its course—observe the arc—to get a grip on the dynamics of disease. In my work at a teaching hospital, I often worry that the current crop of interns, mandated to leave the hospital after a twenty-four shift, is missing out on valuable lessons and is learning a mentality of moderation that is incompatible with the highest ideals of doctoring. Residency may not need to be as painful as it used to be—as it perhaps still is—but it probably has to retain a certain degree of wretchedness to serve its purpose.

Back in my neighborhood, green scrubs and stethoscope necklaces started to appear. I had walked these streets before starting internship, and now, with the promise of a new life at a new institution, it was as if I was seeing them again for the first time. Outside the hospital, interns were walking with their usual bustle, coupled with that slightly vacant stare you noticed if you got too close. Not so long ago, I had been one of them, and though internship had been the toughest year of my life, I was glad that I had gone through it. There was so much in store for these interns, and those who would follow them, such a wealth of experience. For a moment I actually envied them. Like me, they had probably been reading Harrison's textbook of internal medicine. I wanted to tell them that it wasn't necessary. The real learning was going to happen someplace else.

notes

x "No one could ever say what exactly . . ." A third of the patients who spend more than five days in the intensive care unit will experience some form of psychotic reaction. Even if they have never had any psychiatric problems before, these patients may experience anxiety, become paranoid, or hear voices and see things. Sometimes they become severely disoriented to time and place. They may get out of bed and grapple with nurses. Occasionally they become very agitated, even violent.

In recent years, progress has been made to reduce the stressors of the ICU. Many units now have visiting hours. Shifts are adjusted to minimize changes in the nursing staff caring for a patient. Lighting is adjusted to synchronize with day-night cycles. When patients leave the ICU, the problem almost always vanishes. Even in the ICU, the psychosis often resolves spontaneously, with the coming of morning or sleep.

CHAPTER THREE: MEDICAL SCHOOL

39 "Hypothyroid coma has . . ." In 1888, the Clinical Society of London published the first major report on the disorder, calling it *myxedema* and likening it to childhood cretinism. In its most severe form patients can experience a reduced level of consciousness and even florid psychosis with paranoia and hallucinations. Dr. Richard Asher, a British internist and essayist, coined the term *myxedema madness*.

CHAPTER NINE: CUSTOMER SERVICE

117 "When I looked in the medical literature . . ." In 1998, the American Psychiatric Association commissioned a panel to examine hospital violence. According to a psychiatrist who was a member, the group examined many factors that contributed to the problem, including nursing shortages, HMO frustration, long waiting times in emergency rooms, bad medical outcomes, poor staff training, and tolerance for violent behavior. Most cases of violence are preventable, the

psychiatrist told me, if health care providers learn to recognize the signs and avoid inadvertently provoking patients. Most of his suggestions were common sense: Position yourself between the patient and the door. Practice responding to various situations. But one was more controversial. "We thought that institutions should give physicians permission to defend themselves," he said. "If a guy's going to hurt you, you've got to hurt him first."

CHAPTER TEN: FALLING DOWN

121 "If internship was . . ." In his book *Time to Heal: American Medical Education from the Turn of the Century to the Era of Managed Care* (Oxford University Press, 1999), Dr. Kenneth M. Ludmerer, an internist and a medical historian, bemoans the deterioration of the learning environment in teaching hospitals. He writes: "Most pernicious of all from the standpoint of education, house officers to a considerable extent were reduced to work-up machines and disposition-arrangers: admitting patients and planning their discharge, one after another, with much less time than before to examine them, confer with attending physicians, teach medical students, attend conferences, read the literature, and reflect and wonder."

Resident and attending physicians today are running on a treadmill that is moving faster and faster. Attendings are doing briefer consultations. Residents are caring for more and sicker patients, and dealing with quicker patient turnover. This is driven partly by medical advances—only very sick AIDS patients now require hospitalization, for example—but also by the financial bottom line.

It's not just the burgeoning workload, faster patient turnover—the average inpatient length-of-stay has dropped by 50 percent over the past few decades—and a shortage of educational time. There are the protocols. Today, on the wards, there are set standards of treatments for everything: pneumonia, asthma, heart attacks. They serve a useful purpose, employing available data to ensure that all patients receive a basic level of care. But that's not necessarily why they were designed: they cut costs. And they teach residents to follow recipes.

We immediately called a consultation for the man who periodically stopped breathing at night, not just because we didn't know what to do, but because it was the easy way out, passing the problem on to someone who might have more time to deal with it.

CHAPTER FOURTEEN: WINTER BLUES

180 ". . . must have been going through." Doctors are more likely than members of the general public to commit suicide. Female doctors are just as likely as male, even though laywomen are four times less likely than laymen. Only 22 percent of depressed medical students seek help. Only 42 percent of those who are considering suicide seek treatment.

CHAPTER SEVENTEEN: INFORMED CONSENT

223 "Hospitalized patients have . . ." Some doctors argue that obtaining informed consent from patients is a meaningless exercise promoted by ethicists who don't understand the realities of medicine. There are data to support this view. Most studies show that patients recall less than half of what doctors tell them. In one study on informed consent before cataract surgery, for example, only 4 percent of patients recalled more than two out of five risks disclosed to them by their doctors. Only a third remembered later that blindness was a potential risk.

CHAPTER NINETEEN: CODE LEADER

255 "I felt conflicted about this . . ." Swallowing dysfunction is one of the most common problems in the ICU, and it is becoming more prevalent as life spans increase. In 1999, an editorial in *The New England Journal of Medicine* criticized as futile and harmful the routine placement of feeding tubes into patients with advanced dementia who stop eating. "Although the use of feeding tubes is not unequivocally futile in all cases," wrote Dr. Muriel Gillick of the Hebrew Rehabilitation Center in Boston, "balancing the risks and benefits leads to the conclusion that they are seldom warranted for patients in the final stage of dementia."

Feeding tubes, she went on, do not prolong life or prevent aspiration, and they inflict considerable pain and suffering by depriving patients of the pleasure of eating and socializing at mealtimes. "Feeding by hand is an act of nurturing that cannot be accomplished by hanging a bag of nutrients on a pole for delivery through a tube," she concluded.

263 " 'Do you think he'd . . .' " Up to 20 percent of patients in a teaching hospital have DNR orders written. A third of patients who had been resuscitated and left the hospital stated unequivocally that they wished they had not been resuscitated and would not consent to resuscitation in the future.

CHAPTER TWENTY: GENTLE SURPRISES

272 "Our apathy seemed . . ." In fact, the decline may already have begun. For example, in a 1992 study at Duke University Medical Center, one of the country's best teaching hospitals, 63 residents in internal medicine were asked to listen to three common heart murmurs programmed into a mannequin. The results were troubling to medical educators. Roughly half of the residents couldn't identify two of the murmurs, despite being tested in a quiet room and having all the time they needed—hardly conditions encountered in real practice—and approximately two-thirds missed the third. Performance had not improved later in the year, when the residents were retested.

In a later study at thirty-one internal medicine and family practice residency programs on the East Coast, 453 residents and 88 medical students were tested on twelve different heart sounds taped directly from patients. On average the residents got only 20 percent of the sounds right, not much better than the medical students.

275 "With decreasing reimbursement and . . ." Primary care, particularly preventive medicine, is looking more and more untenable in the era of fifteen-minute office visits. A study published recently in the *American Journal of Public Health* estimated that it would take over four hours a day for a general internist to provide the preventive care currently recommended for an average-size panel of adult patients. "The amount of time required is overwhelming," the authors wrote.

In a recent study of family practices in Michigan, only 3 percent of female and 5 percent of male patients over fifty had fully completed age-appropriate cancer screening tests. Nationwide, less than a third of older adults have had their stool tested within the past two years for occult blood, one of the first signs of colon cancer. Only 33 percent have ever had a flexible sigmoidoscopy, even though recent research suggests that performing this test more frequently could detect more intestinal cancers.

276 ". . . roughly a third of my class was . . ." In 2003, 12 percent fewer medical school graduates decided to specialize in internal medicine than in 1998, the year I started internship. That year, fewer seniors chose internal medicine residencies than at any other time in the previous decade. Though I couldn't have known it at the time, our year marked the beginning of a demographic shift.

One of the reasons, of course, is money. The average medical school debt is now $104,000, and internal medicine subspecialties, especially procedure-based ones like cardiology, are more lucrative than primary care. But a more important reason, I think, is that medical students increasingly view primary care physicians as harried and overworked.

acknowledgments

There are many people I wish to thank for their help and support during the writing of this book.

First and foremost, I am deeply indebted to the patients I had the privilege to care for—and learn from—during internship and residency. Knowing you, if only briefly, has made all the difference.

My agent, Todd Shuster, knew I should write a book well before I did. I am grateful for his perseverance and faith.

I owe a tremendous debt of gratitude to my brilliant editor, Paul Elie, who had a clear vision for this book. I will never forget what he told me after the first round of editing. "That's a lot to do," he wrote, "but it's what's needed if the book is to be what it is meant to be." I also want to thank Paul's assistant, Cara Spitalewitz, for attending to so many important details during the course of this enterprise. And I am very grateful to Jonathan Galassi and John Glusman for giving me the opportunity to write the book in the first place.

Writing became a big part of my life during residency. For their contributions to my peculiar career path, I owe a special thanks to the writers and editors of the science section of *The New York Times*: Larry Altman, Laura Chang, David Corcoran, Erica Goode, Denise Grady, Gina Kolata, Barbara Strauch, and the late John Wilson. I am especially grateful to Cory Dean for encouraging me to write about residency and for reading an early draft of the manuscript.

My classmates at New York Hospital lived through the experience of internship and residency with me. I wish to recognize them for their hard work and dedication during that exciting and trying period in our lives. I am especially thankful to Sameer Rohatgi and Sung Lee for their friendship. I also want to thank my present colleagues at Long Island Jewish Medical Center, especially nurse practitioner John Meister, my assistants, Naidra Wilson and Karen Hinds, and my chiefs, Dr. Stacey E. Rosen and Dr. Stanley Katz. I am also grateful for the excellent and extraordinarily industrious cardiology fellows I work with. You make my job easy.

My writing group—Thomas Estler, Bara Swain, and Danielle Ofri—was instrumental in motivating me to complete this book. I am especially indebted to Danielle, an accomplished physician-writer, for her innumerable helpful suggestions during the course of writing and for being such a wonderful role model. Two good friends also stand out for recognition: Ivan Oransky, a physician-editor who read an early draft of the manuscript, and Michael Berry, who proposed titles.

Of course, the narrative has relied on my memory of events that occurred almost a decade ago. If my memory has failed me, the fault is mine and mine alone.

I save my deepest gratitude for my family: my sister, Suneeta, and my mother, for their constant love and support; my brother, Rajiv, for his unflinching determination and for showing me the way; and my father, for all his pushing and prodding throughout my life. He was my first example of an author, and as much as I might not want to admit it, for good or bad, and in so many different ways, I am him. I also want to thank my wife Sonia's family for their advice and support, especially my father-in-law, Madho Sharma, and my sister-in-law, Nina, a writer herself, who lovingly read through the manuscript and made countless helpful suggestions.

Being married to a doctor isn't easy, but being married to an ambivalent doctor can be particularly trying. I am grateful to my wife, Sonia, for being my life partner, for gracing me with a beautiful home, and for sticking by me through the difficult times. The book would not be what it is without her essential advice and support.

Finally, I want to recognize the sunshine of my life, my son, Mohan, who arrived as this project was taking off and provided the necessary pull away from it. He is my angel, a king, the court jester—all in one. I hope one day when he reads this book he'll be proud of his dadda. *Why do I love you so much? Just because!*